Fideism and Hume's Philosophy

Revisioning Philosophy

David Appelbaum
General Editor

Vol. 12

PETER LANG
New York • San Francisco • Bern • Baltimore
Frankfurt am Main • Berlin • Wien • Paris

Delbert J. Hanson

Fideism and Hume's Philosophy

Knowledge, Religion and Metaphysics

PETER LANG
New York • San Francisco • Bern • Baltimore
Frankfurt am Main • Berlin • Wien • Paris

Library of Congress Cataloging-in-Publication Data

Hanson, Delbert James.
 Fideism and Hume's philosophy : knowledge, religion and metaphysics / Delbert J. Hanson.
  p. cm. — (Revisioning philosophy : vol. 12)
  Includes bibliographical references.
  1. Hume, David, 1711-1776. I. Title. II. Series.
B1498.H36   1993   192—dc20   92-30405
ISBN 0-8204-1963-X   CIP
ISSN 0899-9937

Die Deutsche Bibliothek-CIP-Einheitsaufnahme

Hanson, Delbert J.:
Fideism and Hume's philosophy : knowledge, religion and metaphysics / Delbert J. Hanson.—New York; Berlin; Bern; Frankfurt/M.; Paris; Wien: Lang, 1993
  (Revisioning philosophy ; Vol. 12)
  ISBN 0-8204-1963-X
NE: GT

The paper in this book meets the guidelines for permanence and durability of the Committee on Production Guidelines for Book Longevity of the Council on Library Resources.

© Peter Lang Publishing, Inc., New York 1993

All rights reserved.
Reprint or reproduction, even partially, in all forms such as microfilm, xerography, microfiche, microcard, offset strictly prohibited.

Printed in the United States of America.

To

Edward James Hanson

and

Mazie Huston Hanson

Parents who knew the

perfect balance between

guidance and freedom

CONTENTS

CHAPTER		PAGE
1	HUME AND HIS AGE	1
2	THE PROBLEM OF HUME'S BELIEFS	5
	Hume's Skepticism	5
	Fideism and Naturalism	8
	Humean Naturalism and Fideism	12
	Faith and Rationality	18
	Attitudes and Approaches to Rationality	21
	The Plan of the Argument	25
3	HUME'S PHILOSOPHY OF RELIGION	27
	Hume's Treatment of Miracles	28
	Hume and the Composition of the *Dialogues*	37
	The Meaning of "God" for Hume	40
	An Assessment of the *Dialogues*: Their External Background	43
	An Assessment of the *Dialogues*: Norman Kemp Smith's Views as a Typical Interpretation	50
	Gaskin's Assessment of the *Dialogues*	57
	Hume's Beliefs and His Mother's Death	69
	The Immortality of the Soul	71
	Suicide	74
	A Problem and Summary of the Chapter	75
4	HUME'S METAPHYSICAL DOCTRINES	83
	Hume's Pattern of Reasoning in the *Treatise*	85
	Hume's Doctrine of Causation	88
	Causation: The Analytic or Negative Side	90
	Causation and Induction	99

	Causation: The Constructive or Positive Side	105
	The Regularity Theory of Causation	122
	Hume's Doctrine of Self Identity	125
	Substance	137
	The Existence of Material Objects	138
5	METHOD AND PYRRHONISM IN HUME'S PHILOSOPHY	141
	Hume Scholarship and the Fideist Claim	142
	Hume's Reflections on His Philosophy	149
	The Skeptical Tradition Prior to Hume	157
	Hume's Own Pyrrhonism	161
	Hume's Critique of Pyrrhonism	166
	Conclusion	172

NOTES 175

BIBLIOGRAPHY 193

INDEX OF NAMES 203

PREFACE

This book is a product of my course in modern philosophy. As I pored over the texts of modern philosophers I was struck by the fact that often what I found in Hume did not seem to fit what we could call the "orthodox" or standard interpretation of Hume's philosophy. That Hume is a skeptic and engages in skeptical analysis is undeniable to anyone who reads Hume and tries to make sense of his ideas, but it did not seem coherent with what I found to call him a skeptic at the end of his work. He used skeptical, reductive analysis, but he was not satisfied with the consequences of it and expressed himself quite strongly about the distress he felt about his philosophical conclusions. I have dealt in this book with what I see to be Hume's efforts to extricate himself from his rationalist and empiricist philosophical analysis. Consequently, I am trying to make a contribution to Hume studies which will make better sense of that influential figure than the view that Hume was a skeptic and even in some cases, a nihilist. I argue that Hume was not a skeptic in the end. Our conclusions here affect Hume's doctrines of belief and knowledge primarily in his religious philosophy and in metaphysics.

In addition, I have become convinced that the ahistorical approach to studying philosophy short changes our knowledge of past philosophers. Philosophical problems may be perennial, but their particular formulation is closely tied to the times in which the philosophers lived who articulated them. To neglect the historical understanding of important thinkers is to miss the illumination of the philosophical problems which engaged the minds of important thinkers like Hume and the insight which historical understanding can bring to solutions of these problems. Our knowledge of Hume in particular has been hindered in the past by lack of knowledge of the modern Pyrrhonist movement, especially with the pervasive influence of Pierre Bayle, the chief Pyrrhonist influence on Hume. But besides Bayle, too little attention has been paid to the influence on Hume of Descartes, Malebranche, and Leibniz. My understanding of Hume deviates from the view that Locke and Berkeley were the almost exclusive influences on Hume which Hume scholars in the past have been inclined to take for granted. Many philosophers outside circles of Hume specialists hold that view and regard Hume as a final, ultimate skeptic.

I owe debts to many people. Many of my students have been alert readers of Hume and have stimulated me in many ways including their complaints about the length of Hume's treatment of cause and effect in the *Treatise*! I won't name any out of fear of overlooking some names I should mention.

As for my teachers, I want to express my gratitude to Professors John Dreher, Hartry Field, and Brian Loar, all of the University of Southern California. They have been invariably courteous and very generous to me with their encouragement, time, stimulation, and correction of my philosophical views. I want publicly to acknowledge my debt to them for their commitment, care, and thoroughness in doing philosophy.

With respect to this particular project, Professors John Hospers, Wesley Robb, and Dallas Willard have given me a great deal of time and attention. Professor Hospers, for example, gave me copious and explicit criticisms and suggestions. I am very grateful to these men for their astute criticisms and suggestions at many points.

No one of these people can be held responsible for any defects in this book.

My thanks go to Professor Philip Quinn for his work in sponsoring a workshop on Skepticism and Fideism several years ago at Notre Dame where I read a paper on fideism in Hume's philosophy of religion.

My gratitude is due to the editor of the series, Professor David Appelbaum and to Editor Michael Flamini of Peter Lang Publishing, Inc. for their forbearance with the length of time it took to get them the manuscript.

Among my colleagues, I am grateful to my fellow philosophy department colleague, Professor David Ciocchi for his buoyant support and encouragement. I found it indispensable. Professor Leland Wilshire has always been a ready listener. Also, to my boss, Dean Dwight Jessup, I want to express my gratitude for his encouragement and for providing help in reduced teaching hours.

ABBREVIATIONS FOR HUME'S WORKS

Abstract   *An Abstract of a Treatise of Human Nature.* Introduction by J. M. Keynes and P. Sraffa. London: Cambridge University Press, 1938; reprint, Hamden, Conn.: Archon Books, 1965.

Dialogues   *Dialogues concerning Natural Religion.* Edited by Norman Kemp Smith. 2d ed. Edinburgh: Thomas B. Nelson & Sons Ltd., 1947; reprint, The Library of Liberal Arts. Indianapolis: Bobbs-Merrill Co., 1979.

Enquiry   *Enquiries concerning Human Understanding and concerning the Principle of Morals.* Edited by L. A. Selby-Bigge. 3d. ed. rev. by P. H. Nidditch. Oxford: Clarendon Press, 1975.

Nat.His.Rel.   *The Natural History of Religion.* Edited by A. Wayne Colver. And: *Dialogues concerning Natural Religion.* Edited by John Valdimir Price. Oxford: Clarendon Press, 1976.

Treatise   *A Treatise of Human Nature.* Edited by L. A. Selby-Bigge. 2d ed. revised by P. H. Nidditch. Oxford: Clarendon Press, 1978.

CHAPTER 1

HUME AND HIS AGE

There are two dominant motivations in this treatment of David Hume's doctrines and method. The first is cultural. Euphoria over the Newtonian scientific synthesis lasted for most of the eighteenth century and in its wake came revolt from all authority, especially religious and political ones. The eighteenth century was the first truly modern century in that a broad popularization of scientific theory among the masses created a wide thirst for knowledge, a belief in the possibility of comprehending all things, an optimism about the general amelioration of life's conditions, and a secular outlook on life. The revolutionary mood of our own century is in the tradition of the eighteenth, and in many other ways the age of reason, the Enlightenment, has left an indelible mark on our own century. Hume was an eighteenth-century figure and a child of that age expresses and typifies many of the tensions and anxieties of our own time.

"Reason" was seldom if ever defined in that age, but a careful reading of the literature shows that reason was roughly equivalent to the scientific method. For Descartes reason had been mathematical reasoning which he and his followers assumed could be used equally well in other fields than mathematics. Locke, however, whose spirit was an ideal for enlightenment thinkers, understood reason after the fashion in which he used "reason" as a physician. It was the way by which he would make an informed decision about how to treat Shaftesbury. Answers arrived by such reason came not at the end of a long chain of reasoning and with logical certainty; they emerged instead through trial and error and yielded probability only.

This conception on how to arrive at new conclusions must have added to it the enlightenment resistance to the authorities of the past. The philosophes of the eighteenth century had many differences among themselves, but they were united in their opposition to authority and their commitment to autonomy. The two great sources of authority were the church or religious establishment and the king/state/parliament, the political establishment. Furthermore, in their eyes, much of what had passed for knowledge in other centuries was ignorance and superstition, so a totally new beginning had to be made. So, what was going to be the authority for the autonomy of man? Deductive rationalism in the sense of the Cartesian program (or the extreme of Spinozoism with its almost total absence of empirical data) was in eclipse—Descartes was not the hero of the eighteenth century. Something, however, had to replace the dogmatism of the past. The one rallying ground on which they all could agree was science. The great heroes of the age were Bacon for his vision of what induction and discovery could accomplish, Locke for his empiricism, and Newton for his mechanical philosophy.

Eighteenth-century reliance on reason was not uniform, as Rousseau demonstrates; but his revolt against authority was quite consistent with the rest of his age. This stress on reason carried with it a skepticism that still besets us in many areas of life. Belief that human concerns and values were lost or in danger of being lost to the scientific world outlook provoked solutions as desperate as Berkeley's mentalism and Kant's recourse to practical reason. A sense of futility and pessimism about human capabilities lay just under the surface of optimism, and no one felt the short-comings of human logic in all areas more than Hume. Hume's relevance and interest persists because he serves as a bellweather for many of our own misgivings.

Today we have many parallel attitudes. In our revolutionary age we have observed widespread abandonment of belief in our ability to comprehend and give answers to ultimate issues and matters of human significance. Such skepticism has led to emphasis on unconscious drives and compulsions and pessimism about the dignity and worth of human life. In religious thought a common product of this skeptical attitude is fideism, a reliance on faith apart from any rational grounds to preserve beliefs and doctrines which it is believed cannot withstand the illumination of historical facts, the pressure of scientific interpretation, or the close examination of philosophy. Thus a close study of the age of reason, and of the importance of Hume in that age, should be an aid in better understanding our own problems about religion, and in seeking their solutions.

The second motivation is historical. This historical interest concerns two things, the interpretation of Hume's writings and our understanding of Hume's relationship to his intellectual predecessors. With respect to our interpretation of Hume's writings, Hume scholarship has been preoccupied with Hume's "skepticism" and the effects of his analytic techniques. With this preoccupation or fixation, Hume scholars have failed to see how his skepticism is part of a larger epistemological orientation. That orientation is revived Pyrrhonic skepticism, taken from Sextus Empiricus and propagated in early modern times. This issued in a general fideistic outlook which affected both religious and nonreligious issues in philosophy. Fideism helped to retain the doctrines the "skeptic" was loath to lose, avoided the appearance of philosophical nonsense in denying things we all believe in or know, and preserved the philosopher from intellectual frustration.

Hume scholarship has generally overlooked Hume's connection with the skeptical/fideist tradition, especially as this was conveyed to Hume by such writers as Pierre Bayle. Richard Popkin's work has given us the historical background which illuminates many puzzles about Hume, his remarks about skepticism and its futility, and his response to his own conclusions. It has served to place Hume in a larger tradition and to give a better understanding of the skeptical tendencies of modern philosophy. Popkin shows that Bayle gave faith as a basis for the acceptance of conclusions outside the area of religion. Thus, it will be argued here, fideism about nonreligious topics is thoroughly consistent with a philosophical tradition Hume knew and which deeply influenced him.

The historical understanding of the skeptical tradition better explains Descartes' interest in deriving a positive method of philosophy and of seeking certainty in science and philosophy. It also explains why Hume's philosophy propounded some views which appear barren and sterile to us. The interpretation of Hume has been beset with the problem of why Hume would adopt views so unacceptable on so many issues when he is obviously such an astute philosopher. The historical phenomenon of early pyrrhonic skepticism enlarges our understanding of those factors at work in Hume's life and thought. The time seems right now to draw the implications of Popkin's studies in skepticism for all of Hume's philosophy.

Fideism traditionally has been traced to Kant. In this book it is my claim that Hume is the first great user of this epistemological resource in English-language philosophy and though Hume had fideist predecessors who influenced him, like Bayle, these figures have had little or no influence themselves on later philosophers. It is through Hume primarily that fideism has come to us and become a force in the English-speaking world.

This book is, then, a sustained attempt to account for some of Hume's most arresting features and to place him in a much more understandable intellectual and historical situation than does that judgment which stops at David Hume, the Edinburgh skeptic.

CHAPTER 2

THE PROBLEM OF HUME'S BELIEFS

HUME'S SKEPTICISM

Discussions of Hume typically conclude that he was a skeptic. He did not accept the received opinion on the metaphysical doctrines of cause, personal identity, substance, or external objects, or the religious doctrines of miracles, immortality, or the existence of God. He gives his reasons for his conclusions in the *Treatise*, his first *Enquiry*, the *Dialogues concerning Natural Religion*, and his shorter essays. Such an interpretation, however, does not wholly account for his (unexpected) acceptance of those very same beliefs. Instead of rejecting those beliefs and being a skeptic about them, Hume seems to accept them at last on various, though similar, nonrational bases. He thus appears to be a fideist instead of a skeptic, and to accept nonrationally concepts and theses which he had before rejected on a rational basis. Hume's "fideism" was a solution which he found to extricate himself from his "skepticism." This is a substantial expansion of the ordinary meaning of "fideism" and one which we must clarify later on.

Our histories of philosophy generally interpret Hume to be a skeptic. To give a few examples, Wright asks, "In what sense is Hume a skeptic?"[1] Jones writes about Hume's "Philosophical Scepticism,"[2] and Mossner's biography of Hume repeats that theme again and again.[3] Stroud, though dissenting, remarks on the view:

> David Hume is generally considered to be a purely negative philosopher—the arch sceptic whose primary aim and achievement was to reduce the theories of his empiricist predecessors to the absurdity that was contained in them all along. This view, part of which started in Hume's own day, was strongly encouraged by nineteenth-century historians of philosophy who saw all intellectual changes as necessary stages in a predetermined process of the unfolding of something called History or the Absolute. In that scheme of things Hume's assigned role was to carry the empiricist philosophy of Locke and Berkeley to its logical and incredible conclusion, thus setting the stage for Kant and eventually for the final Hegelian liberation. Even today many philosophers not noticeably

sympathetic to that intellectual tradition regard Hume as little more than the third and final step in the downfall of classical British empiricism. No doubt some passages in Hume taken alone, might support this line of interpretation, but it is an extreme and unfortunate distortion of what he actually wrote. Not only is it mistaken; it would make Hume much less interesting and important for us as a philosopher than he actually is.[4]

Current literature continues to emphasize Hume's skepticism, without recognizing Hume's acceptance of doctrines which he (at least to his own satisfaction) had before analyzed into intellectual oblivion. As an example of this we can mention Robert Fogelin, who remarks that "most recent Hume scholarship has either neglected or downplayed an important aspect of Hume's position—his skepticism—and this needs putting right."[5]

Some of the claims that Hume is a skeptic come from Hume's own use of the term. MacNabb[6] discusses Hume's position with regard to skepticism in the *Treatise*[7] and the first *Enquiry*, and Stove[8] discusses the claim that Hume's philosophy is "skeptical" or "negative" or "destructive." Hume's treatment of themes and his use of "skepticism" with regard to his own beliefs has disposed the majority of Hume scholars to view the philosopher this way.

In section XII of the *Enquiry* Hume writes about the skeptic who is an enemy of religion and who provokes the indignation of divines and graver philosophers. He is certain, however, that no one ever met any such person, who had no opinion or principle concerning any subject, either of action or speculation. He then proceeds to answer his own question, "What is meant by a sceptic?" by distinguishing between "antecedent" and "consequent" skepticism.

"Antecedent" or methodological skepticism is the Cartesian variety. It employs doubt as a device or technique meant to preserve us from error or impulsive judgments and to provide an incorrigible basis for knowledge. It is designed to eliminate what is baseless or false and to leave what cannot be successfully doubted. Thus we could avoid philosophy's scandal of divergent opinions and provide a final, definitive, universal (and in a word, infallible) system of knowledge. Hume does not believe very much can come out of the Cartesian program. When taken in its "pure" or rigorous form, it represents an unattainable dream. But when we take that program in a moderate sense and with proper limitations, it is a very productive preparation for the study of philosophy. It preserves a proper impartiality in our judgments and weans our minds from prejudices which we have absorbed from our education and from other people's rash opinions. If we can start with clear and self-evident principles, advance "by timorous and sure steps" (*Enquiry*, p. 150), review our conclusions frequently, and examine accurately all their consequences, then we have a method by which we can attain truth and realize stable conclusions: You have to demolish before you can construct; you have to excavate before you can build. So Hume allows that if the Cartesian variety is a kind of mitigated skepticism it has its legitimate uses:

"by these means we shall make both a slow and a short progress in our systems; [they] are the only methods, by which we can ever hope to reach truth, and attain a proper stability and certainty in our determinations." (*Enquiry*, p. 150)

Consequent skepticism, however, comes *after* science and enquiry. Such skepticism is doubt about the truth or adequacy of conclusions arrived at on some question or issue; and it points to the alleged inability of our sensory capacities and mental faculties, or their unfitness, to reach any fixed conclusions. This is genuine skepticism, for it is a deliberate and systematic doubt about conclusions, and Hume indicates his distress at certain features of this kind of skepticism. For example, he considers the tendency to question our senses because of illusions, etc. as trite, and affirms that people are disposed by a natural instinct to "repose faith in their senses." (*Enquiry*, p. 151)

Consequent skepticism comes in two forms, distinguished by Sextus Empiricus: Academic (Platonic) skepticism and Pyrrhonism. Academic skepticism rejects dogmatism (the claim that we can know anything with certainty), but it holds that people can have *probable* knowledge and that this probability should be the guide to life. Probable knowledge is still knowledge. Pyrrhonism rejects both dogmatism and academic skepticism. According to the Pyrrhonists we can have neither certain knowledge nor probable knowledge. "Academic" acceptance of probable knowledge is only a kind of concealed dogmatism. The Pyrrhonist claims that we must totally suspend judgment and let our lives by guided by nature and custom.[9]

There is considerable disagreement as to whether these two versions of skepticism can be isolated in the *Treatise*.[10] Immerwahr believes that Hume does distinguish them, and that he argues for the academic variety. He claims further that the academic skepticism of the first *Enquiry* differs significantly from the academic skepticism of the *Treatise* and that this difference accounts, in part, for Hume's preference for the *Enquiry*.[11] Immerwahr's claim that Hume comes out in favor of Academic probability rests upon the first paragraphs of the *Treatise*, I, IV, I. Richard Popkin, on the other hand, holds that Hume is Pyrrhonian.[12]

It is possible to admit both views, if we take Immerwahr's statement as based upon what Hume *claims* and Popkin's judgment on what Hume *does*. Hume argues, in the same section to which Immerwahr appeals, that there is no use in accepting a total extinction of belief and evidence, for "Nature, by an absolute and uncontroulable necessity has determin'd us to judge as well as to breathe and feel." (*Treatise*, p. 183) Further, he says in the same place that "Whoever has taken the pains to refute the cavils of this *total* skepticism, has really disputed without an antagonist, and endeavour'd by arguments to establish a faculty, which nature has antecedently implanted in the mind, and render'd unavoidable." This is the strategy of the Pyrrhonic skeptic who holds that, since neither certain nor probable knowledge claims can be defended, we must abandon philosophy, stop loooking for sophisticated reasons, and be guided by nature or custom. Hume talks about this problem in his *Abstract*:

> By all that has been said the reader will easily perceive, that the philosophy contain'd in this book is very sceptical, and tends to give us a notion of the imperfections and narrow limits of human understanding. Almost all reasoning is there reduced to experience; and the belief, which attends experience, is explained to be nothing but a peculiar sentiment, or lively conception produced by habit. Nor is this all, when we believe any thing of *external* existence, or suppose an object to exist a moment after it is no longer perceived, this belief is nothing but a sentiment of the same kind. Our author insists upon several other sceptical topics; and upon the whole concludes, that we assent to our faculties, and employ our reason only because we cannot help it. Philosophy wou'd render us entirely *Pyrrhonian*, were not nature too strong for it. (*Abstract*, p. 24)

Thus the thesis of this book: *Doctrines, conclusions, and beliefs Hume could not rationally hold and defend on either a rationalist or an empirical approach he regained and preserved for himself on nonrational grounds, including nature.*

But if Hume was skeptic, as Hume scholars have claimed and as Hume admits, then why claim that he was a fideist? Doesn't the very idea of fideism involve the idea of *believing* things on a basis of faith (or other irrational basis) instead of doubting them? The answer: *Every fideist first has to be a skeptic or there would be no reason to appeal to an nonrational basis as a way of keeping the esteemed beliefs.* After fideists face their doubts and admit to being troubled by their skepticism, they seek to preserve their beliefs. They retain an item of belief, but not on the basis of logical argument. Logical argument was what produced doubt in the first place. Fideists are inclined not only to adopt what has a weak intellectual basis, or none at all, but also to adopt points which they have explicitly questioned or doubted. Thus, fideism is not only an attitude, but also an act carried out consciously and deliberately. In Hume's case, "skepticism," was an essential stage in his thinking. He starts out in the skeptical manner, but his final conclusions were not very different from the conclusions of those whom he opposed in his skeptical thinking. His atomistic empiricism was quite severe, and it imposed limits upon him which he found difficult to accept, but he passed beyond his negative conclusions to hold these doctrines. So, he does not qualify as a skeptic except in the sense that every fideist is a (preliminary) skeptic. He was motivated to retain his conclusions on a nonrational (or irrational) basis, and thus brought about a saving of these conclusions.

FIDEISM AND NATURALISM

The claim that Hume's philosophy is a fideism requires some examination of that concept together with the concepts of *rationality* and *faith*. Full, systematic examination of these concepts is not required for our task of examining the role of fideism in Hume's philosophy, but something must be said in order to avoid certain confusions.

In recent decades fideism has become a widespread position, and even something of a 'method,' in religious epistemology. It is an epistemological position because it bears upon the relationship of faith and reason in religious beliefs. It is a method because it is advocated as a *way* of coming to believe in the existence of God, or at least of justifying the *assertion* of certain religious statements.

Fideism holds that belief in God or some religious theory or proposition is sustained on the basis of faith alone. Many religious systems claim that their tenets must be held on the basis of faith, and sometimes by faith "alone." But to say "faith alone" in the context of a philosophical discussion means that faith must be exercised without any accompanying or supporting *rational* means, such as arguments or evidence. Paul Edwards contrasts fideistic believers to those he calls "rationalistic" believers.[13] He includes among the latter any believer who justifies his position by reference to one or more of the arguments which are claimed to show that the existence of God (or some other religious theory) is either certain or probable. This believer *would cease* to believe but for those arguments.

Fideism is seldom held consistently, though it comes much closer to consistency in certain philosophers such as Søren Kierkegaard and Emil Fackenheim. It is, therefore, difficult to describe. Fideists often state a fideist position, and then write entire books which do not fit that. For example, John Hick gives a statement of "the religious rejection of the theistic proofs"[14] and then goes on to defend the teleological argument for the existence of God—or at least to cut down the force of the chief objection to it, the presence of evil in the world.

Hick holds out no hope for any factual support for theism in this life. It is not possible to establish the truth of such a claim as "God exists," or "There is a personal God." The theistic and naturalistic alternatives are both equally supportable *in this life*. He does hold out the possibility of "eschatological" verification, however, for though the theistic viewpoint may not be proveable in this life, but it will be *after* this life. This presumes the reality of the immortality of the soul and the possibility of the Christian claim of bodily resurrection, neither of which would be supportable on Hick's principles. Although the empirical evidence for God's existence will be no different in a future life than in this one since God is invisible and otherwise not open to any other of our senses, the survival of the person itself apparently would serve as evidence of the claims of religion. It is hard to understood Hick without such an assumption.

The whole project of eschatological verification bristles with problems. But leaving off his remaining discussion, let us notice how his position is fideistic in nature. First, Hick does not give up any of his religious convictions, however many problems they may bring. Second, he more or less discounts all evidence available to us now, for he holds it to be incapable of establishing the existence of God (or other religious doctrines) either certainly or probably. Third, he asks us to accept as evidence what cannot count as evidence *now*. Hick intended his position on eschatological verification to be an answer to the positivist challenge to religious utterances. As such, his proposal of eschatological verification may save the theistic position from *meaninglessness* in the sense that he satisfied the old positivist demand for verificationist conditions. That was, perhaps, its primary intent, but it does nothing to establish any probability of its truth.

Hick is aware of the questionable nature of his suggestions, and agrees that his reliance on eschatological evidence as a method of verification has always met with disapproval by both philosophers and theologians. His all-important assertion, however, is that it is the proper position to take because "no viable alternative to it has been offered to establish the factual character of theism."[15] He says the same thing in a parallel passage about moral experience. It is alleged to be the primary evidence of a moral order in the world, its source in God, and hence the existence of God, It is suggested that the sense of obligation implies a transcendent, personal Will as its source and ground. But, says Hick,

> This religious analysis of moral obligation (whether true or false) is a corollary rather than a premise of theism. Taken by themselves the facts of our ethical experience are capable of either a naturalistic or a theistic explanation, and our choice at this point is determined by our prior conviction as to the theous or atheous character of the universe.[16]

Terence Penelhum provides another analysis of fideism. He defines fideism as "the insistence that faith needs no justification from reason, but is the judge of reason and its pretensions."[17] Also, "any attempt to show that faith is immune to the demands of reason by using arguments from this source is a form of Skeptical Fideism."[18] These fideisms are called "skeptical" because they urge religious conformity combined with beliefessness ("conformist" fideism), or they despair of our capability of establishing a doctrinal position ("evangelical" fideism). This kind of fideism is not simple faith adopted since the particular adherent cannot make sense of the intellectual or doctrinal content. It is rather a position adopted by some of the educated religious leadership of Europe. Whether on grounds of traditional conformity to church dictates or evangelical espousal of faith, intellectual activity is rejected for faith. Both forms are based on what he calls the "parity" argument, which claims that many of the secular beliefs of common sense or science and the beliefs of faith are intellectually on a par—hence the name of the argument. Neither set of beliefs can be supported, justified, or defended by reason, i.e. no acceptable justification can be given for our convictions about the world, so the beliefs of common sense are just as much in need of faith as are those of religion. In either case, it is claimed that intellectual or rationalist demands for grounding beliefs are misdirected and ineffectual.

Conformist fideism gets its name from exponents who attempt to show the pretentiousness, inconclusiveness, and sterility of rational argument and doctrines based upon it, but nevertheless urge us to continue in the Christian religion, to be dutiful and submissive to the authority of the Church, to celebrate its rites, and to partake of its sacraments. Its representatives, according to Penelhum, are Erasmus, Montaigne, and Bayle. They contend that skeptical indifference will permit simple piety to continue unsullied by sectarian differences. Erasmus in his dispute with Luther insisted that "Christian godliness" does not require us to engage in theological disputation about divine foreknowledge, the efficacy of the will, or other matters which God does not wish us to penetrate but only to contemplate as we do God Himself in mystic silence. Such a claim attempts to represent Christian faith as analogous to the Pyrrhonian conformity to appearances: "This is very close to the skeptic's recommendation to fall in with tradition while avoiding interpretation."[19] For Montaigne, the most famous of these skeptics, faith should not be based upon reason at all though reason can be of great service *within* faith.

Sebond's arguments are inadequate, Montaigne concludes, but so are everyone's, since that is how reason is. When the disillusioned seeker abandons the dogmatist's quest for ultimate truth, he nevertheless can attain to it by divine grace. Erasmus' and Montaigne's (conformist) fideism best fits the Catholic mentality, with its elaborate tradition and authoritative hierarchy. Bayle, though a Protestant, is also placed by Penelhum in this tradition. Penelhum puts him in the conformist camp rather than the evangelical one because, for Bayle, faith serves as the unreflective conclusion of a quest which ends in the abandonment of argument. Bayle, thus understood, is a latter-day advocate of suspension of judgment as a source of quietude. In urging the inadequacies of reason and rational arguments, Bayle encourages his readers to turn away from doctrinal disputes altogether. Faith supplies the calm that Pyrrhonian argument alone cannot supply, but for which it is nonetheless a precondition.[20]

Penelhum's second kind of fideism is the evangelical type. The best representatives of that position are Pascal and Kierkegaard. It is more natural for Protestants than is the conformist type. Evangelical fideism attempts to serve the cause of faith by exposing the inability of human reason to provide grounds for the commitment faith embodies. Advocates of this position believe natural theology to be an attempt to replace faith by argument, so in this approach skepticism is believed to prepare the way for divine grace to generate faith without philosophical obstacles. Skeptical argument functions as a heaven-sent barrier to false philosophical constructions which must be demolished before the true wisdom can be received to convert and empower one's life.

What then are the essential features of fideism? It is not merely the vague awareness we have about many things and for which we can provide few if any good reasons. Thus, F. H. Bradley remarks that "metaphysics is the finding of bad reasons for what we believe upon instinct."[21] This is not a fideism, for it lacks the deliberate repudiation of rational resources and the adoption of a substitute basis instead. Nor is fideism another name for intuition or noninferential insight. It is not another name for faith. Rather, it is stance about the *significance* of faith and about its use as a replacement for reason (thinking) and argument. Nor is fideism simply the claim that we need faith, since faith is an agreed-upon need by those who completely reject the fideist program. Nor is fideism a form of mysticism; for the latter position is a claim about the relation of religious experience to knowledge, not a doctrine concerning the lack of any relation between intellectual matters and belief.

Two things are necessary to have a fideism: First, the claim that rational procedures, evidence, and argument will not suffice for our purposes, whatever those may be. The most persistent claim of fideists has been this contention about cognitive goals. Second, there is the claim that our goals, cognitive, emotional, social, vocational, religious, can come to us by faith alone, even when there is total lack or repudiation of rational support. Thus we need not rest in a state of skepticism with reference to the specific matters concerned. Faith or some other nonrational device will supply our need for belief. If the first point was the negative feature of fideism, this is the positive one. The adoption of these points is a *deliberate* move by those who have taken a fideist position.

Thus, fideism is *not* an *essentially religious* position. Historically, perhaps, most fideisms have been concerned with religious questions. That is not the only area where the fideistic pattern can be found, however. In the centuries immediately preceding Hume's, the use of faith to eliminate rational argument with its doubt, insecurity, and anxiety, and to secure belief, peace of mind, and psychological certitude, was extended by many philosophers to the basic issues of philosophy. Popkin shows that fideism—reliance on faith to establish or defend beliefs when reason cannot succeed—has been adopted by skeptically-inclined thinkers such as Bayle to defend points in mathematics and logic, epistemology and metaphysics, though they have no close or discernible connection with religious claims or beliefs. *It is in this extended or broader sense that Hume's philosophy is fideistic.* Not only do we find fideism in Hume's philosophy of religion, but there are fideistic elements in Hume's *Treatise* and in his first *Enquiry*.

HUMEAN NATURALISM AND FIDEISM

The thesis that Hume is a metaphysical fideist as well as a fideist in his philosophy of religion should not be surprising. Hume scholarship in the last twenty-five years has largely transcended the view that Hume is the skeptic of British empiricism. According to the older conception, Hume represented the end product of empiricism. By showing the inconsistencies and contradictions inherent in empiricism he completed the process Locke started and Berkeley advanced. Russell, for example, contends that Hume is one of the most important philosophers because "he developed to its logical conclusion the empirical philosophy of Locke and Berkeley, and by making it self-consistent made it incredible."[22]

That interpretation goes back at least to Green and Grose, and possibly even back to Reid and Beattie, and is not dead: "There are still well-informed philosophers who find it odd that anyone should even suggest that Hume is not a skeptic."[23]

The claim that Hume is a (final) skeptic has been replaced by many Hume scholars with the view that Hume is a "naturalist." Kemp Smith is responsible for this thesis, published in *Mind* in 1905 and then expanded in his influential book on Hume in 1941. For Kemp Smith, "naturalism" is the position Hume adopted by substituting those forces in human nature which are the real basis for our common beliefs in place of the intellectual reasons which Hume says will not suffice. Penelhum succinctly summarizes Smith's thesis: "A *naturalist*: someone whose prime concern is to show us how human nature provides us with resources, mostly non-intellectual, which enable us to interpret and respond to our experience in ways which rationalist philosophers had vainly tried to justify by argument."[24] Common people give no reasons to justify their beliefs, since they seldom if ever think about such things and produce no writings, and philosophers have not been successful in discovering any. Therefore, it is necessary to abandon rationalist approaches to the problem and to fall back on the natural forces of human nature.

Kemp Smith tells us that he was led to develop this view because of the contradictory data we find in Hume and the conflicting positions to which Hume committed himself: "Why is it that in Book I of the Treatise the existence of an impression of the self is explicitly denied, while yet his theory of the 'indirect' passions, propounded at length in Book II, is made to rest on the assumption that we do in fact experience an impression of the self, and that this impression is ever-present to us?"[25] Almost the same thing was stated to me by Prof. John Hospers: "It is amazing that in the first book of the *Treatise* Hume deals with all these problems and issues and then in the rest of his work he proceeds as if there isn't any problem with any of these things at all."[26]

M. Jamie Ferreira gives us another analysis of skepticism and the naturalism which replaces it. She describes three types of naturalism, "sceptical, reasonable doubt, and justifying." The first type which she attributes to Hume, "Offers merely the counter-description of unavoidability of natural beliefs with no challenge to the sceptic's requirements, and so remain distinctively sceptical."[27] In other words, it remains skeptical because the possibility of rational belief on the basis of evidence and argument is abandoned as a sort of counsel of despair and belief is adopted on grounds which are something else than rational. The other two types of naturalism are anti-skeptical, because they offer a challenge to the skeptic's requirements for justification. Reasonable doubt naturalism draws a distinction between reasonable and unreasonable doubt. It argues that there is no reasonable ground for doubting fundamental beliefs of human nature. The third type seeks to justify beliefs by using a different model of justification from the stringent one demanded by the skeptic.

What is wrong with the naturalist position?[28] The major difficulty in the view that Hume is a naturalist is that it doesn't go far enough. Hume's skepticism (and then the relief he sought from this) is not taken seriously enough. He is not a skeptic pure and simple, according to the naturalists, but he is a skeptic *plus* the natural mechanisms which mitigate this skepticism. In this way his skepticism fails to be acknowledged adequately. Penelhum, who of Hume scholars comes the closest to the position for which we are arguing here, demonstrates this failure of Kemp Smith to accentuate Hume's skepticism:

> I would suggest, then, that Hume is both a skeptic and a naturalist: that he does say that our basic beliefs about matters of fact are devoid of rational justification, that he offers us detailed accounts of how we come to hold them and why we cannot abandon them, and that these accounts are applications of a general understanding of human nature that is applied elsewhere to our emotional lives and to our moral and social evaluations .... Hume's skepticism is not something incompatible with his naturalism. It is an integral part of it.[29]

Robison also states a similar view:

> It is a mistake ... to suppose that Hume, being a naturalist, is not a sceptic. For, first, however causal judgments are analyzed, there are normative criteria for making them, and it is one of the persistent features of Hume's philosophical works that he uses those criteria to assess judgments made by ordinary persons and philosophers alike .... This kind of scepticism is straightforward enough to require no special treatment here .... Second, Hume is committed to some form of inductive scepticism by explicit arguments in the *Abstract* and the *Enquiry* and by implicit assumptions in the *Treatise*. Again, whatever the difficulties, Hume's commitment has often enough been documented and detailed to require no special treatment here .... It is Hume's commitment to a third sort of scepticism which I wish to pursue. For, as I shall argue, Hume's main sceptical point is not that certain concepts do not or cannot apply to experience, but that even though they do not apply, we must apply them. He is, as it were, a metasceptic: in describing the natural operations of the human mind to account for why we make judgments which are unreasonable by the empiricist principle, Hume discovered that the mind's essential nature is such that we must make such unreasonable judgments. This scepticism, clearly emerges from his analysis of judgments regarding external objects .... But its main elements are present in his analysis of causal judgments .... It is a scepticism, as we shall see, which, were it true, would be devastating to our pretensions of rationality.[30]

Some remarks on Robison's statements seem appropriate: Robison sees correctly that Hume's skepticism must be taken seriously, but he fails to see that Hume is a preliminary skeptic who "gets back" the doctrines he questions or gives up on rational grounds by resorting to those natural influences pointed out by

Kemp Smith and other current Hume scholars. Robison fails to recognize Kemp Smith's point that what Hume had questioned he later accepts as real, true, or right. This is the most common failure of attempts to explain Hume as a naturalist. To call him a naturalist is to move in the right direction, but it fails to see that by the use of nonrational ("naturalist") means Hume moves beyond his skepticism and leaves it behind. That is why the issues Hume examines in the first book of the *Treatise* are ignored in later portions of that work and in subsequent works. Hume distanced himself from them; he did not continue to hold them as a skeptic must.

So, Hume *does not remain a skeptic* after resorting to habit, custom, propensity, association, and the like. He believes all the doctrines he had previously analyzed away. If we understand Hume to be fideist, his tendency to accept a doctrine or viewpoint he earlier rejected on logical grounds becomes perfectly understandable. It also explains his disquiet over his skepticism and the intellectual "corner" into which it placed him.

Kemp Smith's claim that Hume's philosophy originated in his preoccupation with moral questions[31] is consistent with the fideist claim. The preoccupation-with-morals claim is an explanation of Hume's motivation in writing the *Treatise*, of how he got started on his project; the fideist claim is an explanation of how Hume carried through his program. Skepticism is an issue only in the first book of the *Treatise*, in the parallel sections in the first *Enquiry*, and in the *Dialogues concerning Natural Religion*. Hume may have had other kinds of skepticism in his work, such as noncognitivism in the ethics of the *Treatise*, but that kind of skepticism is not what is usually meant when Hume scholars talk about it. What they have in mind is the analysis of our concepts of substance, causation, personal identity, and the existence of material objects in Book I of the *Treatise*.

Let's look at Livingston's treatment of the issue. He cites Richard Popkin as working within the main outlines of the Kemp Smith position. Popkin understands Hume as taking the Pyrrhonist position. The ancient Pyrrhonists advocated suspension of judgment and then claimed that the peace of mind he had been seeking came about accidentally in the disposition to suspend judgment. "Pyrrhonism" here is modern, revived Pyrrhonism stemming from Montaigne, Bayle, etc., whose representatives advocated relying on faith, faith in all areas of life. Hume's emphasis is to rely on faith in religion and on the forces of our personality for solving dilemmas in metaphysics and other areas of knowledge. These additional forces act much in the same way as faith is held to do in religion. This is fideism. Livingston summarizes the additional step taken by Hume:

> Popkin shows that Hume deployed Pyrrhonian arguments to show that there is no justification for belief in natural objects, the causal principle, demonstrative reasoning, and probabilistic reasoning. But unlike the ancient Pyrrhonians, Hume did not think that we could suspend judgment on these matters. Like Kemp Smith, he argues that nature compels us to have

beliefs of all sorts including beliefs about ultimate reality which, given the Pyrrhonian arguments, we know are not justified.[32]

The second major defect of the naturalist thesis is that it fails to see that Hume's use of psychological techniques is usually done with a logical goal. Penelhum argues that Hume's primary aims are psychological rather than philosophical:

> Hume's naturalism is a combination or mixture of philosophy and psychology, with the latter predominating. The skepticism is the main thrust of the epistemological part of the philosophical propaedeutic to his psychological account of the sources of our cognitive commitments. Its purpose is to show us that it is not because we have good epistemological reasons to do so that we make these commitments, since ordinary men do not have good reasons and philosophers have been unable to invent any.[33]

We must not hold Penelhum too closely to every word of his text. He did not have much space to argue his point. But it seems reasonable to contrast his position to the one we are arguing. It appears that psychology in Penelhum's comments just quoted here is equivalent to a basis for belief to the nonrational mechanisms stressed here. Also, it is true that Hume claims we do make commitments on things "men do not have good reasons" for. The problem comes with what Penelhum stated a few lines earlier: "Hume's primary aims are psychological rather than philosophical: that his complex and exciting arguments about the rationality of our beliefs are propaedeutic to a psychological examination of the sources of the cognitive and affective commitments our natures cause us to make." Nothing can be gained by a verbal dispute over what "psychological" and "philosophical" mean, but Penelhum seems to be wrong here. Hume is concerned throughout with the issue of the grounds for our beliefs. Hume's psychological approach involves the *reasons why* we may accept some doctrine rejected on a rational basis. It is true that custom, propensity, association, human nature, etc. are psychological mechanisms, but they are introduced in order to provide grounds for our beliefs. The "psychological" elements are used to explain our acceptance of the belief and *to justify* that acceptance. In so far as the psychological elements do that, they have a philosophical use, they are philosophical. If rational "reasons," the philosophical grounds, will not do, nonrational ones, the psychological factors, will serve to give us the basis for our beliefs.

The claim of naturalism fits well into the claim that this mechanism works as a fideism. Hume in the first *Enquiry*, despairing that considerations of reason will not support our ideas, retreats to the idea that the ideas can be accepted as correct and true because nature ensures it:

> This operation of the mind, by which we infer like effects from like causes, and vice versa, is so essential to the subsistence of all human creatures, it is not probable, that it could be trusted to the fallacious deductions of our

> reason .... It is more conformable to the ordinary wisdom of nature to secure so necessary an act of the mind, by some instinct or mechanical tendency, which may be infallible in its operations, may discover itself at the first appearance of life and thought, and may be independent of all the laboured deductions of the understanding. As nature has taught us the use of our limbs, without giving us the knowledge of the muscles and nerves, by which they are actuated; so has she implanted in us an instinct, which carries forward the thought in a correspondent course to that which she has established among external objects. (*Enquiry*, p. 55)

This is the thesis of naturalism—nature is the basis for belief not reason. What the naturalists have failed to see is the essential fideistic nature of this whole process. Natural propensities or tendencies are a nonrational basis which Hume accepts *after* his attempt and failure to find a rational basis.

Is all naturalism or reliance on common sense fideist? The answer has to be negative. Fideism has been historically, and is perhaps by its very nature, a response of despair and rational defeat. The general pattern of fideisms has been to resort to some mechanism or other, faith or other nonrational means, to secure the desired conclusion. Thus, after section IV of the *Enquiry,* "Sceptical Doubts concerning the Operations of the Understanding," Hume entitles Section V, "Sceptical Solution of These Doubts."

"Naturalism" is a general description of those mechanisms Hume uses to retain his conclusions, but it is only a partial account of what Hume is doing. To get the entire story we need to see Hume's essential fideism. Naturalism, in the view argued for in this book, is the particular resource Hume used to escape the confinement of reason.

A third mistake of the naturalist thesis is to regard Hume's nonrational mechanisms as a different sort of reason. This is not a universal view among those who subscribe to the naturalist viewpoint, but Capaldi for one describes them as "informal" reason in contrast to the formal reason which Hume attacked: "All accounts of even the informal rules are informal ... Hume stressed at the very beginning of the *Treatise* that the best we can hope for is the statement of what we find to be the most general rules."[34] Custom, habit, association, propensity, etc., however, are not anything of that kind. They are not cases of reasoning at all, but forces in our personalities which *supplant* reason. They are not different kinds, variant species of reasoning but substitutes for it, replacements of it. The nonrational mechanisms are not another way of going about reasoning to philosophical conclusions. Instead, they are by their very presence and use an abandonment of reason, an admission that reason is ineffective, an acceptance of rational defeat. They do the job of securing our conclusions for us in place of reason. It is an abandonment of the idea that we can understand things and provide answers through reason. We must give up on that and go about it in another way, the way of faith or human nature.

FAITH AND RATIONALITY

In this chapter we have claimed that fideism is a major force in Hume's philosophy. Since faith is the root concept of fideism, and questions of its relation to rationality constantly arise, a brief discussion of these two concepts seems imperative. To attempt to look at all the uses of "faith" is a bewildering task, consequently there is no claim here of giving an exhaustive treatment. Nevertheless, some understanding of the nature of faith is necessary to understand fideism.

The first, and least important, use of "faith" is as a substantive. It can refer to the set of one's religious beliefs when we talk of a person's faith. The term can refer to a religion when we talk of the Christian or Muslim faith. It can be used interchangeably with a branch of that religion when, for example, we talk of the "Catholic" (Roman Catholic) faith. Or we may speak of the Protestant faith. There is one thing in common in all these uses: There is something we can describe by telling what it is and is not, by listing its qualities, relations, dispositions, etc.—by using "faith" to refer to one of the world's abstract things.

We also can use "faith" to say "keep the faith," meaning to stick to what we set out to do whether it is religious or not. To "keep the faith" may have an almost entirely religious meaning when it means to hold to what is believed to be orthodox doctrine. Often the proposed task is entirely secular, such as a social revolution, an economic policy, or a vision for reform.[35] For the most part, however, substantive uses of "faith" help us little since they have no epistemic connection with the issues raised by fideism and rationality.

Psychological uses of "faith" occupy a substantial place in philosophical and theological literature. By "psychological uses" is meant the use of "faith" to designate some state of mind or emotion in the life of a person who is said to have that faith. These psychological states can be called that without attaching any prejudice to that description. There is no reason why someone's state of mind or consciousness should be thought better or worse simply because it is a state of consciousness. Psychological states may be healthy or pathological, but since states of consciousness are simply a part of the world, to describe them as "psychological" is not to assert anything pejorative. In Freudian theory faith is considered a form of neurosis, and wish fulfillment or projection is invoked to explain almost the whole of religious thought and behavior. Taking faith as a psychological state can enable us to understand people who say that they don't have much faith. They believe in God, i.e. they believe that God exists, but they do not feel very positive about it. They feel depressed or disheartened, and so they don't have much "faith": in their own lives there seems to be little effect from what they believe.

One instance of the psychological use of faith is to regard it as equivalent to confidence. Thus, when an employer has "faith" in his employee, he believes the employee will perform his job acceptably and will prove to be a valuable asset to the business. A wife may have "faith" in her husband, believing that he will keep his marriage vows to her. Such confidence may be well-founded or not, but the important thing is her feeling that he will not disappoint her in this respect. If we were asked how we know that someone we work with or count as a member of our family will not attack and kill us, we might say that we have "faith" in them. The question may never have occurred to us and we may never have thought about it, but after some reflection we agree that we *feel* that we have no reason to think that this person would ever do such a thing.

Faith also can have a psychological use equivalent to "believe in." To say that a person has faith in God is certainly to say that he believes there is a God. But to say "A believes that God exists" is not equivalent to "believing in" God, what Christians regard as having "saving" faith. Saving faith is a moral response to the Christian message, resulting in repentance and conversion or a turning from the former way of life with a change of life, attitudes, and feelings towards God (and others). To say "B believes in God" is also distinct from merely believing that God exists, because in our language it often carries the claim that B worships God: lives and thinks differently because of this belief than he would if he didn't have the belief at all.

Since the psychological use of "faith" conveys to us a state of some person's mind or emotion rather than a state of knowledge or belief, this widespread claim of faith does not help us very much in making up our own mind about these issues. These states give us no evidence or argument and do not carry any obvious claim to be the product of discursive or intuitive thinking. Such uses of "faith" do little to help or hinder the rest of mankind in their questions about what is true, good, right, or prudent. So, this use of the word is somewhat irrelevant for epistemology, except as it helps clarify the issues and implications of the use of language, and we must look to another use of "faith" to discover any relevance for those questions.

What is relevant for our purposes is the cognitive use of "faith." This very possibility is denied by some philosophers, but Christians of all stamps have claimed that faith was a *means* whereby they came to believe something (some propositional content) or to believe that such and such is or was the case. Or it was the means whereby they came to know God, to experience Him. In this use, then, faith is a kind of method of knowledge, a way coordinate with other methods such as rationalism, empiricism, intuition, or authority.

Such an understanding of faith involves freedom, some freedom, to believe. Faith must be the exercise of the capacity to believe in what is not proved or logically necessary, since it would see very odd not to believe what is logically or mathematically necessary. We accord no merit to people who believe what we can hardly help believing anyway. This may apply to what is self-evident as the axioms of geometry, tautologies of contemporary logic, or the laws of thought. Or it may apply to metaphysical doctrines such as the belief that all material things have dimension, no thought has a physical shape, or nonliving things have no consciousness. Since it is a regular thing not to exercise faith about things which are certain, the Christian religion characteristically considers belief in God and the creeds of Christendom to be morally praiseworthy.

But how can faith aid knowledge or belief as it is alleged to do? Many a believer has claimed that he is able to believe that God is interested in the small events of his life or that "the steps of a good man are ordered by the Lord,"[36] or that many things are so which other people find it hard to accept and cultic in outlook and expression. This does not daunt the believer because he believes these things "by faith." Faith is the aid or foundation upon which his belief is based, he claims, and because there is this faith, he has no difficulty in believing things which the external evidence at least at the moment would not appear to support.

Parallel to this we find similar claims made about "knowledge." According to William of Occam, for example, it is by faith alone that one finds certain (i.e. not probable) knowledge about God. The arguments of philosophy cannot prove certainly the existence of God because the God philosophers talk about is not the God of ordinary understanding or of Jews and Christians. The God of philosophers is the first conserving cause of this world without those philosophers having any certain knowledge about the nature of that cause. Perhaps that God can be proved, Occam thought, but the God of Christians, the absolutely supreme, perfect, unique, and infinite being cannot be philosophically proved. And since this is the only God Occam is interested in and regards as important we can say that God cannot be proved. Only faith can give us the certainty (certitude?) of God's existence.[37] Here Copleston remarks that from this it seems to follow as historians have argued, that theology and philosophy fall apart since it is not possible to prove the existence of the God whose revelation is accepted on faith. What Occam appears to have meant was that "since the premises of theological arguments are known by faith the conclusions too fall within that sphere."[38] In Occam, then, we have a case where the claim is made that knowledge and certainty about some things come by faith.

Luther is a good illustration of the position which claims that faith is a means to belief or knowledge. He had grave doubts about the ability of reason and philosophy to answer our inner questions. He railed at the empty, arid controversies of the schools which did not and could not benefit the individual who cries for reality and salvation. Faith is the solution, he claimed, for it alone can bring the self-authenticating authority the seeking individual needs, obviating the need for philosophy and bypassing the logic-chopping arguments of monks and scholars. If a person will submit to this faith it can bring the assurance needed to overcome doubt and the attacks of the devil. Faith alone can bring a certainty (and knowledge) beyond anything that reason (or philosophy) can possibly supply:

> When this Word enters the heart by true faith, it makes the heart as firm, sure, and certain as it is itself, so that the heart is unmoved, stubborn, and

hard in the face of every temptation, the devil, death, and anything whatever, boldly and proudly despising and mocking everything that spells doubt, fear, evil, and wrath.[39]

Such a view of faith has traditionally relied upon or used evidence and argument and to some degree "rests" on these things. It certainly did for Luther, for example. Kierkegaard, however, to give an extreme example, repudiates such a view of faith because it is not characterized by the agony, crisis, pain, and struggle of leaping to or adopting a belief. Many others concur with him, but traditionally most of the Christian communions have held that faith in Christ is warranted by historical facts, textual data, and experience and that a religious faith in other persons or things is not warranted. Faith in Christ is justified; faith in the stars or in my rabbit's foot is not. Faith may be a volitional exercise, but it involves a large element of intellectual activity and content. Faith accepts and expects more than the evidence warrants, but the evidence and arguments warrant the placing of faith in the object and then moving beyond that for which there is logical or epistemological justification. The opposite of this is the fideistic position which cuts faith loose from *all* these connections to operate by itself independent of any and all basis and warrant.

It is not a violation of good usage to speak of faith as warranting secular beliefs and convictions. While the main use and locus of faith has been in religion, it is not a violation of the "logic" of "faith" for it to be used of beliefs which we have not and perhaps cannot now rationally justify. This does not imply that there is no possible rational justification of such concepts but instead, that very few people have undertaken or been able to justify them. Penelhum comments on this use of "faith": "This is common, and it is harmless, and even healthy, if it serves to draw attention to the fact that these beliefs are held implicitly, and that even if they *have* philosophical justification, this is unknown to almost all who hold them, and is certainly not the cause of their being held."[40]

ATTITUDES AND APPROACHES TO RATIONALITY

Faith and religion have their perennial critics who press the claim of irrationality in religion. Such claims are accentuated by the presence of fideisms which tend to question and denigrate any rational procedures. Fideists often claim that human rationality is not sufficient and that it cannot but fail to fulfill not only the demands which religious knowledge and beliefs place upon it but secular beliefs as well. Consequently, a few words on rationality.

The nature of the rational, irrational, and nonrational is hotly contested, though we can understand them well enough on a common-sense level. If rationality has to do with thought and intellectual categories that meet the demands of logical procedure, evidence, and argument, we can define "irrational" as the opposite or contradictory of "rational." What violates rational states, procedures, or conclusions would be irrational. "Nonrational" refers to those things which are neither rational nor irrational but simply different in kind from either of these. Many things which affect our thinking and cognitive states are nonrational. Thus, feelings such as a pain, or a reaction to something we ate which did not agree with us, or a cramp in one of our muscles are nonrational. Involuntary reflex actions such as a knee jerk or a blink of our eye would be other cases. Urges such as the craving for sleep, food, or sex would not properly be rational nor irrational but nonrational. A neurosis would be a nonrational thing since such personality disturbances are not the sorts of things which can be rational or irrational. Acts or utterances resulting from a neurosis are often said to be irrational, however, since they violate or go against what a healthy person would be likely to do. They result in behavior "against reason."

In common usage the distinction between irrational and nonrational is not strictly observed and the two are generally conflated. We shall follow that policy here of linking irrational and nonrational together: whatever is not rational is irrational since *the effect of having either the nonrational or the irrational is the same. That appears to be Hume's policy.* He opposes habit, custom, propensity, association, a felt inclination of the mind, human nature, etc. to his rational analysis. In effect, then, the nonrational mechanisms in Hume's thought act against the conclusions of reason. Therefore, though they are in strict character nonrational, in effect they are equivalent to the irrational.

Philosophers display a broad tendency to assume answers to questions about the nature of rationality without seeing any need of elucidating the concept. Adjectives like "rational" or phrases like "rational argument," "rational conclusions," and the like, occur with great regularity in philosophical literature since philosophers as a group have been committed to clarity, reasonableness, truth, and validity. All of these concepts quickly come to the front when we ask questions about rationality. Although we have a rough and ready, intuitive idea of rationality, most of the time it is assumed in the pressure to get on with our work, and it ends up seldom being analyzed, so comparatively little has been written on the subject.[41] More philosophers have been exploring and writing on this topic in the past few years than were writing on the issues thirty years ago. Nevertheless, in comparison to other foundational concepts in philosophy there is a paucity of literature on rationality. Bernard Gert says:

> The concept of reason plays an extremely important part ... in philosophy. It also plays an important role in all the social sciences, particularly political science, sociology, and psychology. It is of crucial significance in psychiatry. It is therefore surprising that there has been relatively little work on this concept. Philosophers and others have generally used the concept of justification, as if these concepts were understood by all. But,

as it will become evident, these concepts are almost universally misunderstood. The general low esteem into which reason has fallen in many circles is due primarily to this misunderstanding.[42]

Philosophy journals abound in essays on rationalism, the method and outlook of Descartes and his followers. When we look for articles on the general concept of rationality, however, we find that the bulk of literature currently available on the topic concerns not philosophy, strictly speaking, but the social sciences. A perusal of *The Philosopher's Index* for the past forty years and particularly since about 1970 shows that the subject of rationality is a chief concern for anthropologists, sociologists, psychologists, and students of public policy. To the extent that these discussions focus upon epistemological concerns, questions of logic, apprehensions of reality, and the relation of one's world view to attitudes and acts, they are philosophical and hence we can understand their inclusion in journals devoted to philosophical discussion. In spite of that, there is a notable disappointment in much of the literature since so much of it focuses upon a particular rite of magic or some social customs which fail to include the generality and explanatory power which philosophical answers are meant to provide.

Rationality as generally treated in the social sciences does not help us very much because in these sciences the model of rationality is that of meaningful action, of purposefulness in the choice of means. It is mainly concerned with acts, and is, therefore, of little help in philosophy where not only acts but thought and reasoning or even emotions and valuations are a part of the concept.

Two areas within traditional philosophy have provided the main sparks of controversy over rationality, natural science and religion. Since the Enlightenment, science, particularly by those of a positivist bent, has been held to be the paradigm of rationality, but religion has been questioned and often dismissed as being irrational. We are not concerned here with a general investigation of rationality in religion, but Burke gives some good clarifications on the question:

> Whether religion is rational, then, will depend on what we mean by the question. In one sense it is never rational, in that its roots do not lie at all in the activity of reasoning, but in the experience of an imperative need. It does not draw its nourishment from theoretical considerations. It is not motivated by curiosity. From first to last it is practical. Its aim is not conceptual satisfaction, but salvation. A toothache may quickly become a concept, but before that it is an experience clamouring for action. The wellspring of religion is the experience that in some respect life is like a toothache. Let the philosopher try to understand man—the task of religion is to save him.
>
> In another sense religion is always rational, in that we assume there are always reasons for it. It has causes, and to the extent those causes are discovered, it can be understood. In this sense religion is rational the way

it is rational for a psychotic to shoot people. There is an explanation for it. That does not make it justifiable, only intelligible.

In a third sense religion is variously rational, depending on the extent to which it is pervaded by reflective thought.[43]

Burke holds that the reasonableness of a belief is not decided by its content but by its foundation.[44] A belief is reasonable when it is supported by adequate grounds, by the best evidence available, even though those two things are relative to the historical situation.

Richard Swinburne has given us the most carfully worked out and comprehensive examination of rationality in religious belief.[45] He gives five kinds of rationality based on probability, inductive standards of investigation, evidence, self-criticism of one's own rational standards, and external criticism. Swinburne's account has the great virtue of recognizing levels or qualities of rationality from minimal to ideal. Although several levels do not come up to to what Swinburne or others would hope for, they are still rational, because the conclusions are adopted on the basis of good reasons.

When we turn from religion to science we find many who have presented science as the paradigm case of rationality. It is claimed that the natural sciences are the single and final arbiter of what is rational or reasonable and even of what rationality is. This idea is current: Robert Jastrow recently remarked in an interview that scientists believe they have the only viable method of knowledge.[46] Among philosophers of science an extensive and frequently acrimonious debate between the logical positivist, Popperian, and Kuhnian models of scientific rationality has expended much thought and printer's ink since Popper published his *Logik der Forschung* in 1934.

The history of philosophy gives us many different models of rationality. Aristotle furnishes one of the earliest in his doctrine that man is a rational animal, that human beings possess the power or faculty of reason and the ability to exercise it: to grasp abstract ideas and hypotheses, to adopt or recognize ends, and to order acts and behavior so as to gain the greatest possible value. As such rationality is both a quality and a disposition of human life.

Philosophers have often urged too restrictive a model of rationality. Putnam believes that too little recognition has been given to "informal" rationality described by him as intelligence and common sense.[47] Informal rationality was necessary for the methodological maxims put forward by physical scientists and philosophers between the fifteenth and seventeenth centuries. Scientific method does exist, he believes, but it presupposes prior notions of rationality. It "is not a method *de novo* which can serve as the be all and end all, the very definition of rationality."[48] If this is the case, as Putnam claims, then our general philosophic conception of rationality is more important than the scientific model of rationality since it is both chronologically and logically prior to scientific rationality and determines many of its features. We would never be able to do the "rational" things we do without rationality already being in place.

So this leads us back to our philosophic or general standard of rationality: a viewpoint is held rationally when there is evidence, argument, or implications to support it, or evidence we believe supports it, and it is rejected rationally when the evidence or arguments (in all their variety and subtlety) support a negative conclusion. The same holds of a suspended judgment, when to the best of our ability to see, the arguments are inconclusive. There can be no general test or external criterion to determine when an argument supports or does not support a conclusion. There is no way of getting past human judgment about rationality, truth, and falsity even though all our logical rules, the tradition of philosophy, and the debates of our time are available for our help.

Our use of "rationality" involves the minimal concept of rationality, not a maximal one. Following the convention in much current epistemology, our use of the minimal concept of "rational" would be parallel to the use of the weak sense of "know": By the weak sense of "know" we refer to the ordinary but less demanding use of the word in which we know a proposition when it is true, when we believe it, and have good reason for believing it. This is in contrast to the strong sense of "know" which contains the condition that we have absolutely conclusive, irrefutable evidence for it.[49] The strong sense of "know" is often used in skeptical denials of knowledge, when we are able to make a perfectly convincing case using "know" in the weak sense. It appears that the weak sense of "rational" or weak conditions for "rationality" are entirely justified because it is the one which successfully guides us in all of life.

Our present concerns allow us to pass up many other interesting questions such as, Is rationality teleological? How should we adjust our model of rationality to deductive and inductive procedure respectively? What role does freedom play in rationality? How is rationality relative to external compulsions (like imprisonment) and internal ones (like chemical addiction)?, etc. A great many other valuable insights by current philosophers on this topic also can safely be left aside as we return to Hume's method and conclusions.

THE PLAN OF THE ARGUMENT

The claim that Hume's philosophy has fideistic elements or even is a genuine fideism will be argued in three steps. For the first step, the attempt will be made to show that Hume's conclusions in the philosophy of religion are fideistic. It will be argued that fideism, not skepticism is Hume's position on religious matters. This use of "fideism" as a description of Hume's position in the philosophy of religion is less debatable than the extension of that claim to other parts of Hume's writings since he does directly discuss the issues of faith, reason, skepticism, evidence for, and arguments against topics of religious significance, and because fideism has been understood as applicable to the issues and claims in religion. His conclusions follow the pattern of fideism because he appears finally to accept certain doctrines on the basis of faith which earlier he had argued against accepting. Thus, the claim of fideism there will be easier to support, will treat an issue which otherwise would continually intrude itself into the discussion, and will justify the attachment of fideism to Hume's other views.

The second step of the argument claims that the general position and method of fideism (or the more modest claim of fideistic elements) in Hume's philosophy can be seen in his metaphysical doctrines from an early period in his life when there was little indication of his views on religious doctrines and issues. This claim and its defense will be the heart of the book.

The third step of the argument consists of an examination of Hume's general statements about his method and conclusions. That chapter will show that Hume was dissatisfied with the nature of his philosophy, and though he persisted in it, he sought relief by resorting to such forces as habit, custom, propensity, association of ideas, a felt inclination of the mind, and human nature. All those nonrational means enabled him to recover the conclusions he had previously discarded through his philosophical analysis. The second part of the chapter follows out some conclusions of Richard Popkin which use different vocabulary and stress the influence of Hume's skeptical predecessors more than is done here. This brief review of Hume's precursors, and the philosophical influences which swayed him, claims that Hume followed a kind of pyrrhonism, the skeptical approach conveyed to us by Sextus Empiricus and then revived in the modern skeptical tradition. Hume attempted to escape from that sterile approach and dead end by giving human nature as a force which conquers the negations of reason and relieves him of his skeptical conclusions and inclinations. Hume argues that this involuntary influence saves us from the skeptical conclusions reason would leave for us. Popkin's historical treatment gives a slightly different approach than we get from an examination of Hume's writings, but one which agrees substantially with and reinforces the claim that Hume "recovered" his conclusions by nonrational or irrational means.

CHAPTER 3

HUME'S PHILOSOPHY OF RELIGION

The Introduction to Hume's *Natural History of Religion* begins with a statement we would not expect to find in Hume:

> As every enquiry, which regards Religion, is of the utmost importance, there are two questions in particular, which challenge our principal attention, to wit, that concerning its foundation in reason, and that concerning its origin in human nature. Happily, the first question, which is the most important, admits of the obvious, at least, the clearest solution. The whole frame of nature bespeaks an intelligent author; and no rational enquirer can, after serious reflexion, suspend his belief a moment with regard to the primary principles of genuine Theism and Religion. (*Nat.His.Rel.*, p. 25)[1]

Two surprising things can be seen in this citation. The first is that the opposition of reason and human nature occupies Hume's mind right at first in a document that is claimed to be an historical treatment of religion and not a philosophical treatment of it. We should not be surprised at his opposing reason and nature because it was an established part of Hume's view of things and so, of course, it is going to show up in any discussion about reality. And it continues to be an opposition to the very end. The *Dialogues concerning Natural Religion*, published posthumously, and the last publication of Hume's writing effort, turn on this prominent distinction.

The second thing is that Hume gives the teleological argument such a favorable comment. The remark is surprising because it does not fit in with the claim that Hume is a skeptic about religious questions. The claim that Hume is a skeptic holds that Hume rejected the teleological argument and was skeptical about the existence of God, the possibility of knowing about a divine being, whether analogies we can furnish could fit the uniqueness of God, and many other questions.

Few Hume scholars appear to have noticed this comment about the teleological argument and even fewer have taken it seriously. Hume's comment neatly focuses attention, however, on the split between one of Hume's responses and the near standard doctrine of Humean scholarship that Hume did not accept the teleological argument. The claim goes that since Hume believed the teleological argument is the best argument for the existence of God, and it cannot support belief in the existence of that being, it follows that if the best argument for God's existence has no value for supporting belief in that alleged fact, then, a fortiori, none of the inferior arguments have any value. Therefore, belief in God is not intellectually, i.e. rationally, justifiable.

Hume's comment from *The Natural History of Religion*, however, states the exact opposite of this conclusion and it seems that this would have caused careful scholars to ask whether their conclusions about Hume's views are justifiable on the basis of Hume's text. Such has not been done, however, at least not very widely. Consequently, this quotation from Hume focuses attention on the puzzling nature of Hume's beliefs especially as they have to do with his skeptical analysis in the *Dialogues concerning Natural Religion* and other places.

The goal of this chapter will be to show that the data of Hume's writings and the facts of Hume's life support the view that he was not a skeptic but something else instead. Skepticism is found in Hume's writings, but it is a preliminary skepticism, preliminary to a fideism on religious matters which follows upon his skepticism and supplants it. With respect to religious belief Hume follows a fideist pattern and not a final skepticism.

For that purpose, Hume's *Dialogues concerning Natural Religion* is the most important source because it is the largest work dedicated to questions about belief in the existence and nature of God. Since some of Hume's writings shorter than the *Dialogues* show the fideist orientation fairly well, I will stress them along with the *Dialogues*. These writings are "Of Miracles," Section X of the first *Enquiry*, and his posthumously published essays, "Of the Immortality of the Soul" and "Of Suicide."

The treatment of Hume's philosophy of religion given in this chapter is the first stage of a sustained argument on the claim that Hume was a fideist, that his skepticism is preliminary only and serves as a stimulus or prod to force him to seek a solution to the dead end or conceptual corner into which his atomistic, reductive empiricism had forced him.

HUME'S TREATMENT OF MIRACLES

Hume omitted the section on miracles when he published the *Treatise*. From his letters we learn that the original first part of the *Treatise* had a critical examination of the evidence for religious miracles, but in order to avoid the displeasure of Bishop Joseph Butler, a leading Anglican divine of the day, he removed this section from the book.[2] Hume later admitted this was "a piece of cowardice" and that he had "castrated the book of its nobler parts." Nine years later, however, he included this controversial section in his first *Enquiry*.

Section X, "Of Miracles," generated controversy; A. E. Taylor suggests that it may have been included precisely for that purpose.[3] Hume's desire for literary fame may have moved him to write as he did. Hume himself tells us that his desire for literary fame was a major preoccupation of his life: "Even my Love of literary Fame, my ruling Passion, never soured my humour, notwithstanding my frequent Disappointments."[4]

Randall claims that though Hume is the ablest British philosopher, Hume's "interest in philosophy was largely to startle Englishmen into recognizing the Scottish writer David Hume."[5] The importance of literary recognition in Hume's life can be seen in his response to the neglect of his *Treatise*. He was bitterly disappointed that the *Treatise*'s publication failed to bring him the fame and fortune he had hoped to receive: "Never literary attempt was more unfortunate than my Treatise of human Nature. It fell *dead-born from the Press*, without reaching such distinction, as even to excite a Murmur among the Zealots."[6]

It is perhaps not recognized often enough that Hume was a man of strong feelings and not given to moderation of expression. Many of his comments must be taken with a grain of salt because of his often seen penchant for drastic utterance. Mossner comments on Hume's stay in London in the late 1760s in connection to English and Scotch politics. John Wilkes had returned to London and the climate of the time brought forth an ongoing anti-Scotch attack. Hume was growing more and more short-tempered about the situation. Mossner says about this that,

> Hume had always held strong opinions on contemporary politics and had always expressed himself forcefully .... It is easy to say that he was becoming more conservative with age and more irascible with the continued onslaught against Scotland.[7]

These feelings were characteristic of more than Hume's political opinions. When we combine with this Hume's admitted thirst for notoriety and a desire for popular acclaim, we can see that the penchant for Hume was to be drastic, skeptical, shocking, and outrageous. We must keep these temperamental features of Hume in mind if we are to put his writings in perspective.

His reputation as an infidel, however, did not come from the *Treatise*. It was to the first *Enquiry* and some knowledge about his shorter essays that Hume owed his bad reputation among the orthodox Presbyterians of Scotland and the high Anglican churchmen of England. The *Dialogues* were not a factor in his reputation because they were not in print during Hume's lifetime. His Scotch clerical opponents to his candidacy for a faculty position at Edinburgh in 1745 accused him of "universal scepticism," but that was based on his metaphysical discussions in the *Treatise*. His opponents worried about his philosophic skepticism on important metaphysical doctrines such as the existence of substance, the existence of the human mind, and his denial of causation. His shorter essays such as "Of Suicide" and "Of the Immortality of the Soul" were published in the 1750s. A few copies were distributed, but the essays, especially the one on suicide, brought such violent protests from certain clergymen that they were prudently withdrawn from the market. Their wide circulation came only after Hume's death, so it is to the essay on miracles in addition to the perceived skepticism on other doctrines such as the existence of the human soul that Hume's reputation as a religious skeptic owed its foundation during Hume's lifetime. The essay on miracles, then, played a major part in the opposition Hume provoked among the orthodox, Scottish presbyterian clergy.

Taylor remarks that the entire section on miracles is superfluous to the purposes of the *Enquiry*, and he regards Hume's bad reputation as undeserved since he was not an anti-clerical zealot, but rather an amiable, easy-going man of the world whose chosen social circle consisted largely of the "moderates" among the Edinburgh Presbyterians.[8] These comfortable, socially prominent men regarded the Christian religion as the bulwark of social order, and they probably took Hume's attack on miracles to mean very much less than it meant on the face of it. Taylor believes that the essay would certainly not have destroyed the faith of the average Presbyterian of the eighteenth century though it should have left a thinking Presbyterian dissatisfied.

If the essay on miracles is superfluous to the argument of the first *Enquiry* as Taylor contends and the essay had originally been planned for the *Treatise*, as Hume tells us, where would it have gone? David Wootton has some instructive comments on this question. According to Wootton[9] it belonged in the *Treatise* at Book I, II, XIII, "Of unphilosophical probability." The last paragraphs of that chapter had prepared the way for the discussion of miracles since the emphasis was on probability theory. Indeed, says Wootton, probability lay at the heart of the *Treatise* and it was in connection with probability that Hume discussed causation. The subject of miracles is a subject which philosophically educated persons would have expected there. After all, miracles are singular incidents whose cause the faithful claim to be able to identify. With all these factors present, Hume's decision to leave out that section may have avoided a controversy with Bishop Butler, but it also removed from the *Treatise* a section which would no doubt have attracted considerable attention and have saved the *Treatise* from being "*dead-born from the press.*" If "Of miracles" had been in the *Treatise*, it surely would have excited "a Murmur among the Zealots."[10]

How does Hume conceive of a miracle? Hume's emphasis lies on the epistemological issue of the attestation of miracles and less upon their character. Nevertheless, he gives in bits and pieces a description of miracles. For an event to be a miracle, it has to be an unusual event, a happening which varies from the regular, expected pattern of things. Ordinary events are regular, but in contrast to these, a miracle has to be an extraordinary and marvelous event, an "irregular" event. (*Enquiry*, pp. 115, 117-118) Being unusual, however, is not enough to pronounce it a miracle for all sorts of unexpected things happen, and these unexpected things can range from a surprise reaction from one of our pets to the flaring of a supernova. Neither of these are miraculous, however, because we presume that our pet has the power of responding and initiating some actions.

Supernovae are considered natural events even though they are not completely understood, and so the close study they are accorded is in line with the view that they are natural processes. Hume remarks that June weather ought to be better than December weather, but it may not be. This irregularity is not a miracle, however. (*Enquiry*, p. 110)

So being unusual is not enough for Hume: A miracle for Hume has to be a violation of a natural law, that is, an event inconsistent with a natural law. Such natural laws or descriptive statements of regularity in the world tell what will happen under certain conditions. If under the conditions the law-like statement encompasses an event occurred which was a positive counter-instance to the prediction of the law, we would have such a violation. Since laws are statements of uniform experience, a miracle would be something that has never occurred in any age or country. (*Enquiry*, p. 115)

How, then, would anyone be able to claim this unusual, law-violating event is a miracle? The answer seems to be that the claimant got an *impression* of that nature since any idea ultimately must be founded on impressions, ideas being the faint images of impressions in thinking and reasoning. (*Treatise*, p. 1) But what is the impression like? Apparently it is here that we have to stop: Hume does not discuss that issue since it is probably not possible to tell what an impression is. "Those perceptions which enter with most force and violence [upon the mind], we may name impressions." (*Treatise*, p. 1) Impressions being primitive sorts of things defy analysis, so we can talk about impressions, state that they exist, link them with our appropriate senses, but we cannot tell what they are since they are not examinable. Hume states that the claim of miracles runs upon against the firm and unalterable experience of human experience, of sensory impressions, so the affirmation of a miracle is prima facie questionable.

Last, the extraordinary event laws must be traceable to the Deity (in a monotheistic religion or a deity in polytheistic ones). Hume does not deal with miracles in pantheistic-type religions like Hinduism or atheistic ones like Jainism or historic Buddhism. Such religions did not compel much interest or attention in eighteenth-century Europe, and probably Hume knew very little about them. Even miracles as those reported of the Emperor Vespasian were due to Serapis and miracles in the Christian religion to God. Without the presence or association of the deity (whether real or alleged) there could not be a miracle. So, its supernatural origin would be both its necessary and sufficient conditions for that would make both its extraordinary and unnatural character possible. Thus he defines a miracle as "a violation of the laws of nature." (*Enquiry*, p. 114) Since all the agents we know are visible, the invisibility of the agent carries a presumption of the presence of God since angels who might also be agents receive no recognition from Hume. If the cause were angels, however, they would still be "supernatural."

The essay itself starts with Archbishop Tillotson's proposition that the evidential value of other people's testimony (considered merely as testimony) is always inferior to the testimony of our own senses. Tillotson had used the argument against the Catholic doctrine of transubstantiation, which the Anglicans rejected. Hume takes the argument as a blow against Old and New Testament miracles because the evidence for them by those who testified of them must diminish in coming from them to us, and because the evidence of our senses is that miracles do not happen.

Hume's essay contains many different arguments which are carefully delineated by such writers as Taylor; retracing each step of the argument is unnecessary but several major points need to be dealt with. The first one is that "A wise man ... proportions his belief to the evidence." (*Enquiry*, p. 110) This means, presumably, that he will count the number of instances in which there is a conjunction of events. Some events are found in experience to be "constantly conjoined"; other conjunctions are more variable. This is Hume's doctrine that there is no "necessary connection" between events. All events are separate, and there is nothing in the character of an event which demands that it should be related in one way rather than in another. Since that is so, it is necessary to determine when the conjunction of the kind in question has occurred, and the number of instances in which one member of the conjoined pair of events has occurred without being continued by the other. The wise man will base his judgment on the probability of the alleged event. Hume judges that if the fact which the testimony endeavors to establish partakes of the extraordinary and the marvelous, then the evidence resulting from the testimony admits of a diminution, greater or less, in proportion as the fact is more or less unusual. And so, Hume implies, miracles must be rejected.

Hume's next major move is to define a miracle as a violation of the laws of nature. (*Enquiry*, p. 114) So this "is one case in which the value of testimony is not merely diminished by the 'conflict of experiences,' but actually reduced to zero."[11] There are several self-contradictory features about this definition, as for example, how we can rule out something for which people, often many of them, claim experience, when experience is the foundation of all our knowledge.

Hume's main idea is that miracles simply do not happen because our experience is uniformly against them. He adds a lengthy footnote which may show that he is a little uneasy about the procedure he used here, and in that footnote he defines miracle again as "*a transgression of a law of nature by a particular volition of the Deity, or by the interposition of some invisible agent.*" (*Enquiry*, p. 115) Nevertheless, Hume stays with his conclusion:

> And as a uniform experience amounts to a proof, there is here a direct and full *proof*, from the nature of the fact, against the existence of any miracle; nor can such a proof be destroyed, or the miracle rendered credible, but by an opposite proof, which is superior.

> The plain consequence is (and it is a general maxim worthy of our attention), 'That no testimony is sufficient to establish a miracle, unless the testimony be of such a kind, that its falsehood would be more miraculous, than the fact, which it endeavours to establish; and even in that case there is a mutual destruction of arguments, and the superior only gives us an assurance suitable to that degree of force, which remains, after deducting the inferior.' (*Enquiry*, pp. 115-116)

Hume gives the second part of his essay to the testimony about miracles which have come from so many ages, religions, and cultures. He attempts to show that no kind of testimony would be adequate because questions about the ability, integrity, intellectual adequacy, etc. of such people cannot be taken seriously. Consequently there cannot have been any miracles, or more accurately,

> no testimony for any kind of miracle has ever amounted to a probability, much less to a proof; and that, even supposing it amounted to a proof, it would be opposed by another proof; derived from the very nature of the fact, which it would endeavour to establish. It is experience only, which gives authority to human testimony; and it is the same experience, which assures us of the laws of nature. When, therefore, these two kinds of experience are contrary, we have nothing to do but substract [*sic*] the one from the other, and embrace an opinion, either on one side or the other, with that assurance which arises from the remainder. But according to the principle here explained, this substraction, with regard to all popular religions, amounts to an entire annihilation; and therefore we may establish it as a maxim, that no human testimony can have such force as to prove a miracle, and make it a just foundation for any such system of religion. (*Enquiry*, p. 127)

So, miracles simply cannot be attested. Furthermore, from the standpoint of Hume's view of the looseness and separateness of events in a world which (at least as revealed to us in experience) has no metaphysical structure, there is no more reason to believe in Newtonian science than there is to believe in miracles since the world is but a series of free and disconnected incidents. Taylor gives a very perspicuous exposition of this part of Hume's logic[12] and concludes that Hume's essay is thus an attack not so much on the credibility of miracles as on the validity of induction.

Why did Hume write such an essay? If the tenth section of the first *Enquiry* is as irrelevant to the argument of that book as Taylor claims that it is, then we must question why a man of Hume's brilliance would include such a thing. He may have wanted to vent his feeling someplace, but why here in a document which was meant to be a more readable version of the *Treatise* and so calculated to have a greater appeal and influence on the literate public? Did he so regret excluding this material from the *Treatise* that he had to include it here?

A part of the answer appears to be that Hume desired literary recognition (even notoriety) and this essay would surely rouse many people. Another reason must appeal to the superstition abroad in Hume's age. It is hard for us, conditioned as we have been by the scientific tradition to remember that the pre-scientific mentality was prevalent in Hume's day. The scientific world-view first emerged as a factor in the popular consciousness during the eighteenth century when the Newtonian synthesis was ready for the popularizers. Popularizing a scientific view of the world among hard-working but uneducated people took a long time, and it was from the "vulgar" that Hume must have observed a great deal of superstition and a susceptibility to stories of the latest "miracle" at shrine A and all the wonder-mongering which opportunistic clergy appeared ready to exploit. Hume did not believe such stories, and with his Protestant reserve about accepting any current miracles, he was willing to do battle against those hucksters of wonder.

This leads us to a third reason: Protestants were anxious to challenge any miracles except those which they believed supported the existence and authority of divine revelation claimed to reside in Old and New Testaments. Samuel Clarke, the Protestant, expressed this viewpoint when he defined a miracle as

> a work effected in a manner unusual or different from the common and regular method of Providence either of God Himself, or some intelligent agent superior to man, in the proof of evidence of some particular doctrine or in attestation to the authority of some particular person. And if a miracle so worked be not opposed by some plainly superior power nor be brought to attest to a doctrine either contradictory in itself or vicious in its consequences--a doctrine of which kind no miracles in the world can be sufficient to prove--then the doctrine so attested must necessarily be looked upon as Divine, and the worker of the miracle entertained as having infallibly a commission from God.[13]

The Protestant reformers opposed "popish" miracles and tried to drive them from the world, because they were regarded as a species of blasphemy on the part of those who stand for false doctrines and a corrupted form of the Christian religion. The proper understanding of miracles, according to those reformers, is that the original ones recorded in the Old and New Testaments were genuine. They were credentials and attestations of new revelation. The history of Old Testament times reports several revelatory epochs and the New Testament one which ended with the apostles, but after the revelatory epochs ended, then miracles ended too since there was no further use for them, the Scriptures having the encapsulated, propositional revelation of God. John Calvin's tract against relics[14] was an unsparing assault upon the popular miracle-mongering and superstition of much of the church of his time. His list of the carloads of wood from the cross, jugs of wine from the wedding feast at Cana, fake bones of the Christian apostles and martyrs, etc., etc., which is an ever-dependent source of guffaws and entertainment, suggests the milieu against which Hume reacted. Hume naturally came by his adversion to miracles from his protestant background. We must not forget this confessional influence on Hume.

Hume's essay, "Of Miracles," seems to attack prophecies as well as miracles with no quarter given, for prophecies too are genuine ("real") miracles, and no miracles either are possible or can be believed. Readers of Hume's essay who come to this conclusion about Hume's intent very early in the essay find some remarks very different from these at the end of essay. He says:

> I am the better pleased with the method of reasoning here delivered, as I think it may serve to confound those dangerous friends or disguised enemies to the *Christian Religion*, who have undertaken to defend it by the principles of human reason. Our most holy religion is founded on *Faith*, not on reason; and it is a sure method of exposing it to put it to such a trial as it is, by no means, fitted to endure. (*Enquiry*, pp. 129-30)

The question of Hume's own beliefs will fit better into the examination of the *Dialogues concerning Natural Religion*. It can be said here, however, that Hume, though not orthodox, was not an atheist in the modern sense. He himself denied that he was the unbeliever people thought he was and affirmed that he held beliefs much more like those of other people than was commonly understood.[15] Curiously, some of the people who knew Hume took this quite seriously and held an optimistic view of Hume's religious views, and tended to discount some of the things which he said. In our time the tendency is to take Hume's words with a heavy pinch of salt!

Hume carried an animosity to a climate of "free-floating" miracles, but more decisive was his suspicion of natural theology. Even if the degree of dependability were dropped to that of probability, Hume was still not satisfied. Reason, he thought, is not adequate to penetrate the mysteries of the divine nature, because religious claims, as matters of fact, cannot be solved by mere thought without the presence of empirical data. Hume repeatedly emphasized the claim that philosophy cannot give conclusive evidence but that he who has faith can accept what the claims of reason cannot give. Exposition of this point will have to wait until later in the chapter.

In section XII of the first *Enquiry*, Hume talks about the "havoc" which his principles must make when applied to any volume of divinity or school metaphysics. He tells us that if it contains no abstract reasonings concerning quantity or number (relations of ideas) or if it contains no experimental reasonings (empirical data) concerning matters of fact, then it must be consigned to the flames for it can contain nothing but sophistry and illusion. Defense of the reality and significance of miracles as things belonging to "matters of fact and existence" cannot, then, be a problem for abstract reasoning, because reason has little to do with miracles. Nor can the existence of miracles be a question of empirical evidence since that has been ruled out by Hume. So there is no reason to believe in their reality at all.

Noxon gives the "standard" interpretation of this essay, that "Hume assailed the stronghold of Christianity, Revelation, by arguing that no miracle can be a fit object of a rational man's belief."[16] Religious beliefs are spurious, and there is no explaining Christian belief outside of insincerity or temporary or chronic localized insanity. Hume alternated between these two hypotheses and eventually fused his hypothesis of hypocrisy and delusion into a theory of self-deception.

Noxon fails to notice the last paragraph of the essay on miracles, however:

> So that, upon the whole, we may conclude, that the Christian Religion not only was at first attended with miracles, but even at this day cannot be believed by any reasonable person without one. Mere reason is insufficient to convince us of its veracity: And whoever is moved by *Faith* to assent to it, is conscious of a continued miracle in his own person, which subverts all the principles of the understanding, and gives him a determination to believe what is most contrary to custom and experience. (*Enquiry*, p. 131)

And Gaskin does the same thing.[17]

Gaskin, the most thorough author on Hume's philosophy of religion, fails to say anything about Hume's phrases in the opening paragraph of the section on miracles. Hume summarizes Tillotson's words ("The apostles ... were eyewitnesses to those miracles of our Saviour by which he proved his divine mission") without any attempt to soften or change them. Nor does Gaskin deal with the last paragraph in the essay beyond extracting the words about a miracle which will subvert "all the principles of his understanding." He gives a summary of Hume as saying that:

> A reasonable man can have a non-natural belief which goes beyond the evidence and may not be due to general pathological [*sic*] causes of the sort Hume examines in the *Natural History of Religion*. But the belief will exist alongside, rather than as part of, the rational man. It will subvert 'all the principles of his understanding' and be brought home to him 'by the immediate operation of the Holy Spirit': an operation which Hume ironically describes as 'a continued miracle'. Another such irrational oddity confirmed by a suspect revelation is belief in personal immortality.[18]

Why is there no change in Hume's use of Tillotson's words? Can we account for all this as "irony"? Or as "irrational oddity"? If Hume is so opposed to miracles, then what about these words? They are a part of the text too. It looks as if these words have to be treated the way Gaskin treats them because the conviction was arrived at previously that Hume is a skeptic which means he could not have accepted the historical reality of any of the miracles or of predictive prophecy. Since that view was settled on long ago, then we have to adequately handle the text to preserve that interpretation. If, however, this interpretation is not able to handle Hume's words as adequately as a good interpretation should do, then perhaps a more comprehensive interpretation or understanding of Hume is in order. That is precisely why the fideist interpretation is adopted here. Does that make Hume a Christian? No, and the discussion of that question is deferred to another place, but what is in order here is to raise the question of the skeptical understanding of Hume. The fideist interpretation of Hume's philosophy of religion goes against much of the "orthodoxy" of traditional Hume scholarship which has forced us into interpretations which tend to overlook or to explain away many of Hume's surprising statements.

The last paragraph in Hume's essay on miracles is not consistent with the skeptical interpretation. Nor is the skeptical interpretation consistent with similar paragraphs in the *Dialogues* and the essay on immortality. The abandonment of evidence in this paragraph and the substitution of faith as a way of saving the conclusion is precisely an example of what fideism is, so the claim made here is that Hume is not rejecting the existence or the reality of miracles, at least the biblical ones, but is saying that reason (with the use of logic, etc.) cannot suffice for the matter. What can suffice is faith, but not a faith of the type that Samuel Clarke or Joseph Butler advocated, based upon evidence and argument, but a faith which abandons argument and exercises itself anyway. It has to be a faith we just adopt and hold fast.

Hume clearly expresses this approach in section XII of the *Enquiry*:

> Divinity or Theology, as it proves the existence of a Deity, and the immortality of souls is composed partly of reasonings concerning particular, partly concerning general facts. It has a foundation in reason, so far as it is supported by experience. But its best and most solid foundation is faith and divine revelation. (*Enquiry*, p. 165)

It is significant that this statement of general position appears only a few pages from the chapter on miracles. "Of Miracles" seems to illustrate Hume's approach: religious matters of whatever kind cannot depend upon reason. They rest instead on faith, a faith which is not joined to reason. Other works by Hume also amplify and illustrate this fideistic pattern.

HUME AND THE COMPOSITION OF THE *DIALOGUES*

Hume worked on the *Dialogues* for many years. He liked the novelty of the dialogue form and carefully refined it to avoid its peculiar pitfalls. Hume began the *Dialogues* in 1751, completed them by 1757, revised them in 1761, and when his health began to fail in 1775, they became the chief preoccupation of his declining energies. This work, then, is the mature, deliberate effort to deal with the problems he perceived in natural theology.

Many writers believe the youthful influences of Hume's Scottish Calvinism were quickly shed; after that, religion was brought to his attention not by his own personal needs and convictions but by the prominence it assumed in the lives of other people. This is the rather negative assessment of Norman Kemp Smith.[19] Nevertheless, whether as a philosopher or historian, Hume was moved by speculative thought upon religion and seemed almost compulsively driven to react to it. He seems unable to leave the matter alone. Hume does not seem to have had that consciousness of sin, that sense of personal alienation from God, so characteristic of Calvinist Christianity, and so far as can be seen did not himself enter into the Calvinist experience of personal conversion. Presbyterian orthodoxy of Hume's time was severe and stressed the darker side of human experience. Calvin's teaching appeared in a distorted and exaggerated form in the ecclesiastical tradition of the Scottish church and apparently had its part in prompting Hume's reactions to Scottish orthodoxy.

After Hume published the *Enquiry* and gained notoriety for his attack upon miracles, providence, and the possibility of a future state, he suffered many attacks by members of the Scottish clergy and became known as "the great infidel." He was gratified in one respect by some of these attacks because at least it meant that he was being read and that his books were selling. Hume informs us that his friends and confidants warned him against publishing certain things and recommended that he leave them out for his own good. He often failed to heed that advice. Early in the 1750s, for example, he published "Of Suicide" and "Of the Immortality of the Soul." Protests launched by leading clergymen against these essays, especially the one on suicide, were a major factor in Hume's 1752 defeat in his attempt to gain a Glasgow professorship. This was his second attempt, the first one being his loss of an opportunity for a professorship at Edinburgh in 1745. Hume's *Dialogues* continue Hume's reputation as a religious skeptic, but they were not the reasons for his reputation as an unbeliever and detractor of Christianity during his life time.

The first relevant consideration for the meaning and intent of Hume's *Dialogues* comes from the preface where Pamphilus says that the dialogue will be on natural religion (natural theology) not revealed religion (dogmatic theology). The *Dialogues*, then, is a conscious treatment of the doctrines and problems of religious philosophy, not of theology, and however much he may have wanted to counter some of the objectional theological views he had heard in church, his focus remains always on his disdain of religious philosophy.

Students of the *Dialogues* have frequently pointed to the similarity of Hume's work to Cicero's *De Natura Deorum*. Hume borrowed from this work much more than merely the dialogue form. Kemp Smith[20] gives the correlation: The three protagonists in Cicero's dialogue are Cotta the Academic or the Skeptic,

Balbus the Stoic who represents orthodoxy, and Velleius the Epicurean. In Hume's *Dialogues* Philo corresponds to Cotta, and Cleanthes to Balbus.

Cicero prefaced his dialogue with an introduction in which he anticipates objections to the free discussion of so sacred a subject. Though he himself had learned from Philo (Cotta's teacher) to be an Academic, that is, to be sure (certain) of nothing, he is present at the discussion only as an auditor with an impartial and unbiased mind. Cicero favors the orthodox teaching though not the argument in its favor and then concludes with words which are apparently the ones Hume used as a pattern for the words of Pamphilus. Hume modifies these words in a manner which enables him to preserve his anonymity and invents the character of Pamphilus especially for the purpose of reporting the discussion and of passing judgment upon the parts played by the three main characters. There is added, then, the mystery of how to interpret the dialogue since Hume did not permit his own views to be directly identified anywhere in the dialogue.

Pamphilus characterized the three antagonists by opposing "the accurate philosophical turn of Cleanthes" to "the careless skepticism of Philo" and both of these to "the rigid inflexible orthodoxy of Demea." Thus there is an indication that Cleanthes may be the "hero" of the *Dialogues*. Smith suggests the problem of interpretation is largely the question of how Hume's intention is to be understood. Is Hume using this device to obscure his intentions further? Is Hume playing and setting up his readers for the full brunt of his satire and irony? Does Hume mean what Pamphilus says at the conclusion of the *Dialogues* that "I cannot but think that Philo's principles are more probable than Demea's; but that those of Cleanthes approach still nearer to the truth"?

Smith concludes that Hume's own teaching is not presented through any one of the characters but is developed throughout the argument as elements of his own beliefs are put into the mouths of all three disputants.[21] Gaskin takes almost the same view: "I shall take it that Hume in the *Dialogues* is any speaker who appears to be making a good philosophical point."[22] This helps some, but it does not untie the knot because we don't know in a particular case exactly who is talking for Hume. Each protagonist says things with which the others agree and to which they would subscribe, yet at other times each one excludes one of the others by something he says or by the "tone" in which he speaks. Smith believes that when they agree, the position is Hume's but when they disagree, it is very difficult to know who represents Hume.

Beginning with Dugald Stewart and continuing to our time, there have been those who believe that Hume's position is represented by Cleanthes and that the final comment of Pamphilus about Cleanthes' position is Hume's. In recent decades the consensus among many philosophers about Stewart's conclusion has been somewhat more guarded, but it still stands.[23] Richard H. Popkin is the most prominent recent holder of this position.[24]

Smith is unable to accept that reading of the *Dialogues*. Although he gives the blanket statement about how all the speakers may represent Hume, he does not stick with that. For Kemp Smith, from start to finish, Philo represents Hume, and Cleanthes can be regarded as Hume's mouthpiece only in those passages in which he is explicitly agreeing with Philo, or in those other passages in which while refuting Demea, he is also being used to prepare the way for one or other of Philo's independent conclusions.[25]

Gaskin gives the most recent discussion of the literature on the issue of who speaks for Hume in the *Dialogues*.[26] He takes Kemp Smith's views for the most part, that Philo speaks for Hume and give a number of additional points which tend to confirm, he believes, Kemp Smith's thesis.[27] The most recent opponent of that claim is James Noxon.[28] Gaskin goes through Noxon's argument point by point and shows that in his opinion the points do not apply, fall short, or are plain mistaken. The final conclusion for Gaskin is that Philo represents Hume.[29] The astonishing thing about Gaskin's position, which is a part of contemporary "orthodoxy" on Hume, is that he never seriously deals with Philo's surprising and contradictory remarks in Part XII of the *Dialogues*. Gaskin seems unable to imagine that Hume could be illustrating here the fideist position.

THE MEANING OF "GOD" FOR HUME

Since the *Dialogues* center on issues about God and especially about the existence of God, it is well to ask, what did Hume mean by "God"? "God" in Hume's *Dialogues* means the existent, personal, supreme being who created the world. There is no indication whatever that the God Hume is considering is anything different than the God of Christian theology and piety whether this is traditional theism or the then-current Deism. The God of Hume's reasoning is not some diverse deity of another religion than Christianity.

Let's look at some of the evidence for these claims. Part XII of the *Dialogues* gives in short compass the conclusions of Hume on God's nature. Demea has left and Philo, the most likely spokesman for Hume, gives his conclusions here in a form which though a part of the dialogue is very nearly a monologue, a perfect device to convey one's views. Is Hume doing that?

This deity is a mind or intelligence, that is, an immaterial, "spiritual" or nonphysical being: "We can properly call him a *mind* or *intelligence* ...." (*Dialogues*, p. 217) The deity bears some resemblance to human beings:

> And here I must also acknowledge, *Cleanthes*, that, as the works of Nature have a much greater analogy to the effects of *our* art and contrivance than to those of *our* benevolence and justice; we have reason to infer that the natural attributes of the Deity have a greater resemblance to those of men than his moral have to human virtues. But what is the consequence? Nothing but this, that the moral qualities of man are more defec-

tive in their kind than his natural abilities. For, as the Supreme Being is allowed to be absolutely and entirely perfect, whatever differs most from him departs the farthest from the supreme standard of rectitude and perfection. (*Dialogues*, p. 219)

This, then, is an informal statement of the doctrine of the *Imago Dei*, that man is made in God's "image."

Philo says: "The existence of a DEITY is plainly ascertained by reason." (*Dialogues*, p. 217) Again: "Supposing there were a God who did not discover himself immediately to our senses, were is possible for him to give stronger proofs of his existence than what appear on the whole face of nature?" (*Dialogues*, p. 215) So God is an existing being.

Cleanthes advocates a "genuine theism": "The most agreeable reflection which is possible for human imagination to suggest is that of genuine theism, which represents us as the workmanship of a Being perfectly good, wise, and powerful; who created us for happiness; and who, having implanted in us immeasurable desires of good, will prolong our existence to all eternity, and will transfer us into an infinite variety of scenes, in order to satisfy those desires and render our felicity complete and durable." (*Dialogues*, p. 224) Philo describes these comments from Cleanthes as "most engaging and alluring; and, with regard to the true philosopher, they are more than appearances." Does Philo represent the "true philosopher"? That may be difficult to determine, but if Philo represents Hume's position better than Cleanthes does, as many philosophers contend, then perhaps this may be taken to show that Hume subscribed to some kind of theism.

Hume had little sympathy with the inadequate "theology" of the vulgar, but appears to indicate that he could accept the God of "philosophical theists" (*Dialogues*, p. 226) who had a suitable view of God's divine perfections. This again falls back on the assumption that Philo is a principle spokesman for Hume's opinions and beliefs. Whoever the Humean scholar may be, it seems agreeable that Philo has good claim to represent Hume's position. Cleanthes and Pamphilus may speak for Hume too, but it is unlikely that any Hume scholar would deny that Philo best and most consistently represents Hume's position. *This requires, of course, that when Philo speaks positively that his positive expressions be allowed as those of Hume just as it is claimed that the negative or skeptical views which Philo expresses in the first eleven books are those of Hume.* This proviso is frequently violated: Philosophers who regard Hume as a skeptic appear to be very willing to quote the skeptical passages, but they either overlook or tend to explain away the passages where Philo appears to express many definite, traditional beliefs of Judeo-Christian theism. Gaskin realizes that we must not let our preconceptions mislead us: "We should beware of so relying upon Hume's irony that we read an often repeated declaration as an often repeated denial, especially when such anecdotes as there are seem to give some backing to a non-ironical reading of the declarations I have just quoted."[30]

Ironically, on the very next page Gaskin illustrates that very bias he warns us about. He says, "So my contention is that Hume gives some sort of genuine assent to the proposition *that there is a god*. This assent that 'lyes in the middle' is between deism and atheism."[31] "Atheism" here is probably radical skepticism or the atheism of the French *philosophes*, whose radical rejection of theism shocked and repelled Hume. And "deism" is probably without need of being defined here. But why the two ends of deism and atheism? Why not have theism as the other end opposite atheism? Or, why can't "lyes in the middle" be between "vulgar" superstition and the respectable civil religion of many of Hume's Edinburgh colleagues? Or, was it in the middle between "papist" superstition and Calvinist protestant suspicions of the supercharged world of freely-occurring miracles? Has Gaskin thought in terms of deism so long that he cannot entertain the idea that it is possible Hume may have been a theist?

Can it be claimed that Hume was a deist? He lived in a deistic age and it would not be surprising to find that Hume shared the freethinker's view of God. It seems clear that he was not an atheist in our contemporary sense of that word. Though he was called a skeptic by his enemies and detractors, Hume never seems to have been called an atheist by his opponents. This may be due to their care with words since they were men of letters. The contemporary distinction between "atheist" and "agnostic" had not yet been made, but "atheists" of Hume's time agreed with theists as to the meaning of "God" though they denied or questioned His existence.

If any of the figures of the *Dialogues*, except Demea, speak for Hume, it would appear that he could have held either to a minimal theism or a deism since deism agreed with theism except on the issues of divine immanence, special revelation, providence, and miracles, matters which are not touched upon in the Dialogues. Hume's mouthpieces speak in such a way that it is hard to deny Hume's belief in God. Many a Hume scholar would claim there is little difference between deism and a "truncated" theism, so the issue is really academic.

It is also possible that Hume does not give us his own views either directly or indirectly. The dialogue style is admirably suited to the task of exploring a topic without disclosing the writer's position. The characters in the *Dialogues* share the traditional, Christian view of God as a supernatural, eternal being. It is that kind of God about whose existence they are discussing the reasons for belief or doubt. So far as the characters of the *Dialogues* are concerned, Hume could have been either a minimal theist or a deist since the existence and nature of God which seems to be supported by the *Dialogues* would fit either position. If Hume did believe some miracles were possible, then Hume's position could better be described as a minimal theism, but if he was merely using the dialogue form as a way of evading the statement of his own personal views on God, then we have no way of knowing what he believed about God. It will be necessary to look at Hume's essay on immortality and to look at some other details of his life before further evidence can be given that Hume was a "minimal" theist.

AN ASSESSMENT OF THE *DIALOGUES*: THEIR EXTERNAL BACKGROUND

A careful examination of the argument, the portrayal of the figures, and a taking of Hume's words at anything near face value suggest fideism to be a more coherent conclusion of Hume's approach than is skepticism, or any other interpretation. The *Dialogues* seem to be critical of religious beliefs or propositions of the Christian faith and are aimed at their destruction. These beliefs represented natural theology not revealed theology, and they were aimed at organized religion, and the assemblage of clergy with all who supported them as agents of authority and "tyranny." Is this a product of Hume's craving for literary fame? Or is this due to Hume's inclination to shock and unsettle people? Or is he merely playing with his readers? However benign Hume's disposition might be as Adam Smith has described him, he enjoyed shocking and upsetting people especially if they belonged to he conservative, traditional, orthodox party. No conclusions about Hume's own beliefs and his purposes in writing the *Dialogues* appear adequate unless these tendencies of our philosopher are taken seriously.

Europe's religion was Christianity, at least "above" ground, for there was the persistent presence of witchcraft in the middle ages, but it was "below" ground or lay hidden from the eyes of religious authorities and casual observers. So "religion" meant Christianity which was viewed by many enlightenment free-thinkers as the product of barbarism and superstition. In that view, it had arisen in the ancient world and had dominated and characterized the dark ages which lay between that time and ours. During the enlightenment medieval times were almost invariably viewed as equivalent to the "dark ages" which we now understand to encompass the fifth to the ninth centuries. In Hume's day, the modern practice of dividing the history into ancient, medieval, and modern ages had not yet come into vogue. There were only two ages, the ancient and modern. The Christian religion was the product of the former and now for about three centuries educated, literate men had been living a divided life. Intellectually they possessed the new scientific world view, but in their emotional life were still ruled by the "superstitions" and authorities of the earlier era. Hume, Gibbon, etc. felt that the pre-renaissance Christian centuries were "dark" ages, in which religion and reason did violence to one another and tried to form an emulsion of incompatible elements. According to this viewpoint the time had now come for men to take responsibility for their own beliefs and destiny. European man had come of age even though other peoples in the world were still groping in darkness and dependence, and religion had to be thrown off as a kind of disease or affliction.

According to Hume, religion arose in polytheism. It was impossible that men got their religions by reasoning on the frame of nature because after worshipping one God as the cause of the world they could not have embraced idolatry. (*Nat.His.Rel.*, pp. 26-28) The reasoning which at first produced "so magnificent an opinion" must have been able to preserve it since the first invention and proof of any doctrine is infinitely more difficult than the supporting and retaining it. Hume seems to have embraced the idea of religious evolution and to have regarded the idea of religious degeneracy as impossible:

> It seems certain, that, according to the natural progress of human thought, the ignorant multitude must first entertain some groveling and familiar notion of superior powers, before they stretch their conception to that perfect being, who bestowed order on the whole frame of nature. We may as reasonably imagine, that men inhabited palaces before huts and cottages, or studied geometry before agriculture; as assert that the deity appeared to them a pure spirit, omniscient, omnipotent, and omnipresent, before he was apprehended to be a powerful, tho' limited being, with human passions and appetites, limbs and organs. The mind rises gradually, from inferior to superior: By abstracting from what is imperfect, it forms an idea of perfection: And slowly distinguishing the nobler parts of its frame from the grosser, it learns to transfer only the former, much elevated and refined, to its divinity. Nothing could disturb this natural progress of thought, but some obvious and invincible argument, which might immediately lead the mind into the pure principles of theism, and make it overleap, at one bound, the vast interval, which is interposed betwixt the human and the divine nature. But tho' I allow, that the order and frame of the universe, when accurately examined, affords such an argument; yet I can never think that this consideration could have an influence on mankind when they formed their first, rude notions of religion. (*Nat.His.Rel.*, p. 27)

Although Europe's religion is Christianity and is decisively theistic even in its popular forms, this has not been an unqualified advantage according to Hume, for Christianity has been the source of three great evils:[32]

1. When God is conceived as single and universal, unity of object calls for unity of faith and ceremony and so furnishes designing men with a pretence for discharging on each other that sacred zeal combined with rancor which is the most furious and implacable of all human passions. Hume's Scotland had many places, prisons, and churches which were living reminders of the harsh conflicts between Catholics and Protestants, and the history of the Inquisition was well known all over Europe. This tendency towards intolerance is aggravated by the character of modern religion which inspects our whole conduct and prescribes universal rules to our actions, words, thoughts, and inclinations.
2. The gods of other religions, superior to men by only a small degree, put men at ease in addressing and emulating them, Hume contends, but modern religion which exalts God as infinitely superior to mankind is apt especially when joined with supernatural terrors to sink the mind into such abasement

that only the monkish virtues of mortification, penance, humility, and passive suffering are acceptable to the Deity. This contrasts sharply, Hume believes, with the activity, courage, magnanimity, love of liberty, and all the other virtues which aggrandize a people.

3. Closest to the argument of this book is Hume's third claim, that Christianity has perverted reason from its true and proper function. Philosophical argument could play but little part in the pagan theologies because the traditional mythology put the gods and their acts on a plain of equality. Religion and philosophy, being so different and being unable to affect each other had to tolerate each other. They made a fair partition of mankind between them. Philosophy catered for the needs of the learned and wise, religion for the no less rightful needs of the simple and illiterate. When we come to the Christian centuries, however, we find a sacred book which with its comparatively consistent teaching is so drilled into people by their early education that when they become speculative reasoners they continue in their assent to it. But how unequal the yoke between religion and philosophy turns out to be. Instead of philosophy regulating theology, as they advance together, she is at every turn perverted to serve the purposes of superstition. Reason is drawn into the cause of drawing the logical consequences of dogmas, but over the dogmas reason has no control at all.

Hume continues his diatribe against organized religion by claiming that when any question arises as to this pattern, reproach always falls on reason. Modern religion, thus, is "fanatical," "intolerant," "grotesque," "scholastic." The last term carries the most opprobrium since anything medieval was the synonym of ignorance, superstition, and oppression. This brief sampling of Hume's criticisms of religion focuses on organized religion with its clerical rank, doctrinal rigidity, and moral authority. Hume also had many scathing criticisms to offer of popular religion as he found it in Scotland, so whether official or popular, religion to Hume appeared to be both destructive and contemptible.

Hume claimed that he had no desire to offend religion. There are many passages in Hume where he says something to derogatory to religion (Christianity) and then gives what we have here in the section on the immateriality of the soul:

> 'Tis certainly a kind of indignity to philosophy, whose sovereign authority ought every where to be acknowledg'd, to oblige her on every occasion to make apologies for her conclusions, and justify herself to every particular art and science, which may be offended at her. This puts one in mind of a king arrain'd for high-treason against his subjects. There is only one occasion, when philosophy will think it necessary and even honourable to justify herself, and that is, when religion may seem to be in the least offended; whose rights are as dear to her as her own, and are indeed the same. If any one, therefore, shou'd imagine that the foregoing arguments are any ways dangerous to religion, I hope the following apology will remove his apprehensions. (*Treatise*, p. 250)

Hume then goes on to explain that his arguments against the immateriality of the soul do not hurt but actually help religion:

> 'Tis an evident principle *that whatever we can imagine, is possible.* Now this is no more true of matter, than of spirit; of an extended compounded substance, than of a simple and unextended. In both cases the metaphysical argument for the immortality of the soul are equally inconclusive; and in both cases the moral arguments and those deriv'd from the analogy of nature are equally strong and convincing. If my philosophy, therefore, makes no addition to the arguments for religion, I have at least the satisfaction to think it takes nothing from them, but that every thing remains precisely as before. (*Treatise*, pp. 250-251)

Should we take this seriously? The *Treatise* as a "youthful" book does not appear to be very conciliatory. Hume had not yet run into the Warburtons or John Browns of Scotland and England and seems to have carried the notion that everyone would welcome his book with open arms and that he would be granted that public approbation in the realm of letters which he so craved. This is why the "stillborn" advent of the first edition of the *Treatise* was so painful to him—little could he have imagined that its publication meant so little to the very people he wanted to influence. Second, Hume shows little awareness of how the learned public might take his skepticism and "atheism." Perhaps that can explain his intention to publish the section on miracles in the *Treatise* and decided against it only on the insistent advice of his friends. It is true that he did not want to offend Joseph Butler, but the only change this seems to have brought about was the exclusion of the one chapter on miracles. There does not seem to be any good reason for not taking this comment seriously. It is one more small indication that Hume was not the aggressive unbeliever and skeptic many scholars have made him out to be. There is the possibility that Hume was simply playing politics, and there is no reason why we should think him to be above such things.

Perhaps many of the things Hume mentioned and which have embarrassed Christians result from the lack of the separation of Church and State. When the two are joined so that the business of one becomes the business of the other, a peculiar kind of oppression and hypocrisy often develops. This point is recognized in the *Dialogues* where in Part XII Cleanthes replies to Philo:

> The reason of this observation, replied *Cleanthes*, is obvious. The proper office of religion is to regulate the hearts of men, humanize their conduct, infuse the spirit of temperance, order, and obedience; and as its operation is silent and only enforces the motives of morality and justice, it is in danger of being overlooked and confounded with these other motives. When it distinguishes itself, and acts as a separate principle over men, it has departed from its proper sphere and has become only a cover to faction and ambition. (*Dialogues*, p. 220)

Philo a short time later argues for a needed separation between the religious and political orders:

> Is there any maxim in politics more certain and infallible than that both the number and authority of priests should be confined within very narrow limits, and that the civil magistrate ought, for ever, to keep his *fasces* and *axes* from such dangerous hands? But if the spirit of popular religion were so salutary to society, a contrary maxim ought to prevail. The greater number of priests and their greater authority and riches will always augment the religious spirit. And though the priests have the guidance of this spirit, why may we not expect a superior sanctity of life and greater benevolence and moderation from persons who are set apart for religion, who are continually inculcating it upon others, and who must themselves imbibe a greater saving game of it, and to prevent their pernicious consequences with regard to society? Every expedient which he tries for so humble a purpose is surrounded with inconveniences. If he admits only one religion among his subjects, he must sacrifice, to an uncertain prospect of tranquillity, every consideration of public liberty, science, reason, industry, and even his own independence. If he gives indulgence to several sects, which is the wiser maxim, he must preserve a very philosophical indifference to all of them and carefully restrain the pretensions of the prevailing sect; otherwise he can expect nothing but endless disputes, quarrels, factions, persecutions, and civil commotions. (*Dialogues*, p. 223)

Such commotions have been aggravated by the tendency of the church since late medieval times to claim a position superior to that of the state since the church represents God whose kingdom is above any earthly kingdom. Since the state becomes the "secular arm" of the church and thus an instrument of the divine kingdom in this world, the church's interests and concerns are paramount to all others. Such potential for tyranny has since been lessened due to the horrendous effects of the wars of religion, the terrors of the Inquisition, the rise and consolidation of national states, the separation of church and state into mutually exclusive spheres, and such influences as Locke's teaching on toleration, etc. Hume did not suffer the worst consequences of such a religio-political order, and he was able to write what he did because he did not live in a Catholic country, such as Spain or Italy, where this philosophy was explicit and aggressive. Hume lived in a relatively free and benign culture; however, the residual effects of the Calvinist divinely-sanctioned moral authoritarianism were still felt.

Hume also strongly disliked popular religion. The Scottish Presbyterian Church was a great public church after the model of Ernst Troeltsch and as such was a broad and necessarily latitudinarian entity. Such churches had to include every person in the community in their influence since there was no other church for these people to turn to. And following Calvin's "Ordinances for the

Supervision of Churches"[33] the churches felt that they had a responsibility to require people to attend divine services since their spiritual (that, religious) needs could only be met thereby.

Calvin's rules were for the government of Geneva, but they tended to become models for Calvinistic churches in other lands, and, we may assume that Hume would not have been ignorant of them and of the influence they exerted among the Presbyterian Church of Scotland. The relationship of such ecclesiastical practices with popular Christianity is that when everyone is required to belong to the church, the matter of individual conformity to the ideals of that ecclesiastical body have to be relaxed. In Calvinistic lands, the populace often were dragooned into "virtue." Virtue being what it is, however, cannot be coerced, and an outward conformity often masks an inward nonconformity.

When everyone is a Christian, then the question centers not on whether A is a Christian or not, but on whether A is a "good" Christian or not. A good Christian is one whose confession and behavior conforms to the Christian ideals so that A is a credit to the Church and to God's name. In free churches, that is, in churches where membership is voluntary, the question tends to be whether someone is a Christian or not a Christian. The issue of whether a person is a "good" Christian would not apply, for in such churches those who are not "good" Christians are usually not considered Christians at all. If a "real," that is, a practicing Christian commits moral lapses in a free church, he stands to be disciplined or released as a member. In state churches and broad, inclusivist churches, some people are and some people are not "good" Christians. Since Scotland had an inclusivist church, Hume would tend to see many nominal and inconsistent people whose religious beliefs were slipshod and hypocritical. Part of the vigor of Hume's attacks can be understood better if this tendency of people in public churches is kept in mind.

Some of the inconsistent behavior was alleviated by the Calvinist doctrine of conversion, but there still was a tendency for hypocrisy to take place since it was advantageous to be a Christian and disadvantageous not to be. Social acceptance and financial advantages depended in part on a person's attendance, confession, and conformity.

Advocates of the separation of church and state point out that when the church is supported by public money and its position is rendered secure, that there is generally a corresponding let down on the part of its members. Why worry when the church has always been there and will always be there, when the government will assist in building new buildings and in keeping the existing ones in good repair? Such situations tend to diminish the individual's sense of responsibility and motivation for involvement in church life. Kierkegaard describes such a situation in nineteenth century Denmark, and John Wesley in Hume's own time vividly remembered the fox-hunting parsons who occupied parishes in England. While Wesley's father, Samuel, was a hard working pastor and carried out his duties in a conscientious way, there were many who did not.

So, for these and other reasons, Hume disliked popular religion. Superstition and fanaticism were its twin diseases, and part of those things by which such religion betrayed its unnatural character. Hume disliked "enthusiasm" and it is likely that Philo speaks for Hume when he says that "in proportion to my veneration for true religion is my abhorrence of vulgar superstitions; and I indulge a peculiar pleasure, I confess, in pushing such principles sometimes into absurdity, sometimes into impiety." (*Dialogues*, p. 219) Kemp Smith holds that if Hume had had to choose between the two types of religion, his choice would have been for the superstitious type not the fanatical, and preferably in its pagan rather than in its Christian variants.[34] Smith reminds us, though, that Hume is not speaking of Greek and Roman religions with nostalgia but is indirectly expressing his distaste for religion as he knew it in his time. Hume talks about "true religion" but he nowhere specifies what that is. Perhaps he expected his readers to know what he thought by leaving out of "true" religion all the things he criticized and felt to be pernicious and destructive.

Hume's reaction to popular and organized religion, that is to the Scottish Presbyterianism which he knew is perhaps best understood in the context of a general reaction to a religious or theological "atmosphere." Geddes MacGregor describes his own experience which may suggest a parallel to Hume's own religious orientation:

> I have never found it difficult, in principle, to be a skeptic, and in the presence of those who seem able to talk as glibly about religion as one talks about breakfast .... In ... a "seminary climate," the vivacity of my skepticism knows no bounds. As soon as I am involved in the whirligig of slick theological chatter, my first reaction (and often my last) is to rebel by every means at my disposal ... the pastime of satirizing theological slickness is open to the same moral objection as bullfighting: however you look at it, it is a cruel sport, for you are up against a ferocious, blind force.
>
> On the other hand, fifteen minutes with even a stuttering, let alone a loquacious, positivist is enough to make me want to get up and sing "Onward, Christian Soldiers." Conversation with positivists and atheists is, indeed, the most effective doubt-killer I know. Whenever I find my faith to be in danger of flagging, I have no difficulty in discovering how to revitalize it. All I have to do is to hunt up an atheist acquaintance and ask him to be kind enough to deliver an attack on theism. If he would care to include a specific attack on the Christian faith, so much the better. In the intense egocentricity of the atheistic personality I unfailingly discover the most telling argument for theism.[35]

It is always risky to engage in psychological digging, but MacGregor's description of his experience and reactions may provide some insight into the mind of David Hume and his reactions. Divine services in Hume's day in Scotland were generally about three hours long. The service included a "lecture" as well as the sermon, and each might be an hour long. (At the same time in England, Bishop Butler was preaching two-hour-long sermons in the Rolls chapel.) In the sermon the tradition of Scottish Presbyterianism required the preacher to cover the essential points of Calvist theology: The Fall, man's present helpless and sinful condition, redemption through Christ, the Mediator, the future of the elect and and the reprobate, and practical applications and exhortations. Hume, therefore, as a boy must have known very well the points of Scottish orthodoxy.

AN ASSESSMENT OF THE *DIALOGUES*: NORMAN KEMP SMITH'S VIEWS AS A TYPICAL INTERPRETATION

To return directly to the *Dialogues*: Hume's letter to Gilbert Elliot states that he made Cleanthes the hero of the *Dialogues*.[36] Join to this Pamphilus' statement: "I confess that, upon a serious review of the whole, I cannot but think that Philo's principles are more probable than Demea's but that those of Cleanthes approach still nearer to the truth." (*Dialogues*, p. 228) Demea's position, then, does not seem to be Hume's for Demea appears to represent popular, unreflective, superstitious religion, the religion of the commoners. Hume had little respect for the "vulgar," the common people, who seldom if ever are swayed by reason. Demea serves to add dramatic interest, to support the skeptic, Philo, and to keep the reader in suspense as to how it is all going to turn out:

> Even at this day, and in Europe, ask any of the vulgar, why he believes in an omnipotent creator of the world; he will never mention the beauty of final causes, of which he is wholly ignorant: He will not hold out his hand, and bid you contemplate the suppleness and variety of joints in his fingers, their bending all one way, the counterpoise which they receive from the thumb, the softness and fleshy parts of the inside of his hand, with all the other circumstances, which render that member fit for the use to which it was destined. To these he has been long accustomed; and he beholds them with listlessness and unconcern. He will tell you of the sudden and unexpected death of such a one: The fall and bruise of such another: The excessive drought of this season: The cold and rains of another. These he ascribes to the immediate operation of providence: And such events, as with good reasoners, are the chief difficulties in admitting a supreme intelligence, are with him the sole arguments for it. (*Nat.His.Rel.*, p. 50)

> We may conclude, therefore, upon the whole, that since the vulgar, in nations, which have embraced the doctrine of theism, still build it upon irrational and superstitious opinions, they are never led into that opinion by any process of argument, but by a certain train of thinking, more suitable to their genius and capacity. (*Nat.His.Rel.*, p. 51)

Assuming that Hume's depreciation for the religion of the common people precludes Demea from being his spokesman, which one of the other two disputants represents Hume? Philo and Cleanthes both appear to be possibilities, but though Cleanthes may qualify as that person, not many philosophers have accepted or even entertained the possibility that Cleanthes fills that role. Cleanthes is presented in the *Dialogues* as the hero and as a possible spokesman for Hume's views, but such claims are not very convincing, and have not had very many advocates among those who turned their attention to the *Dialogues*.

Kemp Smith claims that Philo really represents Hume[37] because Cleanthes is unable to meet Philo's sallies despite Hume's devices to make Cleanthes' arguments appear as strong as possible. In Kemp Smith's view, although Cleanthes is the hero at least for the narrator of the *Dialogues*, it is through Philo, not through Cleanthes, that Hume's personal views are being conveyed. For if Hume's purpose is to show the insufficiency of the argument from design, he must avoid making the argument of Philo so one sided that the dramatic interest of the dialogue is destroyed. To prevent this, Hume has given to Cleanthes and Demea a larger share in the dialogue than their arguments could rightly claim. Demea's views are discredited by their extremities and by the obvious difficulties in which he lands himself, but a counter policy is followed with Cleanthes. He is granted compliments he does not deserve, and the reader is led to think that he has stronger arguments in reserve than those he has so far employed. When the reader comes to realize that Cleanthes is being played with, Hume goes out of his way to conceal the full force of Philo's attack.

There are difficulties with this view: First, throughout Hume's writings the consistent position intellectually is not always the one which Hume himself accepts. Hume accepted conclusions which reason could not support. Second, Hume's fideism depends upon the practice of presenting views which, it is claimed, cannot stand the full examination of reason. Calling Hume a skeptic is plausible, for skepticism is an initial stage for fideists who then accept conclusions on nonrational or irrational grounds. The acceptance of some viewpoint because it is intellectually compelling or rationally consistent would be the very abandonment of fideism. Fideism accepts what intellectual means will not and cannot provide. Third, from one way of looking at it, skeptics have an easier time than those who seek to avoid skepticism. It is easier to ask questions than it is to answer them, to raise suspicions about the possibility of error than it is to show that no errors have been made, to press for a standard of rationality which no one can live by than to show the mistake of demanding such an unattainable standard. Cleanthes accuses Philo of this:

> I must confess, *Philo*, replied *Cleanthes*, that, of all men living, the task which you have undertaken, of raising doubts and objections, suits you best and seems, in a manner, natural and unavoidable to you. So great is your fertility of invention that I am not ashamed to acknowledge myself unable,

on a sudden, to solve regularly such out-of-the-way difficulties as you incessantly start upon me; though I clearly see, in general, their fallacy and error. And I question not, but you are yourself, at present, in the same case, and have not the solution so ready as the objection; while you must be sensible that common sense and reason are entirely against you, and that such whimsies as you have delivered may puzzle but never can convince us. (*Dialogues*, p. 181)

Smith points out that Philo emerges as the winner at the end of Part X and announces that it is so: "Here, *Cleanthes*, I find myself at ease in my argument. Here I triumph." (*Dialogues*, p. 201) So, at the end of Part X Philo triumphs and in the two remaining parts he dominates the argument. "Parts XI and XII are practically monologues placed in the mouth of Philo."[38] How then can Cleanthes in any way be declared the "hero" of the dialogue when Hume makes Philo dominate the last part of the book? The answer has two parts: The first is that in a fideism the skeptic has to win to provide the occasion for the fideistic solution. The second is that Philo changes his stance from skeptic to advocate.

Let's take those in order. In any fideist approach the skeptic is *always* the winner, always unanswerable in whole or in part. Were that not so, there would be no need for a fideism nor any appeal to it. The appeal of a fideism is that it "short circuits" the whole rational approach and makes it unnecessary to meet the skeptic's arguments. Fideism saves the skeptic's opponent a lot of work. He can admit the skeptic's position, but he feels no need to answer his arguments. The fideist needs only to assert his conclusion on some basis which misses the skeptical objection. In that sense, then, Smith's conclusion, that Hume is a genuine skeptic, is consistent with the claim that Hume is not a skeptic but a fideist instead. And the claim that Hume is a fideist can account for Pamphilus' judgment about Cleanthes (and the other two disputants) at the end of the *Dialogues* and for the other small concessions to natural theology made in the *Dialogues* better than Smith can. Demea's anti-intellectual position is not adequate because it cannot face up to the issues. So, fideism is a more coherent explanation of the whole dialogue than is skepticism.

The second part of the answer to the question of how Cleanthes can be declared the hero of the dialogue involves Philo's change of speech. Near the end of the dialogue, Philo changes his approach. The last paragraph of Part X signals the change, and at the beginning of Part XI Cleanthes indicates that he is willing to hear what Philo has to say: "You, Philo, ... I would gladly hear, at length, without interruption, your opinion of this new theory; and if it deserve our attention, we may afterwards, at more leisure, reduce it into form."

The characterization of Philo near the end of Part XI of the *Dialogues* is consistent with the portraits we have of Hume. Here Demea protests that Philo has changed his position to agree more with Cleanthes. Cleanthes responds with surprise and annoyance:

> And are you so late in perceiving it? replied *Cleanthes*. Believe me, *Demea*, your friend *Philo*, from the beginning, has been amusing himself at both our expense; and it must be confessed that the injudicious reasoning of our vulgar theology has given him but too just a handle of ridicule. The total infirmity of human reason, the absolute incomprehensibility of the divine nature, the great and universal misery, and still greater wickedness of men; these are strange topics, surely, to be so fondly cherished by orthodox divines and doctors. In ages of stupidity and ignorance, indeed, these principles may safely be espoused; and perhaps no views of things are more proper to promote superstition than such as encourage the blind amazement, the diffidence, and melancholy of mankind. But at present .... (*Dialogues*, p. 213)

Hume loved to taunt the orthodox and to play the infidel.

At the end of part X of the *Dialogues* Philo says to Cleanthes, "It is your turn now to tug the laboring oar and to support your philosophical subtilties against the dictates of plain reason and experience." Cleanthes does *not* proceed "to tug the laboring oar," however. Instead, he retires into the background and with a few mild protests allows the case to become Philo's by default. Cleanthes does not look like Hume's hero in this situation!

Those who believe Hume is and remained a skeptic on all the matters of religion and natural theology find that this part of the *Dialogues* takes "a very strange and indeed bewildering turn."[39] Philo starts out at the beginning of part XI as the skeptic of the previous parts. He asks what a person who had been informed that the world was the production of a very good, wise, powerful being would expect to find in the world. The answer is that he would be disappointed at the "workmanship" though he would not retract his belief in the existence of God. And then Philo poses the other case: what of a person who came into the world not antecedently convinced of the existence of a supremely intelligent, benevolent, and powerful being and who is left to draw his conclusions from the appearances of things? Philo concludes that such a person would never find any reason for the conclusion that there is a God like the one he has been describing. (*Dialogues*, pp. 204-205)

Philo then gives a four-point theodicy explaining that evil can be understood so that the hypothesis of a good and wise creator becomes a possibility. In one paragraph Philo takes three stances: first he seems to agree with Cleanthes:

> What then shall we pronounce on this occasion? Shall we say that these circumstances are not necessary, and that they might easily have been altered in the contrivance of the universe? This decision seems too presumptuous for creatures so blind and ignorant. Let us be more modest in our conclusions. Let us allow that, if the goodness of the Deity (I mean a goodness like the human) could be established on any tolerable reasons *a priori*, these phenomena, however untoward, would not be sufficient to

subvert that principle, but might easily in some unknown manner, be reconcilable to it.

Then he reverts to skepticism:

> But let us still assert that, as this goodness is not antecedently established but must be inferred from the phenomena, there can be no grounds for such an inference while there are so many ills in the universe, and while these ills might so easily have been remedied, as far as human understanding can be allowed to judge on such a subject. I am skeptic enough to allow that the bad appearances, notwithstanding all my reasonings, may be compatible with such attributes as you suppose; but surely they can never prove these attributes. (*Dialogues*, pp. 210-211)

And then he goes back to natural theology: "Such a conclusion cannot result from skepticism, but must arise from the phenomena, and from our confidence in the reasoning which we deduce from these phenomena." (*Dialogues*, pp. 210-211) A short time later while still keeping up the facade of the bold, perspicuous skeptic, Philo proves to be very surprising by finally embracing what Cleanthes, his opponent, has been arguing for all along:

> So long as there is any vice at all in the universe, it will very much puzzle you anthropomorphites how to account for it. You must assign a cause for it, without having recourse to the first cause. But as every effect must have a cause, and that cause another, you must either carry on the progression ad infinitum, or rest on that original principle, who is the ultimate cause of all things .... (*Dialogues*, p. 212)

This prompts Demea's protest that this is a departure from the principles of reasoning (or the questioning of them) for which Demea had joined forces with Philo, and at the end of part XI of the *Dialogues*, Demea departs from the discussion with a sense of disappointment and frustration.

From the beginning of part XII, the final section of the *Dialogues*, Philo almost completely takes the position which Cleanthes has been arguing. He does not come over entirely to Cleanthes' position, because wherever there is any disagreement between Cleanthes and Philo, Philo will invariably take the more negative and less orthodox position. But despite these differences, Philo finishes with a position so different from the one espoused throughout as the "skeptic" one that it is very surprising.

What can be said of Kemp Smith's position as an example of the standard "skeptic" interpretation of Hume? Has his expectations that Hume would turn out to be a consistent skeptic ill prepared him to understand what Hume does late in the *Dialogues*? Smith finds the central problem in holding his view to be Philo's remark at the beginning of Part XII:

You are sensible that, notwithstanding the freedom of my conversation and my love of singular arguments, no one has a deeper sense of religion impressed on his mind, or pays more profound adoration to the Divine Being, as he discovers himself to reason in the inexplicable contrivance and artifice of nature. A purpose, an intention, a design strikes everywhere the most careless, the most stupid thinker; and no man can be so hardened in absurd systems as at all times to reject it. (*Dialogues*, p. 214)

Smith is puzzled by much of what transpires after Philo declares himself to be the victor, and he discusses parts XI and XII at length: "Obviously the argument has taken a very strange and indeed bewildering turn."[40] After Cleanthes is given the chance "to tug the labouring oar," Philo begins to take positions on final causes and declares that his arguments had been mere cavils and sophisms. Kemp Smith adds that it is here that the case is made by those commentators who find that Cleanthes and not Philo is Hume's mouthpiece. Kemp Smith believes, however, that the whole thing is more "artful" than it appears at first sight, for Philo says to Cleanthes that "no one has a deeper sense of religion impressed on his mind" than he does "or pays more profound adoration to the Divine Being." Then Philo adds the phrase "as he discovers himself to reason" in order to point out that "the Deity thus revealed is not be equated with the God of religion; and so to withdraw nearly all he has seemed to allow."[41] His recital of the views of Galen about the remarkable nature of the muscles and bones in the human body "while in the spirit of Cleanthes' teaching, parodies his own."[42] This is done "with mischievous intent."[43] When Philo says that suspense of judgment is not possible, Smith takes the long paragraph about verbal disputes and the necessity of carefully defining our terms and clarifying the issues added by Hume in the final revisions made in 1776, to be evidence of the emphasis on the "negative and quite general character of Philo's conclusions."[44]

There are several difficulties with Smith's interpretation of the last two parts and especially with part XII. First: Why should we not take Philo's words seriously in part XII, as Smith intimates, when we took them seriously in the earlier parts of the *Dialogues*? Any interpretation of this writing, it seems, should give equal weight to the parts which fit the hypothesis and to those which do not. Our interpretation should fit the text we have and not the other way around. Kemp Smith's writings seem to have a *Tendenz* due to his settling on a hypothesis which is not as coherent as it should be. Second, the phrase "as he [the Deity] discovers himself to reason" is not necessarily a way of withdrawing nearly all Philo has seemed to allow because the topic of conversation is natural theology, not ordinary religion (that is, European official and popular Christianity). Why not take Philo's words in their plain and ordinary sense? If we do, then Philo is saying that no one is more reverent than he is or worships the Deity who reveals Himself in nature more genuinely than he does. There is a concession here to natural theology—surprising only if we are not prepared to receive it.

And why should the recital of Galen's views be with "mischievous intent"? Hume already has had Demea object and take leave of the conversation at the end of part XI because Philo seemed to be allowing some value to natural theology. Hume does not tell us, his readers, just what place all these things have in his dramatic intent. He was very conscious of the pitfalls of the dialogue form, and he sought to avoid these. Awareness of this literary purpose should serve to make us careful about what Hume may do. In addition to these considerations, let me propose that these very large changes in Philo's account may lie in another purpose Hume doesn't immediately make clear: a fideistic purpose. Finally, the footnote which Hume added in 1776 need not be taken to add to Philo's negative conclusions. The footnote is taken to belong to Philo's position because it carries the tone of a dialogue speaker and there is no reason to refer the note to anyone else—unless it is Hume's. Price regards the note as a part of the text on the grounds that Hume, in preparing a final draft of the *Dialogues*, was conscious of the incongruity of a discursive note in a dialogue.[45] That view seems perfectly defensible to me. But back to Philo's negative conclusions: They illustrate good theological and philosophical method and reflect the feeling of all disciplined and trained minds when in the presence of loquacious people who are careless, untrained, and intellectually insensitive. This part of Smith's discussion is the weakest part his work on the *Dialogues* and appears to be due to an interpretation he cannot consistently defend.

What can be "consistently defended" is that Hume follows this strategy in the *Dialogues*: Philo gives all the reasons why a person cannot accept the conclusions of natural theology as presented by the orthodox. The problems are so great that they preclude belief for a multitude of reasons. Hume then has Philo, the apostle of skepticism, heal over the whole thing and recover what the skeptical position had given up. *This is the classic style of fideisms*, and here Hume plays it to the hilt. He even generates the dramatic interest of Demea's protest and departure over a position and a group of answers which his anti-intellectualism would not allow. The skeptic brings up all his objections, weighty as they are, and then at the end, he confesses his beliefs in spite of the objections. It is this that Smith misses.

We may protest that fideism is not intellectual self-consistent, but it is entirely consistent with the fideist approach to religious questions that the "skeptic," Philo, would finish with these words:

> But believe me, *Cleanthes*, the most natural sentiment which a well-disposed mind will feel on this occasion is a longing desire and expectation that heaven would be pleased to dissipate, at least alleviate, this profound ignorance by affording some more particular revelation to mankind, and making discoveries of the nature, attributes, and operations of the divine object of our faith. A person, seasoned with a just sense of the imperfections of natural reason, will fly to revealed truth with the greatest

avidity: While the haughty dogmatist, persuaded that he can erect a complete system of theology by the mere help of philosophy, disdains any further aid and rejects this adventitious instructor. To be a philosophical skeptic is, in a man of letters, the first and most essential step towards being a sound, believing Christian. (*Dialogues*, pp. 227-228)

GASKIN'S ASSESSMENT OF THE *DIALOGUES*

The most important current analysis of the *Dialogues*, and one that has received widespread attention, has been given to us by J. C. A. Gaskin. His first judgment was to take any speaker who made a good philosophical point in places where Hume took pains to conceal his own position (in the *Dialogues* and *Enquiry*, Section XI) as speaking for Hume.[46] Later in his book when he gets to the question of who speaks for Hume in the *Dialogues* he generally agrees with Kemp Smith that the one who speaks for Hume is Philo.

He gives us some additional points which he believes tend to support and confirm his thesis:

> First there is the untutored response of the new reader of the *Dialogues*. Without the prompting of an editorial apparatus I have never yet known any new reader, already familiar with Hume through the *Enquiry*, who did not at once pick out Philo as the hero of the piece.[47]

Gaskin believes this is what should be expected in light of Hume's letter to Gilbert Elliot where Hume proposes that the two of them could take the positions of the speakers. Elliot, he suggested, might take the position of Cleanthes. As for himself, Hume believed it appropriate that "I shou'd have taken on me the Character of Philo, in the Dialogue, which you'll own I coud [sic] have supported naturally enough."[48]

Gaskin continues: "Secondly, if Hume does not for the most part identify with Philo's mitigated scepticism, whatever was the main point in the first place of all Hume's efforts to cover his tracks?"[49] If this means that Hume worked hard to provide balance in the dialogue style or keep up the suspense of the reader to the end of the composition, that is one thing. If, however, it means that Hume was interested in protecting himself from his critics and detractors, that is another, because Hume knew the *Dialogues* was to be published posthumously, and so no one could cause him any trouble of any kind.

Hume had worked on the manuscript for several years and had completed it in its draft form by 1751-1752. He then cirulated it among some of his friends for several years. Many of them advised against publishing the work, and so Hume let it sit unattended from 1761-1776. When he saw his death approaching, he made the final revision, took elaborate steps to ensure its publication after his death, and finally settled upon his favorite nephew and namesake, David Hume, the younger, son of John Home. Hume, then, could hardly have endured any worries about how the publication of the work could affect him.

Apparently Hume scholars have often fallen into the habit of thinking that Hume was as worried about his reputation all of his life as he was when he wrote the *Treatise*, and so while the remark ostensibly has to do with considerations of style and substance, it actually is about Hume's personal prudential concerns.

It appears that Gaskin has in mind the idea that Hume was concerned about protecting himself from his critics:

> If Hume should really be identified with Cleanthes, he had everything to gain from making this absolutely clear in the text, rather than leaving it to an apparently disingenuous comment from a spectator in the last two lines of the work. The *only* character Hume could not publicly avow in the *Dialogues* is Philo; the only friend he could not admit to being himself is the 'sceptical friend' in *Enquiry* XI. In terms of the politics and prejudices of his day all the cover-up loses its point if Hume is *not*, for the most part, Philo.[50]

Noxon asks "why Hume would pay such deference to social convention in a work planned for posthumous publication when he has shown so little in books published during his lifetime."[51] To this Gaskin remarks,

> Hume *had* displayed a great deal of concern with social convention in his publications: he withdrew 'Of Miracles' and possibly other items ... from the *Treatise*, he modified Section XI of the *Enquiry* into a dialogue in which his own opinions are hard to isolate, he withdrew two of the *Five Dissertations* from publication, he modified passages in the *History* and he postponed publication of the Dialogues for twenty-six years out of deference to the offence they might cause, despite their being 'artfully written'.[52]

All of this, however, affected Hume while he was alive, so it seems that Noxon is right here. "Deference" here seems to me not to mean a thing in light of the *expected posthumous* publication of the *Dialogues*.

Gaskin's third reason is the close similarity between the kind of belief Hume revealed himself to hold in his private papers and letters and the skepticism of Philo. Then Gaskin takes the other meaning of Hume "covering his tracks":

> It is these similarities which justify speaking of Hume 'covering his tracks' in the *Dialogues* rather than not knowing where he was going or being so uncertain about his position that he communicates his uncertainty to his readers. Much of Philo and much of Hume is so nearly of a piece that it requires a positive effort not to identify Hume and Philo.[53]

Gaskin's last reason is the support given to Kemp Smith's views that Philo represents Hume by Mossner's "The Enigma of Hume"[54] and J. V. Price's "Scepticism in Cicero and Hume."[55] In his essay Mossner identifies Demea with Samuel Clarke and his followers and Cleanthes with Joseph Butler. Gaskin agrees that this identification is entirely possible which leaves Philo as Hume "if only on the negative ground that there is no one else he could be: Philo has no matrix outside his creator's mind."[56] Price, Gaskin feels, gives a convincing account of the relation of Cotta in Cicero's *De Natura Deorum* and Philo in the *Dialogues*.[57]

The last serious attempt to cast doubt on Smith's thesis, that Philo primarily represents the position of Hume, was by Noxon's well-known article.[58] Gaskin gives a long review of Noxon's points and concludes that Noxon does not make his case.[59]

The general weakness of those who identify Philo with Hume's position in the *Dialogues* and so conclude that Hume was a religious skeptic is to ignore or practically ignore Part XII. Gaskin does this just as Kemp Smith had done. By ignoring Part XII or diminishing its importance, the claim that Hume is a skeptic can be made quite strong. The twelfth part is mentioned but in such a way that it is left out for all practical purposes, because it does not fit the role of Philo as "the careless skeptic" and so cast Hume as the same. Most of the time Part XII is dismissed or glossed over. Few scholars are blunt as Jessop who being unable to see how the section fits into his own interpretation of Hume says, "The conclusion being disconnected from the argued content of the *Dialogues*, I shall ignore it."[60] Noxon objects to this approach and suggests that the last part of the *Dialogues* may provide the clue to the understanding of the book:

> But surely a critic has no right to ignore a twelfth of a book upon which he is commenting most unfavorably. Some attempt must be made to interpret this admittedly unexpected finale. And if one does try to think out the connection of the twelfth Dialogue not only with the other eleven but with Hume's other works, one should find an unambiguous clue to Hume's own position.[61]

To this I can add my hearty approval—the neglect of Part XII of the *Dialogues* is the best evidence that viewing Hume as a skeptic is an incorrect view. And it is incorrect because Part XII brings data to show that a more comprehensive or different interpretation of Hume's views is needed.

It seems clear that Philo is the best representative in the *Dialogues* of Hume's position, and that is one reason why I have come to the fideistic interpretation of Hume's philosophy of religion. Philo says things in Part XII which cannot be squared very well with the skeptical interpretation of Hume.

Gaskin has the tendency to follow Flew and his skeptical reading of Hume. In connection with the *Enquiry* where Hume talks about "mysteries, which mere natural and unassisted reason is very unfit to handle" (*Enquiry*, p. 103) Flew describes the references to "sublime mysteries" as a "smirking genuflexion of piety" and Gaskin remarks "and I do not doubt it is just that."[62] These scholars could be right, but here again there is an inability to ask whether Hume's remark could be genuine. If genuine, i.e. if Hume meant what he said, then this once again can be understood not as a piece of Hume's willingness to admit mystery but his impatience with the self-confident, know-it-all thinkers who spun much of what they said out of their own overheated minds.

In the *Enquiry* (p. 103) Hume deals with an issue parallel to the *Dialogues'* issue of the nature and acts of God. This is the issue of whether God can be the "mediate" cause of human actions without being responsible for what those people do. The issue is instructive because it illustrates that scorn Hume had for the "temerity" of those who chose to speculate in areas where He felt there was no answer available:

> These are mysteries, which mere natural and unassisted reason is very unfit to handle; and whatever system she embraces, she must find herself involved in inextricable difficulties, and even contradictions, at every step which she takes with regard to such subjects. To reconcile the indifference and contingency of human actions with prescience; or to defend absolute decrees, and yet free the Deity from being the author of sin, has been found hitherto to exceed all the power of philosophy. Happy, if she be thence sensible of her temerity, when she pries into these sublime mysteries; and leaving a scene so full of obscurities and perplexities, return, with suitable modesty, to her true and proper province, the examination of common life; where she will find difficulties enough to employ her enquiries, without launching into so boundless an ocean of doubt, uncertainty, and contradiction! (*Enquiry*, p. 103)

CONCESSIONS TO NATURAL THEOLOGY

The standard, skeptical view of Hume's philosophy of religion is that Hume had little use for natural theology and found it full of contradictions and inconsistencies. Natural theology was a tool of the orthodox and conventional religionist, this view suggests, and Hume labored to show that no conclusions about God were forthcoming from such an approach. At worst we can have no beliefs whatever about the existence of God, His nature, providence, immortality, and many other doctrines, and at best while there may be something to these doctrines, we have to suspend judgment since the evidence is inadequate to give us any assurance about all these matters.

This view is not adequate as it stands. On one side there is considerable pessimism in Hume's mind about the applicability and worth of natural theology. From another side, however, Hume makes several concessions to natural theology and reserves his sharpest barbs and contemptuous scorn for those who believe that they know all the answers and that the case for their ideas is entirely clear and finished. The argument here is that Hume makes many concessions to natural theology, allows that it may be useful at times, and that if reasonably used may be an aid in thinking about God.

The first concession is found in Pamphilus' speech in the Introduction to the *Dialogues*. Presumably Pamphilus does some speaking for Hume since he sets the tone for the dialogue between the actors, sums them up at the end, and inserts his own comments where useful to carry on the progress of the talks, to add explanatory material, etc. The importance of natural theology is shown in that the being of God is so important for many other things.

> Reasonable men may be allowed to differ where no one can reasonably be positive: Opposite sentiments, even without any decision, afford an agreeable amusement; and if the subject be curious and interesting, the book carries us, in a manner, into company, and unites the two greatest and purest pleasures of human life: study and society.
>
> Happily, these circumstances are all to be found in the subject of NATURAL RELIGION. What truth so obvious, so certain, as the *being* of a God, which the most ignorant ages have acknowledged, for which the most refined geniuses have ambitiously striven to produce new proofs and arguments? What truth so important as this, which is the ground of all our hopes, the surest foundation of morality, the firmest support of society, and the only principle which ought never to be a moment absent from our thoughts and meditations? But, in treating of this obvious and important truth, what obscure questions occur concerning the *nature* of that Divine Being; his attributes, his decrees, his plan of providence? These have been always subjected to the disputations of men: Concerning these, human reason has not reached any certain determination. But these are topics so interesting that we cannot restrain our restless inquiry with regard to them; though nothing but doubt, uncertainty, and contradiction have as yet been the result of our most accurate researches. (*Dialogues*, p. 128)

If it is possible that Pamphilus can speak for Hume, then Pamphilus' admission displays a concession different from what we would expect from a writer committed to skepticism, for the reader would expect a skeptic to have little or no tolerance for the whole subject. To admit the importance of the subject is an opening, and allows that the *conclusions* of natural theology may be acceptable.

The second concession is the compliment of Cleanthes' "accurate philosophical turn" as compared to the "careless skepticism of Philo" and the "rigid, inflexible orthodoxy of Demea." Cleanthes supports natural theology so the conclusions he holds appear to be strengthened by that comment.

The third concession is from Demea, natural theology's mortal enemy. On the subject of education he says:

> The method I follow in their education is founded on the saying of an ancient, *"That students of philosophy ought first to learn logics, then ethics, next physics, last of all the nature of the gods."* This science of natural theology, according to him, being the most profound and abstruse of any, required the maturest judgment in its students; and none but a mind enriched with all the other sciences can safely be entrusted with it. (*Dialogues*, p. 130)

How is this a concession to natural theology? Its complexity is mentioned and the astuteness of its practitioners is acknowledged.

A fourth concession is Cleanthes' humorous, ad hominem attack on Philo's skepticism, and the assertion that if the pyrrhonist skeptics are serious, they won't be around long; if they aren't, we need not be either. Then, he intimates that as serious beliefs return about life's realities, secure religious belief will follow too:

> You propose then, *Philo*, said *Cleanthes*, to erect religious faith on philosophical scepticism; and you think that if certainty or evidence be expelled from every other subject of enquiry, it will all retire to those theological doctrines, and there acquire a superior force and authority. Whether your skepticism be as absolute and sincere as you pretend, we shall learn by and by, when the company breaks up; we shall then see whether you go out at the door or the window, and whether you really doubt if your body has gravity or can be injured by its fall, according to popular opinion derived from our fallacious senses and more fallacious experience. And this consideration, *Demea*, may, I think, fairly serve to abate our ill-will to this humourous sect of the skeptics. If they be thoroughly in earnest, they will not long trouble the world with their doubts, cavils, and disputes; if they be only in jest, they are, perhaps, bad railers, but can never be very dangerous, either to the state, to philosophy, or to religion.
>
> In reality, *Philo*, continued he, it seems certain that, though a man in a flush of humor, after intense reflection on the many contradictions and imperfections of human reason, may entirely renounce all belief and opinion, it is impossible for him to persevere in this total skepticism or make it appear in his conduct for a few hours. External objects press in upon him: Passions solicit him: His philosophical melancholy dissipates; and even the utmost violence upon his own temper will not be able, during any time, to preserve the poor appearance of skepticism. And for what reason impose on himself such a violence? This is a point in which it will be impossible for him ever to satisfy himself, consistently with his skeptical principles. So that, upon the whole, nothing could be more ridiculous than the principles of the ancient *Pyrrhonians*; if, in reality, they endeavored, as is pretended, to extend throughout the same skepticism which they had learned from the declamations of their school, and which they ought to have confined to them. (*Dialogues*, pp. 132-133)

This sally seems to show that Hume is not taking skepticism very seriously and intimates that the skeptical position can never be adequate *as a conclusion* though he does seem by his practice to allow for it *as a method*.

> Our senses, you say, are fallacious; our understanding erroneous; our ideas, even of the most familiar objects; extension, duration, motion—full of absurdities and contradictions. You defy me to solve the difficulties or reconcile the repugnancies which you discover in them. I have not capacity for so great an undertaking: I have not leisure for it: I perceive it to be superfluous. Your own conduct, in every circumstance, refutes your principles, and shows the firmest reliance on all the received maxims of science, morals, prudence, and behavior. (*Dialogues*, p. 137)

Hume puts these words into Cleanthes' mouth and continues for several paragraphs in part I to show the inadequacy of skepticism as a settled group of answers. This answer appears to give Hume's orientation about epistemology, metaphysics, and religion. Doctrines in these areas can be questioned with all the dialectical resources at one's disposal, but the conclusions of such an approach can never be allowed since they are destructive. Human nature takes over as a nonrational mechanism and restores conclusions reason had challenged: "Your own conduct ... refutes your principles ...." Philo allows as much:

> To whatever length anyone may push his speculative principles of skepticism, he must act, I own, and live, and converse like other men; and for this conduct he is not obliged to give any other reason than the absolute necessity he lies under of so doing. If he ever carries his speculations farther than this necessity constrains him, and philosophized either on natural or moral subjects, he is allured by a certain pleasure and satisfaction which he finds in employing himself after that manner. He considers, besides, that everyone, even in common life, is constrained to have more or less of this philosophy; that from our earliest infancy we make continual advances in forming more general principles of conduct and reasoning; that the larger experience we acquire, and the stronger reason we are endued with, we always render our principles the more general and comprehensive; and that what we call *philosophy* is nothing but a more regular and methodical operation of the same kind. To philosophize on such subjects is nothing essentially different from reasoning on common life, and we may only expect greater stability, if not greater truth, from our philosophy on account of its exacter and more scrupulous method of proceeding. (*Dialogues*, p. 134)

This little "speech" was put into the mouth of Philo whereas the one before was put into the mouth of Cleanthes. They come very close to saying the same thing; therefore, it seems there is warrant in holding that these are Hume's own conclusions since he puts them into both mouths of the *Dialogues'* two main actors. These statements parallel Hume's famous "confession" about his own skepticism and the misgivings he had over that at the end of Book I of the *Treatise* which we will deal with in a later chapter.

A fifth concession to natural theology is Cleanthes' statement that the same suspense of judgment or balance between the arguments "which is the triumph of skepticism" (*Dialogues*, p. 136) works also in the science of Newton. "What would you say [addressed to Philo] to one who, having nothing particular to object to the arguments of *Copernicus* and *Galileo* for the motion of the earth, should withhold his assent on that general principle that these subjects were too magnificent and remote to be explained by the narrow and fallacious reason of mankind?" (*Dialogues*, p. 136) The implication is that no intelligent person does that, and it follows that though other areas are abstruse and remote from ordinary experience that is no reason for rejecting them, and we should not do that even thought the topic is natural theology.

Skepticism should be consistent:

> But the refined and philosophical skeptics fall into an inconsistence of an opposite nature. They push their researches into the most abstruse corners of science, and their assent attends them in every step, proportioned to the evidence which they meet with. They are even obliged to acknowledge that the most abstruse and remote objects are those which are best explained by philosophy. Light is in reality anatomized. The true system of the heavenly bodies is discovered and ascertained. But the nourishment of bodies by food is still an inexplicable mystery. The cohesion of the part of matter is still incomprehensible. These skeptics, therefore, are obliged, in every question, to consider each particular evidence apart, and proportion their assent to the precise degree of evidence which occurs. This is their practice in all natural, mathematical, moral, and political science. And why not the same, I ask, in the theological and religious? Why must conclusions of this nature be alone rejected on the general presumption of the insufficiency of human reason, without any particular discussion of evidence? Is not such an unequal conduct a plain proof of prejudice and passion? (*Dialogues*, pp. 136-137)

There doesn't seem to be any good reason for refusing to allow Cleanthes' comments to represent Hume's own ideas except that doing so flies in the face of the "standard" Humean interpretation.

Another concession to natural theology: "If we distrust human reason we have now no other principle to lead us into religion." (*Dialogues*, p. 139) The use of human reason presumably leads us into natural theology. Then Hume's anti-clerical streak asserts itself: "Thus skeptics in one age, dogmatists in another—whichever system best suits the purpose of these reverend gentlemen in giving them an ascendant over mankind, they are sure to make it their favorite principle and established tenet." (*Dialogues*, pp. 139-140) This anti-clerical assertion is paralleled by the statement Hume made in a letter to Hugh Blair about Reid's philosophy before he had read any of Reid's essays: "I wish that the Parsons would confine themselves to their old occupation of worrying one another, and leave Philosophers to argue with temper, moderation, and good manners."[63] There is no use in expecting anything good from any preacher!

In another concession, Philo refers to the presence of evil in the world, saying, "however consistent the world may be, [that is, that the "inconveniences and deformities" are consistent with the architect] allowing certain suppositions and conjectures with the idea of such a Deity, it can never afford us an inference concerning his existence." (*Dialogues*, p. 205) Then Philo launches into "four circumstances" (or considerations) about the existence of evil in the world.

The four circumstances on which evil depends "may be necessary and unavoidable." (*Dialogues*, p. 205) Thus the case for the existence of God is given a boost from the chief detractor. Philo's "mini"-theodicy has already been given so it will not be repeated here, but that little-noticed move by Hume is a way of supporting what Philo seems to condemn throughout the *Dialogues*. In each case the appropriateness of each circumstance is questioned, but Philo considers each of the four circumstances to overshadow the detracting remarks, so the net result is to take the circumstances as evidence for God's existence. This is not a skeptical procedure.

In another concession to natural theology, Philo states that he is as impressed with "natural religion" as Cleanthes is:

> I must confess, replied Philo, that I am less cautious on the subject of Natural Religion than on any other; both because I know that I can never, on that head, corrupt the principles of any man of common sense .... A purpose, an intention, a design strikes everywhere the most careless, the most stupid thinker; and no man can be so hardened in absurd systems as at all times to reject it. *That nature does nothing in vain* is a maxim established in all the Schools, merely from the contemplation of the works of nature, without any religious purpose; and, from a firm conviction of its truth, an anatomist who had observed a new organ or canal would never be satisfied till he had also discovered its use and intention. One great foundation of the *Copernican* system is the maxim *that nature acts by the simplest methods, and chooses the most proper means to any end*; and astronomers often, without thinking of it, lay this strong foundation of piety and religion. The same thing is observable in other parts of philosophy; and thus all the sciences almost lead us insensibly to acknowledge a first intelligent Author; and their authority is often so much the greater as they do not directly profess that intention. (*Dialogues*, pp. 214-215)

Hume here has Philo making confessions which are all that Cleanthes could expect, and this continues for the rest of part XII. If Philo represents Hume's position as Smith contends, then Hume held to far more doctrines and beliefs of Christianity than the traditional interpretation of Hume can admit. This is true whether "skeptic" is used in the pejorative sense of an unbeliever or the more complimentary sense of someone who is in a state of suspended judgment. In any case Hume has his skeptic confessing to more beliefs than one might expect if Hume is a skeptic and Philo represents his position.

Philo says "the existence of a DEITY is plainly ascertained by reason ...." (Dialogues, p. 217) and so seems to indicate that he does not esteem his suspense of judgment to be possible. So, Philo does not agree to a skepticism, and if Philo represents Hume, then Hume looks very much like a believer.

No Humean scholars argue that Demea represents Hume. There is a group of scholars who believe that Cleanthes represents Hume's position. Cleanthes, however, is presented on every page of the *Dialogues* as a believer, so if he represents Hume, Hume must have believed far more than he has traditionally been thought to believe. It is here that Hume's historical situation offers some good reasons for understanding Hume as a fideist, a believer of sorts. With that background we have some warrant for understanding Hume in this way. Without that background Hume would have been even more puzzling than many philosophers find him to be.

The concessions to natural theology which, it is argued are Hume's, weaken slightly the claim that Hume is a fideist in his religious thought, because a person who accepts the good and acceptable arguments of natural theology as evidence for the conclusions is not a fideist in the sense in which it has been defined here, although this definition of fideism is descriptive not normative. The concessions to natural theology noted here, *weaken the claim that Hume was a skeptic*, for admitting the relevance and value of the arguments of natural theology is evidence of belief, not evidence of unbelief (skepticism).

Hume gives his reasons for this through Philo: "All men of sound reason are disgusted with verbal disputes, which abound so much in philosophical and theological inquiries ...." (*Dialogues*, p. 217) Controversies concerning the degrees of any quality or circumstance are particularly hard to settle, and "that the dispute concerning theism is of this nature, and consequently is merely verbal, or, perhaps, if possible, still more incurably and ambiguous, will appear on the slightest inquiry." (*Dialogues*, p. 218) The theist and atheist, Hume contends, will agree on many things, but argument breaks down on the issue of degree:

> While the theist, on the one hand, exaggerates the dissimilarity between the Supreme Being and frail, imperfect, variable, fleeting, and mortal creatures; and the atheist, on the other, magnifies the analogy among all the operations of nature, in every period, every situation, and every position. Consider then where the real point of controversy lies; and if you cannot lay aside your disputes, endeavor, at least to cure yourselves of your animosity. (*Dialogues*, pp. 218-219)

Hume added a footnote after his "Finis" on the concluding page of his 1776 manuscript. In the view of several of the editors of Hume's text, he intended that the footnote be inserted here:

> It seems evident that the dispute between the skeptics and dogmatists is entirely verbal, or, at least, regards only the degrees of doubt and assurance which we ought to indulge with regard to all reasoning: and such disputes are commonly, at the bottom, verbal and admit not of any precise determination. No philosophical dogmatist denies that there are difficulties both with regard to the senses and to all science, and that these difficulties are, in a regular, logical method, absolutely insolvable. No skeptic denies that we lie under an absolute necessity, notwithstanding these difficulties, of thinking, and believing, and reasoning, with regard to all kinds of subjects, and even of frequently assenting with confidence and security. The only difference, then, between these sects, if they merit that name, is that the skeptic, from habit, caprice, or inclination, insists most on the difficulties; the dogmatist, for like reasons, on the necessity. (*Dialogues*, p. 219, note)

Cleanthes believes that even a corrupted religion is better than none, so we should preserve even such a religion, but both Cleanthes and Philo agree that we ought not to throw out the good with the bad though Philo as usual is a bit more negative than is Cleanthes:

> Take care, *Philo*, replied *Cleanthes*, take care: Push not matters too far: Allow not your zeal against false religion to undermine your veneration for the true. Forfeit not this principle, the chief, the only great comfort in life and our principal support amidst all the attacks of adverse fortune. The most agreeable reflection which it is possible for human imagination to suggest is that of genuine theism, which represents us as the workmanship of a Being perfectly good, wise, and powerful; who created us for happiness, and who, having implanted in us immeasurable desires for good, will prolong our existence to all eternity, and will transfer us into an infinite variety of scenes, in order to satisfy those desires, and render our felicity complete and durable. Next to such a Being himself (if the comparison be allowed), the happiest lot which we can imagine, is that of being under his guardianship and protection.
>
> These appearances, said *Philo*, are most engaging and alluring; and, with regard to the true philosopher, they are more than appearances. But it happens here, as in the former case, that, with regard to the greater part of mankind, the appearances are deceitful, and that the terrors of religion commonly prevail above its comforts.
>
> It is allowed that men never have recourse to devotion so readily as when dejected with grief or depressed with sickness. Is not this a proof that the religious spirit is not so nearly allied to joy as to sorrow? (*Dialogues*, pp. 224-225)

Philo's claims about the effect of religion upon people is another issue than the one about belief, because the effect which things have on different people often is little more than an influence of their temperament. It may be that the doctrines of religion can be believed and cause "terrors" or be believed and cause "happiness." Hume puts Philo in the role of putting a slightly more negative cast on what Cleanthes says (as is usual) but in the main there is agreement that "true" religion which is described here by Cleanthes is genuine theism. The view of natural theology resting on the design argument is "more than appearances." This does not fit the description of skepticism!

The *Dialogues* do not present Hume as an unbending skeptic. Instead they seem to indicate that Hume believed far more than most of his contemporaries or ours generally admit. This should not be surprising to us, for fideists *do end up* believing. They may have used skeptical procedures *at first* to destroy the basis for belief but they come around on whatever nonrational or irrational basis they have chosen to believe *at last*. So, to talk about what Hume may have believed, in contrast to the orthodox, conventional view that Hume is a skeptic should not be surprising at all. When we talk about his beliefs we are talking about the beliefs Hume ended up holding after going through his rational analysis, abandoning that as inadequate, and then turning to faith. Faith is his mechanism here in contrast to the other mechanisms we have already located because the issues here are religious matters. For them Hume invokes not habit, custom, propensity, or association, but faith. Mentioning Hume's beliefs is not something irrelevant or extraneous to our thesis. Hume's beliefs are a result we would expect to find if Hume followed a fideistic approach. This is not to say that Hume was a Christian, but it is to say that having religious beliefs, some beliefs, whatever they are, is a natural consequence of being a fideist.

Donald Livingston comes to a parallel conclusion. His comments given here appear in his discussion of politics and providential history. Hume did not think that history is moving inevitably to a state of perfection and Livingston believes Hume's comments on this run parallel to Hume's beliefs about God's existence:

> Hume's rejection of the idea [that history is inevitably moving to a state of perfection] on mere theoretical and empirical grounds may appear as the mark of a small an ungenerous mind. There is a parallel with belief in God. Hume did not think that empirical canons could support belief in an intelligent author of the universe, but he did allow that the belief admits of a post-Pyrrhonian justification analogous to that which can be given for belief in external objects and causal connections. No one can approach the universe in a scientific spirit and not arrive at a strong belief in an intelligent author of the universe, a belief which is not only causally consequent upon scientific inquiry but, logically, is an ultimate belief guiding it. Belief in philosophical theism is a *virtue* and is socially reinforced by the scientific as well as by the religious community. It is for this reason that Hume thought there really are no "speculative atheist[s],"

(EU, 149). One could reject this or that form of popular theism, but Hume thought it extremely unlikely that anyone could, upon reflection, fail to have the beliefs of "philosophical theism." Consequently, anyone who would reject theism merely because there are no good empirical reasons for it would betray a disingenuous mind.[64]

This section is confusing and paradoxical because Livingston says in it that "Hume did not think empirical canons could support belief in an intelligent author of the universe." Then, a few lines farther along he says, "no one can approach the universe in a scientific spirit and not arrive at a strong belief in an intelligent author of the universe, a belief which is not only causally consequent upon scientific inquiry but, logically, is an ultimate belief guiding it."

If empirical canons cannot support belief, then, how can we have science? It is in the scientific spirit that one is supposed to approach nature and "arrive at a strong belief in an intelligent author of the universe." Science is not entirely empirical as the presence of mathematics shows, but if it is not empirical in the sense of "looking around" at the world, then, what is it? Bacon's naive inductive method may not work, but its attempt was to consult the world instead of consulting authorities. "Consulting the world" is generally what has been taken to be empiricism. We can consult the world only by the use of our senses. If this is not empiricism (using "empirical canons"), then what is empiricism?

By "empirical canons" does Livingston mean Hume's atomistic empiricism outlined for us in the first pages of the *Treatise*? If that is what is meant, Livingston gives us no reason for so understanding it.

The last matter from Livingston's comments comes from this sentence: "Hume did not think that empirical canons could support belief in an intelligent author of the universe, but he did allow that the belief admits of a post-Pyrrhonian justification analogous to that which can be given for belief in external objects and causal connections." It seems astonishing that Livingston is here talking about the fideistic approach to belief in God and to secular convictions, and yet fails to see that he is describing the fideist way of belief.

HUME'S BELIEFS AND HIS MOTHER'S DEATH

Joseph Home [sic], David's father, died in 1713 after only five and a half years of marriage. David's mother was left to raise three children of whom David was the youngest. She could have remarried but decided against it and David held her in the highest regard as an honorable woman and a committed mother to her children. David was very fond of her.

In 1745 while Hume was staying in London his mother died, and this news was conveyed to him. An incident took place there which has considerable bearing on the question of Hume's beliefs. The story has been passed on to us by Alexander Carlyle of Inveresk who got it from the Honourable Patrick Boyle, minister of Irvine, Ayrshire and the second son of John, Earl of Glasgow. The account "bears every evidence of the truth" according to Mossner[65] "and was indeed accepted as fact by the philosopher's nephew, Baron David Hume." As related by Carlyle, here is the story:

> When David and he [Patrick Boyle] were both in London, at the period when David's mother died, Mr. Boyle, hearing of it, soon after went into his apartment—for they lodged in the same house—when he found him in the deepest affliction and in a flood of tears. After the usual topics of condolence, Mr. Boyle said to him, "My friend, you owe this uncommon grief to your having thrown off the principles of religion; for if you had not, you would have been consoled by the firm belief that the good lady, who was not only the best of mothers, but the most pious of Christians, was now completely happy in the realms of the just." To which David replied, "Though I threw out my speculations to entertain and employ the learned and metaphysical world, yet in other things I do not think so differently from the rest of mankind as you may imagine."[66]

Boyle and Carlyle, intimates of David Hume, persuaded themselves that Hume was a good Christian at heart, and Mossner thinks it is perhaps the greatest compliment to Hume that so many others attempted to persuade themselves similarly. Nevertheless, Mossner remains unconvinced because Hume had long since renounced the Christianity of revelation and acknowledged "the character of an infidel." And Hume's retaining the characteristics of a good and moral nature is no evidence to the contrary, Mossner maintains, nor is his remark recorded here, presuming that it has been accurately reported.

Boyle and Carlyle as contemporary interpreters of Hume, however, felt that the incident does illuminate Hume's beliefs. The event was reported by people who were on good terms with Hume, so there is no evidence that they had an interest in hurting his reputation. Nor is there evidence that these men had any personal interest in changing Hume's reputation. These men were not regarded as "skeptics" and free-thinkers like Adam Smith. Rather, they were intellectually qualified to "get things straight" without any misunderstanding. Their assessment may not be correct, but they surely were in as good a position to know as anyone could be.

For the most part, this incident in Hume's life has gone unnoticed among Hume scholars. So far as I have been able to determine, no reference to Hume's experience or the response to it given by Patrick Boyle occurs in the writings of Norman Kemp Smith, Lewis W. Beck, Nelson Pike, Charles Hendel, Donald Livingston, David Fate Norton, J. C. A. Gaskin, James King, Richard H. Popkin, Antony Flew, Terence Penelhum, Nicholas Capaldi, John Passmore, Barry Stroud, or G. P. Morice. The absence of any notice of this event in the writings of recognized Hume scholars is very surprising especially when Mossner gives it a sufficiently prominent place in his *A Life of David Hume*. The report of Patrick Boyle (and the favorable notice given to it by Alexander Carlyle) is just another of a whole group of things overlooked, downgraded, or dismissed by many Hume scholars presumably because of their preoccupation with Humean skepticism.

I am not advocating an overemphasis on this incident, but surely it is as important as some of Hume's letters which have received close attention.

THE IMMORTALITY OF THE SOUL

Hume wrote his short essay on immortality in the 1750s, but some of his friends urged that publication be withheld. A few copies were printed and before they were withdrawn from circulation, a few copies fell into the hands of some orthodox clergymen who determined to raise trouble for Hume over it. They were more concerned about Hume's defense of suicide, which they regarded as a sin, but they were exercised over "Of the Immortality of the Soul" as well. Hume prudently withdrew this essay (and the essay on suicide) from the market and made provisions for their posthumous publication along with the *Dialogues*.

The short essay on immortality is divided into three parts with a short introduction and a slightly longer conclusion. The three parts are a bare-fisted, no-holds-barred attack on the philosophical arguments for immortality. The first part he entitles "metaphysical topics," an examination of the arguments that the soul is immortal from the claim that the soul is immaterial and that thought (or memory as the test of personal identity) cannot belong to a material body. Hume's analysis of metaphysical concepts shows he believes that our ideas of material and immaterial substance are confused and contradictory, that our analogies are inconclusive, and that what is incorruptible is ingenerable. If it proves immortality, it also proves the pre-existence of the soul, which is more than Christians want.

Hume titles the second group of arguments "moral topics," arguments that we must be immortal because God is interested in rewarding the virtuous and punishing the vicious and the rewarding is not done in this life. He argues, however, that we have no reason for these conclusions. Our philosophical knowledge is limited to this life and what we can judge by natural reason. Or, to take another approach, reward and punishment presuppose but two types of men, the good and the bad, but the greatest part of mankind float "betwixt vice and virtue." Hume's analysis is calculated to show that the concepts are incoherent, contradictory, and self-refuting.

The third division of arguments, "physical topics," gives arguments which aim to show the immortality of the soul from the analogy of nature, and Hume admits that these at least might have some relevance to the question of the immortality of the soul, because they come from nature which is our only (philosophical) source of knowledge. The question of the immortality of the soul is a question of fact, and no question of fact can be decided but by experience of nature. In summary, this third section suggests that the analogies of nature do not give us the assurance we want, but "prove" the wrong things, lead us into contradictions and absurdities, and become allied with our passions. There is no help to be found in these analogies for the insistent question of immortality.

The result of the whole discussion from the three divisions of the essay is that there is not a shred of a reason to believe in immortality, and there is simply no such thing as immortality at all. That is not Hume's final conclusion, however, for he concludes that we cannot establish immortality on the basis of reason and philosophy alone. If we are going to establish it or have any defensible reasons for believing in it, there must be another basis than that of reason.

Hume begins his essay with these words:

> By the mere light of reason it seems difficult to prove the Immortality of the Soul. The arguments for it are commonly derived either from metaphysical topics, or moral, or physical. But in reality, it is the gospel, and the gospel alone, that has brought life and immortality to light.[67]

He ends the essay with these words:

> It is an infinite advantage in every controversy, to defend the negative. If the question be out of the common experienced course of nature, this circumstance is almost, if not altogether, decisive. By what arguments or analogies can we prove any state of existence, which no one ever saw, and which no wise resembles any that ever was seen? Who will repose such trust in any pretended philosophy, as to admit upon its testimony the reality of so marvellous a scene? Some new species of logic is requisite for that purpose; and some new faculties of the mind, that they may enable us to comprehend that logic.
>
> Nothing could set in a fuller light the infinite obligations which mankind have to divine revelation; since we find, that no other medium could ascertain this great and important truth.[68]

The immortality Hume is talking about here is the survival of the soul after the death of the body (classical view of the matter) plus the Christian, Jewish, and Islamic conviction that that soul will be united with a resurrected body sometime in the future.

But why should we take these statements seriously? After all, doesn't the overwhelming tradition of scholarship on Hume view him as an unbeliever on religio-metaphysical issues? Gaskin, to give one example, is very blunt about it:

> At no time in his adult life did Hume ever believe in any form of personal immortality. This biographical fact, so challengingly at variance

with the professed beliefs of most of his contemporaries, is given little expression in his philosophical writings.[69]

This comment by Gaskin could be repeated with individualistic variations from a variety of sources. Gaskin makes many astute points and give a valuable critical assessment of the essay. For example, he reminds us that "Of the Immateriality of the Soul" (*Treatise*, pp. 232f [I, IV, V]) is highly relevant for the discussion of immortality, but Gaskin's skeptical interpretation of Hume carries here as well as elsewhere. As he began his analysis of Hume's essay, so he ends it: "Hume did not believe in any form of personal immortality. His reasons for this negative belief are as complete as the nature of the case will permit."[70]

But what about the opening paragraph of the essay and two closing paragraphs? Surely they must count for something? Gaskin says: "In light of what he had written about the credentials of revelation in the *Enquiry*, Hume's final flourish in the essay can only be read as sarcastic irony."[71] He also says a few lines farther on: "Since not even divine revelation could substantiate an incoherence, Hume is presumably not referring here to immortality via an immaterial soul but to some other characterization of immortality such as the survival of disembodied experiences or the resurrection of the body complete with soul."

Gaskin misses the point here: The doctrine of immortality is not incoherent; it is incoherent on the basis of rationality. Hume's animus against popular ("vulgar," "superstitious") religion was equalled by his hatred of rationalistic, self-confident natural theology. He saved his most powerful invective for these two unbearable things.

It is not clear at all that Hume's comments at the beginning and end "Of Immortality" are no more than "sarcastic irony." That is Humean orthodoxy, but it is achieved at the price of having to overlook or explain away uncomfortable statements like those at the beginning and the end of the essay. It is the fashionable position on Hume, but it helps to be able to overlook some unpalatable things if we cling to that conclusion.

It seems fairly clear that we have here another clear instance of Hume's fideism. He doesn't use "faith" here, but the pattern which appeared before in Hume's writings on the philosophy of religion is here just the same. The difference is that he announces at the beginning what he is going to argue for or "leap" to at the end. In the three parts of the essay he consistently demolishes sample arguments which had been given for immortality from the time of Plato to Hume. None of these will support immortality. None can guarantee the conclusion that the soul is immortal.

The desired conclusion can be had, however. It is through revelation, through the gospel that we can establish "this great and important truth," because it is clear that we have nothing without that: "The want of argument, without revelation, sufficiently establishes the negative."[72] If philosophy represents reason and rationality for Hume, then the gospel and revelation represent the nonrational or irrational. By abandoning the rational and taking the nonrational, Hume can arrive at the conclusion he wants. *This is a very clear case shown to us in very short compass, so it comes as near to an ideal instance as anyone could hope for.*

Several other times Hume indicates that if we stick to this world and the evidence we derive from it, our judgments on the arguments for immortality are a foregone conclusion. We must stay with this world; rationally we have nothing else. He says, "Reasoning from the common course of nature, and without supposing any new interposition of the supreme cause, which ought always to be excluded from philosophy ...."[73] "These arguments are grounded on the supposition, that God has attributes beyond what he has exerted in this universe, with which alone we are acquainted,"[74] and "... if any purpose of nature be clear, we may affirm, that the whole scope and intention of man's creation, so far as we can judge by natural reason, is limited to the present life."[75] There is then a sharp contrast by Hume on the resources of rationality and the other resources, so this is a particularly clear instance of fideism. The only other hypothesis which seems possible is that Hume was playing: either with us or just for his own amusement. There is nothing whatever which we can discover either in his own life or the comments of others which would support this conclusion. Hume seems to be serious about the issue he discusses in this essay.

SUICIDE

Hume's other posthumous essay, "Of Suicide," is not central to the issue because it is properly a treatise on ethics and does not contain any comments which have a bearing on fideism as an epistemological issue. Some of Hume's unexpected comments, however, are very useful in detecting his attitudes, because he gave them without indicating to us any feeling that some great challenge to him might hang on them. Hume inserted one footnote at the very end which affects our understanding of his own personal beliefs and gives us the flavor of his views:

> It would be easy to prove that Suicide is as lawful under the *Christian* dispensation as it was to the heathens. There is not a single text of Scripture which prohibits it. That great and infallible rule of faith and practice which must controul all philosophy and human reasoning, has left us in this particular to our natural liberty. Resignation to providence is indeed recommended in Scripture; but that implies only submission to ills that are inavoidable, not to such as may be remedied by killing of others over whose life we have no authority. That this precept, like most of the Scripture precepts, must be modified by reason and common sense, is plain from the practice of magistrates, who punish criminals capitally, notwithstanding the letter of the law. But were this commandment ever so express against Suicide, it would not have no authority, for all the law of *Moses* is

abolished, except so far as it is established by the law of Nature. And we have already endeavoured to prove, that Suicide is not prohibited by that law. In all cases *Christians* and *Heathens* are precisely upon the same footing.[76]

If Hume is the skeptic he has been described to be in his philosophy of religion, it seems that he would first reject the scriptures of the Old and New Testaments. He does not do this, at least here. Instead he says what to philosophers is very surprising, that "That great and infallible rule of faith and practice must controul all philosophy and human reasoning." It is surprising, because the philosophical tradition claims that the human mind is an authority unto itself and is under no authority except the realities of the universe and the necessities of logic. Hume here seems to indicate that he regarded the Scriptures of the Old and New testaments as carrying authority and he regarded them seriously. He might rail at popular and organized Christianity with all its shortcomings of rigidity and pettiness, and he might detest official Christianity with its theological wranglings and its lust for position and power, but "divine revelation" as he referred to it in the essay on immortality and "Scripture" as he referred to it here, appear to assume more importance for Hume than the tradition of Humean scholarship would admit—Scripture has an authority and presumably a truth which here Hume feels is appropriate and which the philosopher must take into account.

There is no more reason to take this essay as a piece of satire than there is to take the one on immortality that way since both of them were published posthumously when Hume neither expected to receive any credit he could use nor reactions of "the zealots" he could relish. There is scarcely a comment to be found on this footnote, but it must be a factor in any thinking which seeks to determine what Hume's personal views were. It accords with the judgment expressed earlier that though Hume was neither orthodox nor an atheist he believed far more than the "skeptical" description would allow. For Hume to appeal to Scripture at all as an authority is surprising and puzzling.

A PROBLEM AND SUMMARY OF THE CHAPTER

The claim that David Hume believed far more than is generally thought and was a fideist in his epistemology has some problems, for certain of his friends and confidants describe him as a genuine unbeliever in some particular or other. Popkin repeats one incident for us:

> His close friend, the economist Adam Smith, said in his account of Hume's last illness that Hume had stated that the only reason he had for wanting to

remain alive was to see the elimination of the strange superstition, Christianity, that pervaded the world. Then, in his usual skeptical manner, Hume added that even if he could carry on his efforts in this direction, he doubted that Christianity would ever be eliminated.[77]

This could be a case where Hume continued to play his skeptic role with another friend who also was known to hold similar views about religion. Could it be that Hume was just keeping the same pose? That is possible, but this story can be so understood that it is consistent with the interpretation of this chapter. That is, by referring to "that strange superstition, Christianity," Hume had in mind organized, official religion as he found it in the British Isles, or popular Christianity, the superstition of the "vulgar," and perhaps both of these. If we take this interpretation, then "true religion" would be excepted. That Hume had no interest in eliminating genuine religion but only the counterfeit is warranted, it appears, by other statements in Hume's writings and the things we know about his life. This difficulty posed by Adam Smith's account, then, appears resolvable consistent with the thesis of fideism in Hume's position.

In addition, Boswell reports that Hume stated on his death bed that immortality was a doctrine with many contradictory and troublesome consequences which he found to be unattractive and repulsive. Boswell had gone to see Hume with the purpose of quizzing him about his views of immortality in light of his impending death. He asked Hume if he were not made somewhat uneasy about the thought of personal annihilation, and Hume is reported to have said that it did "not the least; no more than the thought that he had not been as Lucretius observes."[78] Boswell did not think that Hume was serious and did not put any stock in those comments but we have his report. Boswell's story is a more formidable difficulty in the complete picture of David Hume as a sort of freethinking theistic believer, a person who did not like the kind of popular religion which he had seen in Scotland but who nevertheless believed in God and advocated a fideistic approach towards the whole question.

It is more formidable because it was not issued for popular consumption and was given at a time when we would not expect Hume to be constructing jokes. Hume may have been offended by what he considered an insensitive and inappropriate intrusion into his intimate life and decided to give Boswell an answer which would set him back a little. Since Boswell expected a skeptic answer, Hume would oblige him by giving it! We simply don't know enough about the incident to know how to understand it and that appears to be about all anyone can say meaningfully about it.

What conclusion seems justified by the facts of Hume's life? It is clear that Hume was not an orthodox Christian. Nor, at the other end of the matter, could we say that Hume did not believe in God, creation, providence and the rest of central Christian doctrines including what Locke called "the Messiahship of Jesus." Hume never seems to have talked about Jesus, so caution is in order, but there are too many expressions in the *Dialogues*, pieces of conflicting evidence like Hume's testimony to Patrick Boyle, and unexplained statements in print and to listeners to accept the "infidel" description of Hume.

It is fashionable to regard Hume as a deist or a deistic skeptic. That is the majority view among Hume scholars. He was not an orthodox Christian in belief, associations, or practice, and he was a religious free thinker as deists were. His associations were mostly with people of wide philosophical and theological latitude and it was this group which appreciated Hume and applauded his work.

The whole issue is complicated by Hume's penchant for dramatic overstatement and inflammatory rhetoric. Too little attention has been paid to the effect of Hume's youth on the *Treatise of Human Nature*. What reason is there for thinking that Hume did not have to learn some hard lessons from experience like all young men? Philosophic genius brings no guarantee with it that lessons other people have to learn will be known in advance. Young people in the eighteenth century were expected to be more mature in their youthful years than are young people in our day. Nevertheless, Hume was a very young man when he wrote the *Treatise* and he laments that he published the book before reaching suitable maturity. He may have regretted also that his early pronouncements disposed people to view him as a destructive, skeptical, disintegrating influence. "A Letter from a Gentlemen to his Friend in Edinburgh" reflects his dismay that he was interpreted so negatively. We should not forget, either, his desire for literary fame or the effect of Hume's Scottish roots in a world that downgraded Scotch ancestry, traditions, and attainments. In short, many powerful psychological forces can be seen in the life of David Hume, and these surely must have affected his statements on religion.

The only view which seems coherent is that Hume was a free thinker who picked and chose his beliefs. He was a theist, a minimal theist, "theism" taken here to be the belief that there exists a personal, ethical, self-revealing God who is both immanent in and transcendent over the world and that this God both created the world and exercises providential influence over it. I take this position because Hume seems to leave open the possibility of belief in miracles on the ground of faith. What Hume believed on specifically Christian doctrines is not clear. He had separated himself from Christian associations and speaks very little about them. In this respect he differed from Locke who despite his freethinking ways regarded himself as a good Anglican Christian and sought to maintain contact with other confessing Christians. Hume was not as generous as Locke towards these Christians. Hume despised popular Christianity, the religion of the "vulgar," because it was superstitious, intellectually contradictory, and morally hypocritical. He detested official, organized Christianity because of the drive for power and control over others he discovered in the clergy and its willingness to use political means for creating conformity and compliance with its dictates.

Did Hume accept revelation? He does not speak with a consistent voice on this. Many places indicate that he believed in special (that is, supernatural) revelation. In other places he lampoons the miraculous dimension of the book of Genesis, for example, which the Christian doctrine of special revelation entails, and in effect leaves the reader of his chapter on miracles with the impression that he really doesn't believe in revelation at all.

Hume may have been overwhelmed by the Newtonian view of the world which regarded the world as a superb machine, the product of God, the supernatural clock maker. Hume seems to have wanted to believe in the design argument, or at least he wished "that Cleanthes' argument [the design argument] could be so analys'd as to be render'd quite formal and regular."[79] He has his reservations about it, however, because unless our propensity to believe it were as strong and universal as that which causes us to believe in our senses and experience, the argument would be considered an undependable ("suspicious") foundation for belief. Here we have another case of his resort (or attempted resort) to the fideistic mechanism of human nature.

Livingston takes somewhat the same position: "The ultimate system which Hume officially adopts is 'pure theism.'"[80] Then he quotes Philo in the XIIth book of the *Dialogues* (p. 214) to the effect that "A purpose, an intention, or design strikes everywhere the most careless, the most stupid thinker," and cites also the first paragraph in *The Natural History of Religion*. He equates Philo with Hume, but he concludes, "These passages [*Dialogues*, p. 215 and *Nat.His.Rel.*, p. 25] show that Hume accepted, in some form, the argument from design."[81] "As early as the *Treatise* itself Hume had argued that 'The order of the universe proves an omnipotent mind.'"[82]

Too little attention has been paid to Hume's "A Letter from a Gentleman to His Friend in Edinburgh." This letter, written when Hume was 34 and had been turned down on his attempt to secure an open faculty position at the University, represents one of the very few times that Hume broke his vow of public silence to respond to the attacks of his critics. In this letter Hume specifically disavows the accusations of "universal scepticism," "Principles leading to downright Atheism," "Errors concerning the very Being and Existence of a God," etc. He states forthrightly that he has accurately stated the charges, all of them, exactly as they were given, and then he takes up each point in order and specifically repudiates holding (or tending towards) beliefs his opponents had listed. He is not a pyrrhonian, his attacks on reason are aimed only to destroy the pride of reason, his frame of mind is in no way prejudicial to piety, and on and on.

It is no wonder that Hume has been misunderstood. His terminology and way of doing philosophy were not traditional, and combined with some brashness, exaggeration, and vigor of style, they led to misinterpretation. At least misinterpretation is what he claims and the level of moral outrage and outright denial of the charges are *highly* interesting.

Pyrrhonism and the fideism which is part of the program of this skepticism appears not to have been known very well in England. Pyrrhonist principles were better known and had been fairly common in France since Montaigne, and

Pyrrhonism may have been more compatible with the Gallic temperament. Hume appears to have been the introducer of this attack upon the pretensions of reason and the resort to nonintellectual resources to the British Isles. We should not forget the barrier which the Channel represents to the English character!

Turning from the *Treatise* which is all Hume's critics had in 1745 to the *Dialogues*, which is the main source for our ideas on Hume's views towards religion, we find that readers in our day are in a similar position to that of Hume's readers in his day. How can Hume's consistent attacks on the traditional natural theology, his sarcasm, his visible glee in taking the radical (or, at least, nonorthodox) position, and his seeming to favor Philo, the skeptic, be taken in any way but as the slashing attacks of an enemy of Christianity? Although he followed the English style in raising doubts rather than the atheism of so many of the French philosophes, the net result seems to be an underground attack on everything Christian and everything traditional. So, the skeptic interpretation of Hume is understandable, but it is opposed by contrary evidence, and by Hume's specific disavowals and protestations.

Perhaps the hardest thing is to answer the question, why anyone would attack the things he believes? (If Hume did believe?) Why would someone destroy the things he values? How could Hume attack the religion that had nurtured him? Why would Hume hold up to ridicule the intellectual enterprise of natural theology or raise questions about the Christian claims of the goodness, wisdom, or power of God? What is there to be gained from constantly pressing doubts and questions about one's religion? These and many other questions can be asked about Hume's whole treatment of religion.

Of course, we just don't know, but this is not the first time this has come from people who claim to be believers. The answer lies in the mysteries of the human mind and soul, but the phenomenon is not limited to Hume. In our own day the financing of the radical left has often been done by the rich and privileged. Extreme and romanticized environmentalism is being funded by those who would be destroyed if the radical program should succeed. Pornography, cultural and artistic anarchy, educational decline and many other distressing tendencies are supported by the most unlikely people and by people who though they decry such things also state that they support such inappropriate things because they are afraid of losing freedom of speech or have a commitment to human rights, etc. Near-totalitarian restrictions on talk about race, gender, ethnic matters, sexuality, and even physical handicaps, etc., etc., occur in places where free inquiry has been a tradition and with the support of people who believe of all people that they are the most free.

The example most ready-to-hand and most useful for us is Bayle. He is especially important for us because of his influence on Hume, and the intellectual methodology, the epistemology, he modeled. Bayle, the member of a Dutch Reformed church in Rotterdam, regularly and aggressively claimed to be a Christian. He was a descendant of a French Huguenot family, had studied in France, knew

Catholic as well as Protestant Christianity, confessed during one period of his life to being a Catholic, and then returned to his Protestantism. He was a realist about the ecclesiastico-political realities of the late seventeenth century, so he lived in Holland for his own personal freedom and safety.

Bayle's approach was to attack the theology or philosophy of anyone, everyone, always, and ever. An attack on anyone's position was used as an occasion to generalize the attack to all theories and to show the hopeless dead ends and fathomless abysses to which human reason leads. Richard Popkin has described Bayle at much greater length than we are doing here, so we will refer the reader to Popkin's writings for the details on Bayle. Our question, like that of Hume, is how anyone could dissect, defame, and destroy the things he holds sacred. Bayle did this as his life's vocation while confessing at the same time to hold to the Christian creeds, and while participating in Christian rites and ceremonies.

Bayle's church associates in Rotterdam had their doubts about Bayle's protestations of faith and of his program of preparing others to exercise faith. Throughout the work, Bayle's dictionary claims that his skepticism was a preparation for faith, but his smutty and salacious stories on the biblical patriarchs and his assigning of unworthy motives to whatever person and to whatever incident from their life which he examined caused his own fellow church members to struggle over his affirmations of Christian faith. The members of his congregation found it extremely difficult to accept his claims and their examinations of Bayle's writings provided them an ongoing struggle in trying to understand how they fit into Christian ideals and purposes.

Bayle's treatment of religious themes and his appeals to the Bible appear to Popkin to lack a genuine religious spirit and to be devoid of all religious concern and passion. The Old Testament seemed always to be regarded as fair game for Baylean analysis, exaggeration, and ridicule. The content and the spirit of his literature seem remote from the point of view of those who are deeply committed to their religious faith and passionate about the elements of their confession.

I will leave the reader to pursue this interest further, but how does this relate to Hume? It was suggested that Hume's smirking style in the *Dialogues*, particularly with Philo, might not express Hume's actual views. Hume gives many evidences of being a religious fideist and his own personal religious views may have been different from what we seem to find in his printed text. Nevertheless, the question is asked as to how a believer can seem to take such delight in bringing embarrassment to religious teaching and in throwing into question the things he claims to believe.

Bayle fits in here as a specimen who claimed to be a Christian believer but whose words, attitudes, and publications do not in any appear to be consistent with this. So, it may be the same with Hume. We, of course, don't know Bayle's heart; neither do we know Hume's. But if Bayle could hold views and write things which appear inconsistent with his own personal religious confession, then why can't that be the case with Hume? Hume's readers may still not be convinced, but they must remember Bayle and observe his patterns and then realize that as it was with Bayle, that so it could have been with Hume. We may not be able to believe it was this way with Bayle and we may not be able to believe this with Hume. We may find it hard to countenance such religious inconsistency any more than we can accept a parallel inconsistency in another area, and we may view our inability to accept such inconsistency and contradiction as a virtue. Let us not forget Hume's protestations, however. Our interpretation must somehow fit that.

Back to Hume's letter: It does not fit the portrait of the slick underminer of the faith. He mentions "Tribes of Hereticks, the *Arians, Socianians* [sic] and *Deists*" as people whose views he rejects![83]

According to the "official, orthodox" view of Hume, such groups, with the exception of the Deists, were so preoccupied with theological matters and so philosophically naive as not to merit any of Hume's attention. But Hume mentions them as groups he regarded as wrong, and wrong because they so trusted human reason that it got them into trouble. Hume indicates in the letter that he did not want to be linked with them. In effect, he did not regard himself a heretic. He says, "And can one do a more essential Service to Piety, than by showing them that this boasted Reason of theirs, so far from accounting for the great Mysteries of Trinity and Incarnation, is not able fully to satisfy itself with regard to its own Operations, and must in some Measure fall into a Kind of implicite [sic] Faith, even in the most obvious and familiar Principles?"[84] So we are back to Hume's old business of claiming some beliefs while appearing to attack those very beliefs.

Well, what about the Deists? Hume has been interpreted many times as belonging to that group. Surely that group of free thinking, culturally-aware, self-assured theological rebels would best fit Hume's position? According to an account passed down to us,[85] Hume specifically denied being a deist. He, according to Lord Charlemont, who passed the story on to us, attended a social event in London where Hume was boldly approached by Mrs. (David) Mallet who introduced herself and remarked that "We Deists ought to know each other." Hume's answer was, "Madam, I am no Deist. I do na [sic] style myself so, neither do I desire to be known by that Appellation."

While not himself a deist, Hume inherited the heady sense of freedom from the past and of independence from authority, whether political or clerical. Although Hume was a forceful man and could harbor strong feelings, he retained much of British moderation and was shocked and repelled by French atheism and extreme forms of cultural and religious rebellion. Despite his revulsion over the radical pronouncements of the French philosophes, he often sounds like them because of his life-long penchant for shocking people and upsetting their equilibrium. He also acknowledged his desire for literary fame, an all-important force in his life. He played skeptic for the notoriety this brought and in the *Dialogues* we see both the continuing legacy of this and an attempt to tone it down.

Whenever Hume denied a point held by religious radicals and free-thinkers of his day or the uncritical, naive devout, at all times he had a tendency to say repellent, shocking things. In denying that God has human passions Hume says: "It is an absurdity to believe that the Deity has human passions, and one of the lowest of human passions, a restless appetite for applause." (*Dialogues*, p. 226) It is hard to see how this could create anything but indignation on the part of orthodox believers. It seems inconceivable that a believer in God the creator, provider, and savior could make a remark as disparaging of God as that one since Christians believe that praising God is only rendering to God what is due by His nature and grace. So it would appear that Hume is not a Christian believer but was a minimal theist who was far more conservative in his theologico-philosophical views than most interpreters of Hume have thought.

A considerable amount of his more abrasive and noticeable skepticism on matters of natural theology can be explained this way: Hume felt that a prerequisite for being a good believer is to have all intellectual aids destroyed and rationalist pretensions eliminated. Such a assertion is consistent with my claim that Hume was pursuing the fideist program. Butler summarizes the matter thus: "Philo's entire criticism of the argument from design should be viewed as an attempt, not to deny that God exists, but to break down Cleanthes' initial opinion that theological beliefs may find rational support in the recognition of evidence."[86]

This understanding of Hume is furthered by a little-noticed description attached to Philo who claims to be a mystic. (*Dialogues*, p. 199) This also is consistent with the fideistic interpretation: according to the traditional undertanding of this word, a mystic seeks immediate, intuitive, noninferential religious and moral enlightenment because of the impossibility of getting by any other way the facts, knowledge, or understanding about God or anything related to God. This abandonment of rational procedures and resources for nonrational or irrational ones is precisely what the fideist program advocates. This word chosen by Hume is another small point in the entire collection of evidence which shows that the skeptical interpretation of Hume is inadequate. The fideist understanding of Hume is better able to explain such things as Philo's reference to himself as a "mystic" than is the traditional skeptical interpretation of Hume.

Referring to Philo as a mystic is unalloyed fideism which Hume first brought into prominence. It is displayed here rather clearly in his religious writings. It is necessary to turn to his metaphysical works for further examples of this approach to knowledge.

CHAPTER 4

HUME'S METAPHYSICAL DOCTRINES

Fideistic thinking appears in Hume's earliest writings, so it is not a product of his old age or of his last published works. His first work, *A Treatise of Human Nature*, which Hume intended as a technical statement of his philosophical position, shows the fideistic epistemological position and method.

The previous chapters of this book have produced a background against which to appreciate the claims presented in this chapter. On the premise that fideism is a possibility in the *Dialogues concerning Natural Religion*, it may also be a possibility in Hume's other philosophical works. That is the minimal claim of this chapter. The full claim, of course, goes far beyond that.

The *main* emphasis here will be on the *Treatise*. The first *Enquiry* will be of secondary importance. This is in keeping with the assessment given to the *Treatise*, and the study of Hume for the past century. Hume intended that his *Treatise* would be the major vehicle for the introduction of his philosophical views. He had second thoughts about this in the years following the publication of the *Treatise*, and he tells us that he published this work at a time when his maturity was not sufficient for the task, so he decided to supply a more mature account, according to this advertisement printed in the *Enquiry*:

> *Most of the principles and reasonings, contained in this volume, were published in a work in three volumes, called* A Treatise of Human Nature: *A work which the Author had projected before he left College, and which he wrote and published not long after. But not finding it successful, he was sensible of his error in going to the press too early, and he cast the whole anew in the following pieces, where some negligences in his former reasoning and more in the expression, are, he hopes, corrected.* (p. 2)[1]

A few lines farther on he calls the *Treatise* "that juvenile work," expresses outrage at some of his critics, and makes it clear he wanted to be judged by the *Enquiry*. Recent philosophers have not viewed the *Treatise* in that way, and many believe Hume's first work was a masterpiece which deserves the closest study and attention. This study takes the latter perspective, and will concentrate on the *Treatise* and appeal to other Humean material including the first *Enquiry*.

Is it possible to use "fideism" or talk about "fideistic elements in Hume's thought" when talking about doctrines which have nothing to do with religion? Is this not a stretching of concepts, an abuse of words, a case of ignoring the conventions of our language? That will have to be answered in several steps. The fideistic procedure abandons rational means or method and rational basis or argument for something which is nonrational (or irrational) in believing an assertion, adopting a conclusion, or deciding on an action. Often these tendencies are found in religious faith and practice, but they do not belong there exclusively. An arbitrary decision, leap, or commitment to any object of belief or a particular doctrine would be a fideistic act or have a fideistic character whether or not the word "faith" ever appeared. In this usage, fideism is a logical or epistemological approach which abandons a methodology based on rational considerations for one which leaves out rationality largely or altogether. It is an attempt to hold or a way of holding to certain conclusions without having to have reasons or an epistemic ground to support the belief. So, conscious (and even unconscious) reliance on nonrational or irrational bases are marks of fideism. This can be illustrated by a person who found that he didn't understand the issues of a political campaign or the candidate's position on these and who gave up on these only to follow a candidate because he had a large and vocal following, he was receiving a great deal of attention from the news media, he used the right political language, or he was otherwise charismatic. Failure to assess what the politician says, to ascertain his qualifications and experience, to probe for evidences of integrity (or the lack of it) would be an illustration of abandoning rationality in making a choice of political support. Fideism is not a fallacy of irrelevancy, because something irrelevant is not taken in place of the (logically) relevant due to confusion or the attempt to confuse someone else. Instead, the rational and relevant considerations are *passed over* or *let go* only to adopt a nonrational basis for coming to the conclusion.

Hume's procedure for adopting beliefs about metaphysical issues is essentially fideistic. This conclusion is made more likely by the appearance of an explicit fideism in his philosophy of religion since, apparently, he employs "faith" as a way of recovering many doctrines of religion which his previous analysis was calculated to destroy. Since Hume's philosophy of religion appears to support such a method it should not be surprising to find this same epistemological method used elsewhere.

Besides this inherent likelihood, current usage of the term in Hume's time seems to support such a practice. "Fideism" is used by Popkin and other writers about the pyrrhonist skeptical tradition in the expanded sense it is receiving here. References to this are given in a later chapter, and to avoid repetition the reader will be referred that treatment, but prevailing use by prominent philosophers preceding Hume and even during Hume's age supports the use of "fideism" as a means of gaining concepts outside the sphere of religion. The tradition running through Montaigne, Bayle, and many other lesser-known figures to Hume supports this use of the word. French Pyrrhonism used faith in the general, secular, nonreligious sense as providing the basis for belief in all areas of knowledge and intellectual activity and on all kinds of nonreligious topics. It accords with seventeenth and eighteenth century usage to employ faith in this general sense, and we are doing that in applying fideism to Hume's nonreligious doctrines. So, it seems to be entirely appropriate to refer to a fideism in light of Hume's practice, the culture of his day, and recent scholarship on early modern Pyrrhonism. In Hume's metaphysical views, there is an implicit instead of an explicit fideism since he nowhere resorts to "faith," yet the pattern is the same. For those reasons it seems justifiable to refer to his position and method as a fideism or as having fideistic elements. *The fideism employed here is a general, not a religious one.*

HUME'S PATTERN OF REASONING IN THE *TREATISE*

The *Treatise* contains a noticeable pattern of reasoning which is repeated again and again. Hume analyzes some concept such as the concept of substance, causality, or self identity, and his analysis goes something like this little imaginary train of reasoning: Some philosophers claim that we have an idea of A. But if we have such an idea it must be derived either from the impressions of our sense or from reflection. Let us suppose that our idea of A is from impressions of sensation. If the idea is conveyed to us by our senses, I would ask which one of them gives it to us, and how it gives it to us. For example, if it comes to us by our eyes it must be a color. If it comes to us by our ears it must be a sound. If it comes to us by our tongue and palate it must be a taste. If it comes to us by our nose it must be a smell. But the idea of A is none of these. It is not any color, sound, taste, or smell, so it must not come from any impression of sense. And if it is not from impressions of sense that we have the idea of A then it must be from an impression of reflection that we have the idea if it really exists. But our impressions of reflection resolve themselves into our passions and emotions, and none of these can possibly represent the idea of A to us. We have, therefore, no idea of A nor have we any meaning when we either talk or reason concerning it.

Some minor liberties have been taken with this brief imaginary account of a Humean analysis. Nevertheless, the form it takes is familiar to readers of Hume. Hume uses just such a kind of analysis several times in the *Treatise*.[2]

Hume makes the arresting, even shocking, statement that we have no idea of A. Are we to take Hume seriously here? Is this hyperbole or does he have something else in mind? Is this just one of the shocking elements we find in Hume's youthful work? What are we to do with it? This much is clear about Hume's claim: for Hume to make the claim that "we have ... no idea of A," he must have an idea of A or he could not comment on it as he does. He brings A to our attention, analyzes the concept, and goes on to deny it for all kinds of reasons. For Hume and his readers there must be the conception of A, that is, the cognitive awareness of the matter together with some understanding for there to be any kind of a "meeting of minds." Hume's reader, of course, has some idea of what Hume is talking about because he has been watching Hume introduce the topic, examine it, and reject it on some epistemic ground. So, Hume must have the idea, too, for his analysis to be meaningful and relevant.

This may seem to be a trivial problem in Hume's philosophy, but it does not receive much attention and is seldom commented on by Hume scholars. This is surprising in light of the fact that he uses this expression over and over again. Livingston comments on the phrase in his discussion of Hume's doctrine of cause:

> When Hume says we have no idea of causal power, he means that we do not have an internal mastery of the concept; that is, we have no image of power. This does not prevent us, however, from having an external grasp of the concept, that is, knowing the public criteria for applying the expression "causal power" in some linguistic convention.[3]

This treatment of Hume's judgment is highly questionable. First of all, it is hard to imagine what an "image" of power would be. We have images of visible things, but how can we have such a thing when there is nothing to see? The causal relation is not a visible thing. By "image" does he mean concept? If so, then an internal mastery of the concept would be to have a concept, and that is not very enlightening. Second, what would an "external grasp" of a concept be? He applies it to knowing how to use a word, but that is not very useful either. Furthermore, there is no evidence that Hume ever had in mind linguistic usage as a criterion of understanding or the adequacy of a concept

The comment (that we have no idea of A) seems inherently contradictory so that we would expect some notice to be taken of it, but with the exception of an infrequent reference like that of Livingston that seldom happens. Although we are not up against the major problem of the *Treatise*, Hume felt the need to address that very issue. He says: "Now 'tis certain we have an idea of extension; for otherwise why do we talk and reason concerning it?" (*Treatise*, p. 32)

What Hume means by "we have ... no idea of A" must be that we have no justification for having an idea of something or other, or of holding to proposition A. We may have no impressions of what the name designates. Or, there is no logical basis, no adequate reasons, for holding to A—we have no arguments to enable us to hold to the existence of it. Intellectually, it is not possible to defend believing in A to anyone else (or even to one's self). This kind of explanation seems inevitable, because for Hume to say, "We have ... no idea of A" appears to be inconsistent with his very astute treatment of some metaphysical concepts such as causation, substance, or personal identity. How can someone name, analyze, and make pronouncements about something of which he has no idea?

In addition to Hume's analysis of all the ideas he says we don't have, there is the persistent tendency to use the idea later as if the thing it was about had had its existence substantiated and all objections to its acceptance had been answered. Thus, he appears to accept all the ideas (or concepts) he questions and believes the doctrine he analyzes. To do this, Hume is forced to resort to some irrational (or nonrational) basis, and though that point is not the central issue right now, it does add weight to the claim that he in fact *does* have the idea he denies. He believes it at last (after his analysis) because he possessed the idea at first or else there would be little reason for it occurring in his discussion at all. This accords best with the claim that Hume's judgment, "We have, therefore, no idea of A," means that we have no logical justification for the acceptance of the idea.

Explanation for Hume is fundamentally genetic or developmental. He is inclined to engage in this kind of explanation: Since we have no idea of B which is not derived from impressions there must be some one impression which gives rise to the idea of B. Hume then attempts to show that there is no impression which could account for the idea and hence there is no idea. Then Hume begins his explanation on how he retains the idea he has examined and rejected, and his treatment, though not uniform, is like this: "'Tis the constant conjunction of objects, along with the determination of the mind, which constitutes a physical necessity." (*Treatise*, p. 171) Or, "When the mind forms a reasoning concerning any matter of fact which is only probable, it casts its eye backward upon past experience, and transferring it to the future, is presented with so many contrary views of its object, of which those that are of the same kind uniting together, and running into one act of the mind, serve to fortify and inliven it." (*Treatise*, p. 140) Or as this more complete third example elaborates:

> We have a distinct idea of an object, that remains invariable and uninterrupted thro' a suppos'd variation of time; and this idea we call that of *identity* or *sameness*. We have also a distinct idea of several different objects existing in succession ... a notion of *diversity*, as if there was no manner of relation among the objects. But tho' these two ideas of identity, and a succession of related objects be in themselves perfectly distinct, and even contrary, yet 'tis certain, that in our common way of thinking they are generally confounded with each other. That action of the imagination, by which we consider the uninterrupted and invariable object, and that by which we reflect on the succession of related objects, are almost the same to the feeling, nor is there much more effort of thought requir'd in the latter case than in the former. The relation facilitates the transition of the mind from one object to another, and renders its passage as smooth as if it contemplated one continued object. This resemblance is the cause of the confusion and mistake, and makes us substitute the notion of identity, instead of that of related objects .... Our propensity to this mistake is so great from the resemblance above-mentioned, that we fall into it before we are aware; and tho' we incessantly correct ourselves by reflexion, and

return to a more accurate method of thinking, yet we cannot long sustain our philosophy, or take off this biass from the imagination. Our last resource is to yield to it, and boldly assert that these different related objects are in effect the same, however interrupted and variable. (*Treatise*, pp. 253-254)

The *Treatise* has many more such comments, and many such pronouncements are found in the *Enquiry*, for example: "All inferences from experience ... are effects of custom, not of reasoning." (*Enquiry*, p. 43) These statements from Hume show how on philosophical grounds we can come to a skeptical conclusion and how on a psychological basis we can believe that same conclusion. The psychological explanation is a part of Hume's entire approach at metaphysical or epistemological questions, and he sees it as the final reason for the adoption of the doctrine. Hume employs appeals to the tendencies of human nature to arrive at his fideistic conclusions.

CAUSATION AND PHILOSOPHY

The doctrine of causation is the most far-reaching and momentous issue which Hume treats in Book I of the *Treatise*, and Hume scholars have given it more attention than any other doctrine with the possible exception of the doctrine of ideas. Annette Baier comments that Hume's account of causal inference has been written about so much that "it takes a rash person to add another word" let alone add two chapters as she does.[4] Galen Strawson's recent book[5] provides such an outstanding treatment of the topic that it is questionable how much could be added here. Strawson argues against the "regularity" theory of causation, and indicates that it still is the standard view.[6] He cautions us that his book is not just about Hume, but since Hume is the first philosopher to raise questions about the nature of cause, he looms very large in his treatment, and we can be grateful for Strawson's full examination of the regularity view. The book is also quite refreshing in its candor and Strawson's willingness to pronounce judgments on certain philosophical positions in unvarnished terms!

Causation underlies processes, states, and relations of material things, ideas, in fact, almost all else. Metaphysically, then, the doctrine of causation is important not only because cause is of great interest in itself, but because it is so closely linked with the way things are and their place in the world. Analyzing cause and effect as a basic, unavoidable idea (even an assumption) of our lives entitles Hume to recognition for his astute insight. If Hume had brought into question nothing more than our belief in cause and effect, he would have been assured of a place of honor in the history of philosophy for seeing a problem that other thinkers of lasting influence passed over or failed to see.

The doctrine of causation is important also for epistemology because it raises questions about the relations among our thoughts and the relations of our thoughts to the world. The relations of thoughts to each other involve several "bonds of union" for Hume, all of which are part of the association of ideas. Cause and effect is one of these relations (or "relaters"). Since simple ideas may be separated by the imagination, according to Hume, and may be united again in whatever form the imagination pleases, there must be some universal principles which guide the "operations of that faculty" (the imagination) and render it in some measure uniform with itself in all times and places. Ideas are not entirely loose and unconnected or else they would be "joined" entirely by chance. They do have some bond of union, some associating quality, by which one idea naturally introduces another. The mind is not under any sort of compulsion in connection with these uniting forces because it is a very free faculty, more free, in fact, than any other faculty, so one must regard these forces as "gentle" ones which commonly work in the mind. (*Treatise*, p. 10) These common forces are the reason why, Hume believes, different languages so nearly correspond to one another.

Of the three "qualities," from which association arises, resemblance, contiguity in time or place, and cause and effect, the last is claimed to be the most important: "'Tis sufficient to observe, that there is no relation, which produces a stronger connexion in the fancy, and makes one idea more readily recall another, than the relation of cause and effect betwixt their objects." (*Treatise*, p. 11) "The examination of the idea [of causation] bestows a like clearness on all our reasoning." (*Treatise*, p. 75) In addition, Hume uses another classification where cause is treated as one of the seven relations. In that list, cause and effect is a seventh philosophical relation as well as a natural relation, or one which operates as a "matter of fact" and not solely within the sphere of the "relation of ideas." In other words, causation is a relation among objects and not only among ideas, so it has scientific significance and is not of importance only in philosophy, but also in theology, mathematics, or any other discipline where abstract matters relieve us of the necessity to look around for perceptions which will give us authority for our beliefs.

Since causation has such far-reaching implications as a doctrine, and the negative ("skeptical") conclusions Hume held have had such an effect on philosophers who followed him, it seems advisable to take the doctrine of causation for the first case study in which to analyze Hume's fideistic tendencies. Our account here will not include a minute description of all Hume's points since they are quite well known and are readily available from almost any book on Hume or history of philosophy, and many extremely fine treatments of causation are available. Since our purpose here is to show how Hume's position fits into a general fideist position, I intend to present what appears to be relevant to that purpose and to leave out discussion of many tempting issues.

To carry through such a goal it will be necessary as a minimum to talk of Hume's reductive analysis, his negative doctrine, in which he leaves the appearance subscribed to by legions of Hume's readers that he is a skeptic, that we "have no idea of" causation. These readers have understood Hume as one who does not believe in the reality of, in the presence of, a cause or that it is mere regularity between what comes first and what follows, etc. Multitudes of Hume's readers have been astonished that he would question something about which we are so convinced.

The negative doctrine of Hume, his "destructive" program, must be followed, then, by his positive doctrine of causation, his "constructive" side, and by an account on how it is that Hume can believe in such a thing when he took such elaborate steps over scores of pages to cast the concept of cause into doubt. It is with Hume's positive side that I claim that Hume's acceptance of the causal relation is a fideism, an acceptance of things not allowable on rational grounds on other, replacement grounds instead. This fideism is not a religious one but a general fideism involving cause and effect as metaphysical entities in a matter that has nothing to do with religious issues at all. And so Hume allows that there is cause and effect though he previously cast the whole issue into doubt. This dual emphasis and how it fits into the pattern of a general fideism will be the goal of our discussion.

CAUSATION: THE ANALYTIC OR NEGATIVE SIDE

Hume lays out his epistemological method at the very beginning of the *Treatise*, and gives impressions, whether sensory or outer ones, or the reflective or inner ones, the dominant role to play in his theory of knowledge. Not everything which goes on in the mind or is important for human life is a case of perceiving either as impressions or as ideas, however. People have beliefs about all sorts of things which neither are immediately perceived nor are derived from these immediate perceptions. Some beliefs are about things which no one has observed and so there are no impressions to be had about them, and Hume agrees that resemblance or analogy can work to produce ideas for which we have never had an impression. (*Treatise*, p. 3) This is best illustrated by our complex ideas of say, a city like Paris for which we could not have a specific impression. Nevertheless, this holds for all simple ideas which are derived from simple impressions: "*all our simple ideas in their first appearance are deriv'd from simple impressions, which are correspondent to them, and which they exactly represent.*" (*Treatise*, p. 4) Letting several things go which are not of central relevance for us, Hume affirms that the mind possesses great freedom in dealing with these ideas. The imagination is very free to deal with these ideas. Since the imagination is very free to separate and unite ideas there would be no accounting for them were not the imagination guided by some universal principles which render it uniform with itself in some measure in all times and places.

The "gentle force" of association involves resemblance, contiguity in time or place, and cause and effect. By these "qualities" association arises in the mind, and "after this manner" the mind is "convey'd from one idea to another." (*Treatise*, p. 11) Association unites ideas so that the appearance of one idea naturally introduces another. Imagination, Hume says, runs easily from one idea to any other that resemblances it and "this quality alone is to the fancy a sufficient bond and association." (*Treatise*, p. 11) Hume states that "of the three relations above-mention'd this of causation is the most extensive." (*Treatise*, p. 12) "All reasonings concerning matter of fact seem to be founded on the relation of *Cause and Effect*. By means of that relation alone we can go beyond the evidence of our memory and senses." (*Enquiry*, p. 26) Causation, then, lies at the very center of Humean epistemology and explains to us why Hume emphasizes it so strongly: "The examination of the idea [of causation] bestows a like clearness on all our reasoning." (*Treatise*, p. 75)

Hume lays out his analysis of cause by describing the "ingredients" as contiguity of time and place of cause and effect, (*Treatise*, p. 75) the temporal priority of cause before effect, (*Treatise*, p. 76) and necessity or the necessary connection between cause and effect. (*Treatise*, p. 77f) Contiguity and succession do not afford the "compleat" idea of causation because without necessary connection we do not have a causal situation at all. So, necessary connection is the indispensable element in cause. Otherwise we have things like day and night or inhaling and exhaling, both cases where the contiguity and succession fit Hume's analysis without either being the cause or the effect of the other.

Hume has no doubt that his readers do have an idea, a complex idea, of necessary connection which will serve adequately for discussion. Along with these three elements of cause which Hume introduces together, we find a fourth one, constant conjunction, which he introduces slightly later. The introduction of constant conjunction at this place complicates Hume's analysis. He says in the *Treatise* (p. 87) that

> "We have insensibly discover'd a new relation betwixt cause and effect, when we least expected it, and were entirely employ'd upon another subject. This relation is their CONSTANT CONJUNCTION. Contiguity and succession are not sufficient to make us pronounce any two objects to be cause and effect, unless we perceive, that these two relations are preserv'd in several instances."

His words here indicate that cause and effect must be conjoined so that constant conjunction is a relation of these two things. It is not contiguity and temporal priority of cause before effect that must be conjoined but the "thing" called cause and the "thing" called effect. Hume clarifies this detail for us in his *Abstract* when he lists constant conjunction as a third circumstance between cause and effect. This together with necessary connection would give us a list of four relations between cause and effect. Using his model for cause of the striking of two billiard balls, when one strikes the other, says that,

> *Contiguity* in time and place is therefore a requisite circumstance to the operation of all causes. 'Tis evident likewise, that the motion, which was the cause, is prior to the motion, which was the effect. *Priority* in time, is therefore another requisite circumstance in every cause. But this is not all. Let us try any other balls of the same kind in a like situation, and we shall always find, that the impulse of the one produces motion in the other. Here therefore is a *third* circumstance, *viz.* that of a *constant conjunction* betwixt cause and effect. Every object like the cause, produces always some object like the effect. Beyond these three circumstances of contiguity, priority, and constant conjunction, I can discover nothing in this cause. (*Treatise*, pp. 649-650)

Hume's treatment of the causal relation differs considerably in Section VII of the first *Enquiry* from what he gives in the *Treatise*. The *Enquiry concerning Human Understanding* is approximately 59 percent of the length of Book I of *A Treatise of Human Nature*. Some things had to slip in his shorter work, but it is surprising how much Hume shortened his examination of cause and effect in the *Enquiry*, because it was the topic which took the most pages of all in the *Treatise*. Perhaps the inclusion of his long chapters on miracles and providence forced further economies of space than Hume otherwise might have made, because the two chapters on miracles and providence represent one quarter of the *Enquiry*!

The most cogent reason we can give for the shorter treatment of cause and effect in the *Enquiry* was that after several years of reflection, Hume saw that the real issue of cause and effect was the necessary relation between them. The other elements of his analysis of cause and effect were disposable. Hume set out to clarify our ideas on cause and effect much as he did in the *Treatise*, but there is a difference in tone. In the *Treatise* there is more of the spirit of the examination of a metaphysical reality, the influential relation of cause and effect and how this impinges on the association of ideas, reasoning from the past, and drawing conclusions beyond the range of our experience.

Gone from the *Enquiry* is any analysis of contiguity, temporal priority, or constant conjunction such as that given in the *Treatise*. Hume saw that he could leave out an examination of the other "parts" or elements of cause without loss. Since the crux of his whole discussion is necessary connection between cause and effect, he puts his whole emphasis on necessary connection and the terms which serve to express that difficult-to-describe relation.

The *Enquiry* was written at the height of Hume's powers and after he had had sufficient time to reflect upon the *Treatise* and its failure in the academic "market." He may have treated necessity as he did in the *Enquiry* because he regretted making the previous discussion in the *Treatise* so long and drawn out.

Or, he may have realized that the problem was how we can know about, find, and give a basis for believing in necessity since necessary connection was the central issue. Or, there may be other reasons such as the crush for space brought about by sections X and XI. At any rate, the *Enquiry* both simplifies the issue of the nature of this necessity and focuses more sharply on the issue of our knowledge of cause and effect.

Back to the *Treatise*. A difficulty arises quickly when Hume begins his list of the elements of cause and effect, because we have no impression of necessary connection. We have impressions of contiguity, of temporal priority of cause before effect, and of constant conjunction of cause and effect, but not of necessary connection.

> When I cast my eye on the *known qualities* of objects, I immediately discover that the relation of cause and effect depends not in the least on *them*. When I consider their *relations*, I can find none but those of contiguity and succession; which I have already regarded as imperfect and unsatisfactory. Shall the despair of success make me assert, that I am here possest of an idea, which is not preceded by any similar impression? (*Treatise*, p. 77)

It seems to follow that if we never get an impression of the necessary connection between cause and effect in any particular instance, then Hume's main empiricist methodological principle would have to be abandoned. We can certainly disbelieve that many events are causally connected, but however we think about it, we cannot bring ourselves to disbelieve in the existence of cause. Neither could Hume. But the necessity, the necessary connection, is the indispensable element which distinguishes causal situations from other situations which have contiguity and temporal priority. If we don't have necessary connection, then we don't have cause. Hume may be right about the claim that we don't have an *impression* of the necessary connection, the force, power, or "causiness" when we find a case of causal connection. As it works out in our lives, regular succession, constant conjunction may be all that we *see*. The impression we receive may not coincide with our concept, our concept of cause in this case, but that does not mean there is no cause. So, if that is the claim that Hume is making, it is much less objectionable. A broad group of Hume scholars have taken Hume to mean that since we do not have any impression of necessary connection there is no such thing as cause. Claims about our impressions and about what is the metaphysical reality of the world are two very different things.

Is this comment by Hume a counter example to the principle that all ideas arise in the mind as the result of their corresponding earlier impressions (whether of sensation or reflection)? Hume is aware of the threat to his method that this case presents but sticks to his approach "since the contrary principle has been so firmly establish'd, as to admit of no farther doubt; at least, till we have more fully examin'd the present difficulty." (*Treatise*, p. 77) If the question brings up the possibility of an idea without a corresponding impression, the "contrary principle" would be "no impression, no idea" which he regards as "firmly establish'd."

Stroud contends that Hume regards the "no impression ... no idea" principle as contingent:

> If we never get an impression of the necessary connection between cause and effect in any particular instance of causality, it would seem that Hume's main methodological principle must be abandoned. The idea of causality appears to be a counter-example to the principle that all ideas arise in the mind as the result of their corresponding earlier impressions. Hume is aware of the threat this poses, and admits, albeit somewhat disingenuously, that the principle will have to be given up if the impressions from which the idea of causality is derived cannot be found (p. 77). This gives some further evidence that he regards the principle as contingent.[7]

Hume previously has made these assertions:

1. *"All our simple ideas in their first appearance are derived from simple impressions, which are correspondent to them, and which they exactly represent."* (*Treatise*, p. 4) (His unsensed shade of blue allows that there may be exceptions.)
2. "Impressions of reflexion are only antecedent to their correspondent ideas; but posterior to those of sensation, and deriv'd from them." (*Treatise*, p. 8)
3. "Simple perceptions or impressions and ideas are such as admit of no distinction nor separation. The complex are the contrary to these, and may be distinguished into parts." (*Treatise*, p. 2)
4. There are no innate ideas because "ideas are preceded by other more lively perceptions, from which they are derived, and which they represent." (*Treatise*, p. 7)
5. "Many of our complex ideas never had impressions, that corresponded to them, and that many of our complex impressions never are exactly copied in ideas." (*Treatise*, p. 3)
6. "Complex ideas ... are the common subjects of our thoughts and reasoning, and generally arise from some principle of union among our simple ideas." (*Treatise*, p. 13)

These epistemological assertions make it difficult for Hume at this place because we infer causes from effects and vice versa. When we engage in that ineradicable habit of our lives, we do that and there are only two options open to us. We must do it,

> either by an immediate perception of our memory or senses, or by an inference from other causes; which causes again we must ascertain in the same manner, either by a present impression, or by an inference from *their* causes, and so on, till we arrive at some object, which we see or remember. 'Tis impossible for us to carry on our inferences *in infinitum*; and the

Hume's Metaphysical Doctrines

> only thing, that can stop them, is an impression of the memory or senses, beyond which there is no room for doubt or enquiry. (*Treatise*, p. 83)

So, this is the issue: We do not possess any idea unless there is an impression to account for it (psychologically) or to support it (philosophically). The tension of "no impression ... no idea" arises again. We have the idea of necessary connection but no way to get it by Hume's method. "When I consider their *relations*, I can find none but those of contiguity and succession." (*Treatise*, p. 77)

> I immediately perceive that they are contiguous in time and place, and that the object we call cause precedes the other we call effect. In no one instance can I go any farther, nor is it possible for me to discover any third relation betwixt these objects. (*Treatise*, p. 155)

So: "We never have any impression that contains any power or efficacy. We never therefore have any idea of power." (*Treatise*, p. 161)

What is necessary connection? What would we have to see, feel for us to recognize it? What could introduce that term into our vocabulary? Why is the idea so obscure? The term so ambiguous? What makes "necessary connection" so vague? Hume attempts to answer that difficulty:

> There are no ideas, which occur in metaphysics, more obscure and uncertain, than those of *power, force, energy,* or *necessary connexion*, of which it is every moment necessary for us to treat in all our disquisitions. We shall, therefore, endeavour, in this section, to fix, if possible, the precise meaning of these terms, and thereby remove some part of that obscurity, which so much complained of in this species of philosophy. (*Enquiry*, pp. 61-62)

After a brief rehearsal of his doctrine that ideas are derived from impressions of force, power, efficacy, necessary connection, Hume turns to the possibility that we derive the idea from our own persons where physical actions follow immediately upon volitions. In this case the nature of necessary connection is mysterious and unknown: "But the power of energy by which this is effected, [motion in one's body following 'the command of the will'] like that in other natural events, is unknown and inconceivable." (*Enquiry*, p. 67) In a footnote attached to this last sentence Hume attempts to give the meaning of "necessary connection" by referring to the resistance we meet with in bodies:

> It may be pretended, that the resistance which we meet with in bodies, obliging us frequently to exert our force, and call up all our power, this gives us the idea of force and power. It is this *nisus*, or strong endeavour, of which we are conscious, that is the original impression from which this idea is copied. But, first, we attribute power to a vast number

of objects, where we never can suppose this resistance or exertion of force to take place; to the Supreme Being, who never meets with any resistance; to the mind in its command over its ideas and limbs, in common thinking and motion, where the effect follows immediately upon the will, without any exertion or summoning up of force; to inanimate matter, which is not capable of this sentiment. *Secondly,* This sentiment of an endeavour to overcome resistance has no known connexion with any event: What follows it, we know by experience; but could not know it *a priori*. It must, however, be confessed, that the animal *nisus*, which we experience, though it can afford no accurate precise idea of power, enters very much into that vulgar, inaccurate idea, which is formed of it.

Hume does not give a definition of necessary connection precise enough to please anyone with the habits of rigor characteristic of the analytic tradition in philosophy. For the most part he simply claims that it is impossible for us to define necessary connection. It certainly won't do to resort to a group of synonyms. (*Treatise*, p. 157) It doesn't help to invoke terms such as *efficacy, agency, power, force, energy, necessity, connexion,* or *productive quality* since these terms are as mysterious in their meaning as is "necessary connexion." Most of Hume's attention is concentrated on the question of how we know, believe in or recognize the presence of necessary connection. His answer is: "'Tis the constant conjunction of objects, along with the determination of the mind, which constitutes physical necessity: And the removal of these is the same thing with chance." (*Treatise*, p. 171) How do we know when there is physical necessity or necessary connection? What would it be like? The answer is given in Hume's list of *"Rules by which to judge of causes and effects."* (*Treatise*, p. 173f) When those rules lead us to recognize the presence of cause then necessary connection is present. When we do not have cause, there is no necessary connection.

It is possible to exclude some meanings of necessary connection which Hume did not mean. Hume does not have in mind the "formal" world of mathematical and logical relations which are timeless and exceptionless. That being a triangle *necessarily* involves being three-sided, that $2+2=4$, or that if the premises are true and we follow modus ponens reasoning that the conclusion "must" be, that is, *necessarily* is true is not what Hume has in mind. So necessary connection is *not* logical necessity. Such necessity partakes of the relations of ideas which includes "every affirmation which is either intuitively or demonstratively certain." (*Enquiry*, p. 25) Hume is clear that the question of causation is a matter of fact, and is about necessary connection in the world of sensory experience, of spatio-temporal objects, of material things where the conceivable is the measure of the possible, and where it is possible to have a contrary to every matter of fact. Matters of fact do not involve only spatio-temporal, material objects, in Hume's view, however, because necessary connection and cause and effect are concepts in our mind and involve the joining of ideas.[8]

In matters of fact there is no prior assurance that such-and-such will be. We can only look and see whether there is any necessary connection present. It is not a priori necessary. Nor is it the mere regularity of C before E. If it were, then Hume would not have needed to mention necessary connection since he had previously listed temporal priority of cause before effect and the constant conjunction of the two. Nor is it our sort of volitional sense of power shown in cases where we believe our decision to raise our arm actually results in the elevation of that arm. (*Enquiry*, pp. 64-67) Third, it is not any one of the three other conditions of cause either alone or in some combination with the others. Hume lists necessary connection as a separate, a fourth, ingredient of cause. Fourth, it is not the imperative or legal sense of necessary when it is said that we must obey stop signs or detours. These are prescriptive necessities and not the natural or descriptive necessity which Hume is analyzing in his treatment of cause, for no commands are given to cases of cause and effect. Fifth, it is not the moral must when someone says he must keep the promise he made or the sense of personal obligation in returning what they borrowed. Such cases require agents who are capable of contrary action. Causes and effects have no moral consciousness or ability.

Necessary connection is present and can be recognized when the other three conditions of causal connection are present between two things or "objects" and the effect does occur. Necessary connection is not present when the other three conditions of causal connection are present between two things or "objects" and the effect does not occur.

In fact, Hume does not inform us of the meaning of "necessary connection" and leaves the job of discovering that meaning to us. Anthony Flew remarks upon this in regard to Section VII of the *Enquiry* that

> What ought to appear remarkable at this point is not the inadequacy of Hume's account of necessity, but rather the absence from his definition of any reference to it. The whole Section is officially devoted to tracking down the original of the idea of necessary connection, which is supposedly involved in that of causation. Having at last now found that original Hume becomes, on Humean principles, fully justified to employ the word *necessary* and its derivatives in this context. We should therefore expect his definitions to speak both of constant conjunction and of something more, namely necessity. Instead he writes rather as if he had shown: not that talk of necessity does after all have some sense here, and what sense it has; but that really it has little or none, and arises from a misconception—the projection of a mental association out on to a physical conjunction. In the Treatise (*sic*) when he comes to write 'Of liberty and necessity' he claims: 'According to my definitions, necessity makes an essential part of causation ....' (THNI (iii) I, 407). But in neither the *Treatise* nor the *Inquiry* does he in fact find any place in his explicit definitions for the word necessary or for any of its derivatives.[9]

It is difficult to avoid placing our own words in Hume's treatment. Necessity, or necessary connection, when discussed with relation to cause is nowhere observable in the world because it is not a feature of objects. It is rather a feature of the mind and its "projection" of its own nature upon reality:

> Thus as the necessity, which makes two times two equal to four, or three angles of a triangle equal to two right ones, lies only in the act of the understanding, by which we consider and compare these ideas; in like manner the necessity or power, which unites causes and effects, lies in the determination of the mind to pass from the one to the other. The efficacy or energy of causes is neither plac'd in the causes themselves, nor in the deity, nor in the concurrence of these two principles; but belongs entirely to the soul, which considers the union of two or more objects in all past instances. 'Tis here that the real power of causes is plac'd, along with their connexion and necessity. (*Treatise*, p. 166)

So, what "necessary connection" would mean as a part of the analysis of causal connection and what cause there is for our having such an idea are two entirely different things for Hume.

> Recent analytic philosophers would concentrate on 'analysing' or 'defining' necessity, and so would tend to deviate from the spirit of Hume's programme. They would focus, not on what 'having the idea' of 'logical' necessity consists in, or on what makes it possible for us to regard some things as necessary and others as contingent, but simply on what 'necessary', or 'contingent' *means*. But the prospects of genuine illumination in that direction seem dim; terms like 'possible' or 'must' in which any such 'definition' would presumably be expressed 'are all nearly synonymous' with the term to be defined. If we find necessity and our thought of it puzzling we are not likely to get the kind of understanding we want by tracing its fairly obvious connections with other notions we find equally puzzling for the same reasons. At least that is not the kind of understanding Hume seeks in his science of man. He recognizes the dead-end represented by the appeal to 'power', 'efficacy' or 'productive quality' in the clarification of the idea of causal necessity, and the same pessimism would undoubtedly have carried over to an analogous account of 'absolute' necessity if he had pushed his investigation more resolutely in that direction.[10]

Our reading of Hume's analysis of causal connection so far comes to this: Cause involves as a very minimum a relation between two things (cause and effect respectively) which Hume calls necessity or necessary connection. While it may exist in the world (and at this point Hume leaves that question unanswered) our knowledge of it has no foundation. Why? Because ideas must have for their rise, their origin, impressions to warrant their being accepted by us, and we have no impression of necessity. "No impression ... no idea," or else we have an idea without support from experience. It seems highly questionable to challenge the relation between ideas and experience so we are forced to the conclusion that we have no logical foundation for our idea of necessary connection, that is, of cause. That is a skeptical conclusion, and it may not be what we would like to have in the world, but that is all that the facts of our experience will support.

CAUSATION AND INDUCTION

There is one remaining problem with Hume's negative or analytical treatment of causation. It is how Hume's statement of the problem of induction fits into his analysis of cause. Hume tells us that the issue of cause is connected to the problem of induction: "All our reasonings concerning the probability of causes are founded on the transferring of past to future." (*Treatise*, p. 137) Impressions and reflections about cause are about past causes both for Hume and his readers; otherwise we could not talk about cause or impressions. How could we talk about something which had not come into our experience unless these things were purely matters of imagination and speculation? Causes and effects do not have that status in Hume's thought. He is not imagining or speculating but describing and analyzing; thus we are left only with the past, its relation to the future, and the elements of cause that make considerations of past and future meaningful.

The epistemological issue is whether on the basis of past experience it is possible to find, recognize, and defend our beliefs about cases of cause and causal connection in the future. The instances of causal involvement about which Hume was interested, however, were still future. That is, unless Hume had a purely antiquarian interest, and he gives us no indication of any such preoccupation, his interest or concern was with the future for those causes and causal situations which he and his readers were likely to encounter. In past causal situations, Hume contends that there has been no impression of causal necessity; hence there is no (justification for) such an idea as cause, and there will be none in the future.

Any talk then about past causes would bring up the problem of whether the past could carry into the future and whether observed instances apply to unobserved ones. This is the problem of induction. So, whenever talk about past instances of things lead us to consider future instances of those same things, the problem of induction crops up; hence the problem of induction is a logically necessary subpoint or subdivision in the discussion on causation, and that is why it occurs in the middle of that discussion.[11]

The introduction of issues about the transition from the past to the future is epistemological. Hume is worried about ideas and the place that reason plays in these. Induction is like cause and effect in that both go from the past to what is future to it:

> Since it appears, that the transition from an impression present to the memory or senses to the idea of an object, which we call cause or effect, is founded on past *experience*, and on our remembrance of their *constant conjunction*, the next question is, Whether experience produces the idea by means of the understanding or the imagination; whether we are determin'd by reason to make the transition, or by a certain association and relation of perceptions. If reason determin'd us, it wou'd proceed upon that principle, *that instances, of which we have had no experience, must resemble those, of which we have had experience, and that the course of nature continues always uniformly the same.* (*Treatise*, pp. 88-89)

If reason be allowed as the basis for concluding that past instances could lead us validly to infer future instances and that the course of nature would continue uniformly the same, then Hume comes down on the side of belief and rationality. If reason is not allowed for these same conclusions, then Hume comes down on the side of skepticism and irrationality.

What Hume means by "instances" is so vague that it is impossible to know exactly what he has in mind. Even allowing for the degree of generality which must be present in philosophy, one wishes Hume had been more specific. Do "instances" include conditions? Or whole causal situations? Or events which display causal connection? Or mechanical causation? Or personal agency? Even with this ambiguity of reference or vagueness of application, it is easy to see that Hume has fastened on a major epistemological problem: One cannot experience everything; thus, how can one reason to those "things" not experienced? This issue applies whether "thing" refers to object, event, process, or anything else that is part of nature.

Hume provides a parallelism of expressions here which helps clarify what he conceives as rational and irrational. In the passage just cited, he says the "question is, whether experience produces the idea by means of the understanding or of the imagination; whether we are determin'd by reason to make the transition, or by a certain association and relation of perceptions." He contrasts these two sets of "producers":

understanding	imagination
reason	association and relation of perceptions

Since Hume makes the contrast he does, it appears that we are justified in concluding that understanding and reason are to be grouped together and imagination and association are also connected. Hume does not tell us exactly what reason is in the *Treatise*. Perhaps it is one of those "simple ideas" which are too elementary to describe and so must be left to be apprehended or grasped intuitively. He does say it is "nothing but a wonderful and unintelligible instinct in our souls, which carries us along a certain train of ideas, and endows them with particular qualities, according to their particular situations and relations." (*Treatise*, p. 179)

Although Hume is not very clear about the nature of reason he is more explicit about the uses of reason. In the *Treatise* he distinguishes human reason into three kinds: that from knowledge, from proofs, and from probabilities.

> By knowledge, I mean the assurance arising from the comparison of ideas. By proofs, those arguments, which are derived from the relation of cause and effect and which are entirely free from doubt and uncertainty. By probability, that evidence, which is still attended with uncertainty. (*Treatise*, p. 124)

In the first *Enquiry* he arrives at his mature position: "All reasonings may be divided into two kinds, namely, demonstrative reasoning, or that concerning relations of ideas, and moral reasoning, or that concerning matter of fact and existence." (*Enquiry*, p. 35) When Hume lists "moral reasoning" as that concerning matter of fact and existence, he is using "moral" in a sense different from current usage. Kemp Smith explains this sense:

> This broad use of the word 'moral' is connected with Hume's view of our knowledge as determined throughout by the natural beliefs, and as possessing no absolute metaphysical truth. Cf. the *Oxford Dictionary* on this wider application of the term: "Used to designate the kind of probable evidence that rests on a knowledge of the general tendencies of human nature, or of the character of particular individuals or classes of men; often, in looser sense, applied to all evidence which is merely probable and not demonstrative."[12]

Hume discusses the advantages and disadvantages of the mathematical and moral sciences in the first *Enquiry* (pp. 60-61). When everything is separated and shaken down, he concludes that the two fields are roughly equivalent:

> The great advantage of the mathematical sciences above the moral consists in this, that the ideas of the former, being sensible, are always clear and determinate, the smallest distinction between them is immediately perceptible, and the same terms are still expressive of the same ideas without ambiguity or variation. An oval is never mistaken for a circle, nor an hyperbola for an ellipsis. The isosoceles and scalenum are distinguished by boundaries more exact than vice and virtue, right and wrong. If any term be defined in geometry, the mind readily, of itself, substitutes, on all occasions, the definition for the term defined: Or even when no definition is employed, the object itself may be presented to the senses, and by that means be steadily and clearly apprehended. But the finer sentiments of the

mind, the operations of the understanding, the various agitations of the passions, though really in themselves distinct, easily escape us, when surveyed by reflection; nor is it in our power to recal [*sic*] the original object, as often as we have occasion to contemplate it. Ambiguity, by this means, is gradually introduced into our reasonings: Similar objects are readily taken to be the same: And the conclusion becomes at last very wide of the premises.

One may safely, however, affirm, that, if we consider these sciences in a proper light, their advantages and disadvantages nearly compensate each other, and reduce both of them to a state of equality. If the mind, with greater facility, retains the ideas of geometry clear and determinate, it must carry on a much longer and more intricate chain of reasoning, and compare ideas much wider of each other, in order to reach the abstruser truths of that science. And if moral ideas are apt, without extreme care, to fall into obscurity and confusion, the inferences are always much shorter in these disquisitions, and the intermediate steps, which lead to the conclusion, much fewer than in the sciences which treat of quantity and number. In reality, there is scarcely a proposition in Euclid so simple, as not to consist of more parts, than are to be found in any moral reasoning which runs not into chimera and conceit. Where we trace the principles of the human mind through a few steps, we may be very well satisfied with our progress; considering how soon nature throws a bar to all our enquiries concerning causes, and reduces us to an acknowledgment of our ignorance. The chief obstacle, therefore, to our improvement in the moral or metaphysical sciences is the obscurity of the ideas, and ambiguity of the terms. The principal difficulty in the mathematics is the length of inferences and compass of thought, requisite to the forming of any conclusion. And, perhaps, our progress in natural philosophy is chiefly retarded by the want of proper experiments and phaenomena, which are often discovered by chance, and cannot always be found, when requisite, even by the most diligent and prudent enquiry. As moral philosophy seems hitherto to have received less improvement than either geometry or physics, we may conclude, that if there be any difference in this respect among these sciences, the difficulties, which obstruct the progress of the former, require superior care and capacity to be surmounted.

If "reason determin'd us," that is, if reason were the decisive instrumentality in the matter, one could accept the principle of induction, but Hume does not think that there can be any demonstrative arguments which will do that. We can conceive a change in the course of nature, and to Hume, since conceivability is natural possibility, this means that such a change is not absolutely impossible. "To form a clear idea of any thing, is an undeniable argument for its possibility, and is alone a refutation of any pretended demonstration against it." (*Treatise*, p. 89)

Hume doesn't give any more hope to the possibility that we can empirically establish the principle of induction on the grounds that induction belongs to the world of fact and existence. All our experimental conclusions proceed upon the supposition that the future will be conformable to the past. (*Enquiry*, p. 35) Consequently, no experiential justification can be given for the principle of inductive uniformity. "To endeavour, therefore, the proof of this last supposition by probable arguments, or arguments regarding existence, must be evidently going in a circle, and taking that for granted, which is the very point in question." (*Enquiry*, pp. 35-36)

Stroud comments on that:

> Therefore, any experiential justification for the uniformity principle must consist of a justified inference from what *has* been observed to the truth of the principle. But according to the first step of the argument *every* inference from the observed to the unobserved is 'founded on the supposition' that the uniformity principle is true, so by instantiation it follows that any inference from the observed to the truth of the uniformity principle is true.[13]

Hume, then, comes down on the issue of induction precisely as he had in his analysis of cause: We are not justified in holding to the principle of induction or the regularity of nature. We have no reason, no rational basis, for believing in the principle of induction.

Since Hume disposes of the principle of induction by holding that there is no *rational* basis for holding to the doctrine, we are brought back to the issue of causation, because causation, or "cause and effect," is the only connection or relation of objects which can lead us beyond the immediate perceptions of our memory and senses. We must go beyond our memory and senses if we are going to be able to hold to inferences from one "object" to another. But belief in cause and effect is derived from experience which informs us only that such particular objects in all past experience have been conjoined to each other and that we have no rational reason to include the reality of necessary connection.

Such considerations belong to the contrast between "relations of ideas" and "matters of fact." The *Treatise* has such phrases as "the real relations of ideas" and "real existence and matter of fact," (*Treatise*, p. 458) but it is in the *Enquiry* where Hume begins Section IV with this well-known distinction. Cases of this distinction in the *Treatise* are not made clearly and probably would not have been noticed had Hume not made this distinction a major point in the *Enquiry*. In addition to the instance cited from the *Treatise*, Hume uses the phrase "matter of fact" in some places in the *Treatise*[14] and "relations of objects" (*Treatise*, p. 413) in contrast to the "abstract relations of our ideas."

Causation is unaffected by considering relations of ideas, for these relations work only in such areas as geometry or arithmetic, and though they deal with any "affirmation which is either intuitively or demonstratively certain," they have nothing to do with the world we experience. Since the relations discovered are involved in the ideas we compare and cannot be changed without a change in those ideas, their truth is guaranteed by the law of non-contradiction. The relations revealed in that way are, Hume declares, those of resemblance, contrariety, degrees in quality, and proportions in quantity or number. Since the mathematical sciences of arithmetic, algebra, and geometry involve only those relations, they are rendered possible by such discursive analytical thinking.

> *That the square of the hypothenuse is equal to the square of the two sides*, is a proposition which expresses a relation between these figures. *That three times five is equal to the half of thirty*, expresses a relation between these numbers. Propositions of this kind are discoverable by the mere operation of thought, without dependence on what is anywhere existent in the universe. Though there never were a circle or triangle in nature, the truths demonstrated by Euclid would for ever retain their certainty and evidence. (*Enquiry*, p. 25)

The world of our experience, of "matters of fact," is a different matter, however. It is the world of everyday life, of business and commerce, of Newton's science, of cause and effect. It is the world of experience not of reason. And experience can at best give us probability which for Hume is a variation of skepticism. When we seek by means of inference to extend our knowledge of real existence, we encounter a world where reason dealing as it does with relations of ideas has no use. It can criticize, analyze, and destroy our cherished ideas, but it can contribute nothing to our beliefs. In that role reason is impotent.

There is something else at stake in Hume's discussion. If we ask why Hume believes we must have some reason to believe in the principle of the uniformity of nature, it can be answered that he sees it reflecting on the basis of experience for all our knowledge. He says:

> For all inferences from experience suppose, as their foundation, that the future will resemble the past, and that similar powers will be conjoined with similar sensible qualities. If there be any suspicion that the course of nature may change, and that the past may be no rule for the future, all experience become useless, and can give rise to no inference or conclusion. (*Enquiry*, pp. 37-38)

For that to happen to an empiricist would be grave, indeed.

So Hume believes reason can give us no help in trusting in induction. When we look at experience we find it alike is impotent. So, our examination of induction gives us no basis for believing in the uniformity of nature.

Hume's doctrine of causation clearly indicates that on the basis of his analysis we have no reasons for believing in the existence of cause. First, we have no impression of the relation of necessity. Second, the nature of cause as a matter of fact shows that there can be no demonstrable argument to show the existence of so important a relation. Third, we have no basis in reason or experience for accepting the principle of induction which would allow us to believe in a nature uniform from past to future for causes and effects.

CAUSATION: THE CONSTRUCTIVE OR POSITIVE SIDE

Readers of Hume have felt that Hume gives plenty of good reasons for the skeptic interpretation of his writings especially for such a doctrine as cause and effect. Livingston remarks that Hume is best known for his analysis of causality and the theory of causal explanation and that there has always been a remarkably uniform opinion as to what that analysis is:

> It is generally believed that, in Hume's view, to say that A causes B is to say (1) that A-like things and B-like things are constantly conjoined and (2) that the mind on the appearance of an A feels a determination to expect that a B will occur and on the appearance of a B feels a determination to believe that an A has occurred. This interpretation is usually given a phenomenalistic twist to include the thesis (3) that the events conjoined must be analyzable without remainder into impressions. From these theses a theory of causal explanation follows: to give a causal explanation of an event is to cover it with an empirical regularity.
>
> We may call this the positivist interpretation not only because it resembles very closely the concept of causality and causal explanation given by contemporary positivists and logical empiricists but also because contemporary positivists have presented Hume as a precursor of their own view and have been influential in establishing the interpretation. There is, as we shall see, much in the text that appears to support it, but, in the end, it must be rejected because too much is left out.[15]

Although this account of Hume's beliefs is extreme, as are positivist interpretations of Hume's views, it is, nevertheless, a skeptic view. Most of Hume readers have not been positivists, but the skeptical understanding of Hume's treatment of causation has been the majority position.

In spite of the large number of readers who have viewed Hume as a skeptic, there has been a growing realization in recent decades that Hume is not a skeptic about causation, or, if he is a skeptic, we have to have a very special understanding of what his skepticism includes and how he regarded it. For a start on Hume's positive analysis of cause, let's look at three brief points which support the view that Hume did believe in cause and was not a skeptic. The first is Hume's comments in a letter of protest he wrote to John Stewart in 1754, six years after the publication of the *Enquiry*. Hume says in this letter, "Allow me to tell you, that I never asserted so absurd a Proposition as *that anything might arise without a Cause*: I only maintain'd that our Certainty of the Falshood [*sic*] of that Proposition proceeded neither from Intuitionism nor Demonstration; but from another source."[16] His concern is epistemological not metaphysical.

For a second point, Galen Strawson has collected a group of statements from the *Treatise*, the most pronounced source on Hume's alleged skeptical metaphysical doctrines, which Hume made about causation. These pronouncements question our *knowledge* of the causal relation. Strawson points out that without irony and with what look like perfectly straightforward expressions, Hume remarks on the causal relation, its intricacies and mysteries, and gives a distinct impression to the reader who does not demand a skeptical conclusion that Hume himself accepts cause and effect as real things in the world.[17] The net effect of these statements culled from the *Treatise* is that, given the most natural interpretation of Hume's locutions, we are left with the strong impression that Hume was not a skeptic at all about causation. These comments do not carry the main weight of his argument, Strawson tells us,[18] but he considers them very significant.

The third of the patent inconsistencies with the view that Hume did not believe in cause and effect which we will give here is his list of "Rules by which to judge of causes and effects." This section is surprising, even shocking, if we are looking for a consistent development of Hume's negative views on causation to the very end.

Even though reason cannot give us the existence of cause, Hume cannot get along without it. He believes in the existence of cause as surely as does anyone else though his method will not allow him to do this rationally. Rational or irrational, however, Hume is forced to take account of the reality of cause and therefore gives some rules by which to judge of causes and effects. (*Treatise*, pp. 173-176) Rules of discovery or detection make no sense unless there is something to be discovered or to be detected. No one does an assay unless there is something to be tested and determination to be made as to amount and quality. The idea that Hume would give some suggestions or rules for finding something that doesn't exist, and that he does not believe exists, is odd. A natural and unaffected examination of the rules would lead any reader to believe that Hume thought there was cause to be detected.

Some of these rules such as numbers five, six, and seven anticipate Mill's "four methods of experimental inquiry." Other rules from his list repeat what he so often had included in his negative analysis. Along with his eight rules for causes and effects, Hume, ever astute and incisive, offers some comments on how hard it is to establish causal connection:

> Our scholastic headpieces and logicians shew no such superiority above the mere vulgar in their reason and ability, as to give us any inclination to imitate them in delivering a long system of rules and precepts to direct our judgment in philosophy. All the rules of this nature are very easy in their invention, but extremely difficult in their application; and even experimental

philosophy, which seems the most natural and simple of any, requires the utmost stretch of human judgment. There is no phænomenon in nature, but what is compounded and modify'd by so many different circumstances, that in order to arrive at the decisive point, we must carefully separate whatever is superfluous, and enquire by new experiments, if every particular circumstance of the first experiment was essential to it. These new experiments are liable to a discussion of the same kind; so that the utmost constancy is requir'd to make us persevere in our enquiry, and the utmost sagacity to choose the right way among so many that present themselves. If this be the case even in natural philosophy, how much more in moral, where there is a much greater complication of circumstances, and where those views and sentiments, which are essential to any action of the mind, are so implicit and obscure, that they often escape our strictest attention, and are not only unaccountable in their causes, but even unknown in their existence? I am much afraid, lest the small success I meet with in my enquiries will make this observation bear the air of an apology rather than of boasting. (*Treatise*, p. 175)

Here Hume seems to be concerned about the causal connections of natural science, and he does not question the existence of cause and effect. What happened that made these remarks so different from his analytic treatment? How can Hume appear to admit belief in cause here when he questioned it so thoroughly earlier? How can we have rules for discovering the existence of causes when it was claimed earlier that "we have no such idea"? The answer appears to be that Hume, after "banishing" belief in cause or excluding such belief from our legitimate ideas on the basis of reason or rational activity, "brings back" belief in it on the basis of nonrational grounds. Prior to Hume's discussion of induction in the *Treatise*, he makes a remark which a later perspective shows to be prophetic. He says, "Perhaps 'twill appear in the end, that the necessary connexion depends on the inference, instead of the inference's depending on the necessary connexion." (*Treatise*, p. 88) In the next paragraph, he states it slightly differently:

> Since it appears, that the transition from an impression present to the memory or senses to the idea of an object, which we call cause or effect, is founded on past experience, and on our remembrance of their constant conjunction, the next question is, whether experience produces the idea by means of the understanding or the imagination; whether we are determin'd by reason to make the transition, or by a certain association and relation of perceptions.

The answer to this question is given by Hume's analytic or negative analysis of causation in which he says that our belief in causation is not a product of reason. Since we are not "determin'd by reason" to make the judgment of cause and effect (which is one of the two possibilities which Hume gives), the other possibility must give us the answer. And that in fact is what we find. On p. 88 of the *Treatise* Hume lists imagination and on the next page, "association and relation of perceptions" as the reasons why we believe in cause. This is one way of expressing what it is among our natural inclinations by which we are able to "get back" our belief in the reality of the causal situation which Hume's rational analysis had banned.

In I, III, XIV Hume turns to his systematic examination "of the idea of necessary connexion." (*Treatise*, p. 155) Previous discussions in the *Treatise* suggested what Hume's position is likely to be, and after having carefully read his discussion on cause and effect we can see a regular, even uniform, approach to these questions. He says, for example, that "according to my system, all reasonings are nothing but the effects of custom," (*Treatise*, p. 149) so if Hume is consistent at all we should not be surprised to find that approach used here as well.

We get no help from the suggestions of other philosophers, says Hume. For all that "prodigious diversity" which is found in the opinions of philosophers, they have only "pretended to explain the secret force and energy of causes." (*Treatise*, p. 158) Whatever explanation is given must fit all causes because "all causes are of the same kind." (*Treatise*, p. 171) There have been many protests to Hume's claim that all causes must be of the same kind. For example, Prof. Hospers protests that proportioning one's belief to the evidence is surely *not* the same as counting the number of instances in which there is a conjunction of events:

> When you say, "I know that *that* bit of reasoning that Smith presented to me was what caused me to change my mind on this issue," you are not counting any instances—there may be only one. "That's what made me do it" is not verifiable by counting instances. The Humean conception of causality, whatever its merits in physical science, is hopeless when it comes to "human causation."[19]

Appealing to substantial forms will not do. Perhaps the decline of Aristotelian natural philosophy was strongly aided by the claim that all causes are efficient ones and that material, formal, and final causes are not causes at all. They do not stand in the required temporal relationships to what they are "causes" of. Likewise the claim that bodies operate by their accidents or qualities will not do either. Neither will the claims that cause is brought about by matter and form conjoined, by their form and accidents, or by certain virtues and faculties distinct from all this. To trace these ideas to their likely proponents and to see what influences they had on Hume would take us beyond the allowable bounds of this chapter, but Hume believes the traditional answers cannot offer us any help. The myriad mixtures Hume finds in these ideas carry the presumption of their complete inadequacy. None of them come with evidence.

This presumption must encrease upon us, when we consider, that these principles of substantial forms, and accidents, and faculties, are not in reality any of the known properties of bodies, but are perfectly unintelligible and inexplicable. For 'tis evident philosophers wou'd never have had recourse to such obscure and uncertain principles had they met with any satisfaction in such as are clear and intelligible; especially in such an affair as this, which must be an object of the simplest understanding, if not of the senses. (*Treatise*, p. 158)

The ultimate force and efficacy of nature is "perfectly unknown" to us and the example of the Cartesians can show us the elusiveness of our search for the nature of cause. They concluded that we know the nature of matter and found it to be completely inert or inactive. It has no power which can produce, continue, or communicate motion. But we are aware of these precise things in our experience, so since there must be some power in things which causes effects and it does not come from the things in the world, it must come from the actions of the Deity. So God is the prime mover of the universe not only in the sense that at first He "wound up the great clock" but also now in that He is at present providentially bestowing on things their qualities, configurations, and motions (including causes). Hume rejects this argument on his principle of "no impression, no idea" (for we have no impression of any such active principle in the Deity) and on the empiricist doctrine that there are no innate ideas.

Repetition, however, may be responsible for the idea of cause. We see repeated cases of the same object being joined to another object and it is this repeated connection of objects which gives us the presence of cause and effect. Hume is willing to countenance this suggestion provided that we make some distinctions about our ideas.

We must distinguish the actual tie between cause and effect on the one hand from our idea of the "tie" between cause and effect on the other. The issue here is not with the metaphysical problem of the nature of the connection or link between cause and effect. It is rather with the epistemological issue of why we believe in the existence of cause and effect and just how Hume conceived of that.

For the first thing, repetition of "like objects in like relations of succession and contiguity" does have something to do with why we believe there is cause and effect. Repetition does not "discover" anything new in any one of them, because the particular instances of cause and effect which we see are entirely independent of each other. Cause and effect A is totally separate from and independent of cause and effect B, and C, etc. The motion and shock we observe when one billiard ball hits another is separate and distinct from similar cases, but the repetition somehow influences us to get the idea of necessary connection: (*Treatise*, p. 163)

> Suppose we observe several instances, in which the same objects are always conjoin'd together, we immediately conceive a connexion betwixt them, and

begin to draw an inference from one to another. This multiplicity of resembling instances, therefore, constitutes the very essence of power or connexion, and is the source, from which the idea of it arises. In order, then, to understand the idea of power, we must consider that multiplicity.

Hume says the same thing a number of time. So, here we have it: Similar instances, parallel cases, are still the first source of our *idea* of power or necessity even though they do not have any influence on the nature of things, that is, on other instances (of cause and effect) or on any external object. The *idea* of power is brought about by the observation of resemblances in the particular instances of causal connection.

Hume uses a number of different terms to refer to our inclination to attribute causal force or necessity when we invariably see two "objects" united by the constant conjunction of contiguity and temporal priority. Hume talks of "a determination of the mind"[20] to pass from one object to its usual attendant. We feel this, he claims.

It is hard when dealing with the English empiricists to keep the psychological issues of knowledge distinct from the philosophical ones because these empiricists themselves are so much inclined to shift from one to the other. Sometimes the psychological question of the empirical development of belief is taken to satisfy the logical question of the basis for belief: (*Treatise*, pp. 165-166)

> The idea of necessity arises from some impression. There is no impression convey'd by our senses, which can give rise to that idea. It must, therefore, be deriv'd from some internal impression or impression of reflexion. There is no internal impression, which has any relation to the present business, but that propensity, which custom produces, to pass from an object to the idea of its usual attendant. This therefore is the essence of necessity. Upon the whole, necessity is something, that exists in the mind, not in objects; nor is it possible for us ever to form the most distant idea of it, consider'd as a quality in bodies.

Hume supplies us with plenty of statements of this kind. *This is his doctrine as to why we believe in cause or the presence of necessity when reason, his rational procedure, cannot allow us the idea.*

There is an analogy, Hume feels, between relations of ideas and our idea of cause. Both are the result of our understanding, of the tendency of the mind: (*Treatise*, p. 166)

> Thus as the necessity, which makes two times two equal to four, or three angles of a triangle equal to two right ones, lies only in the act of the understanding, by which we consider and compare these ideas; in like manner the necessity or power, which unites causes and effects, lies in the determination of the mind to pass from the one to the other. The efficacy

or energy of causes is neither plac'd in the causes themselves, nor in the deity, nor in the concurrence of these two principles; but belongs entirely to the soul, which considers the union of two or more objects in all past instances. 'Tis here the real power of causes is plac'd, along with their connexion and necessity.

This is a remarkable statement because so far as Hume is concerned the essential feature of the causal situation has a subjective rather than an objective warrant, and a nonrational rather than a rational one. Reason, the main court of appeal of the French philosophes and of the continental rationalists during Hume's time, is inert. Reason itself cannot supply anything that will give warrant for believing in cause. Only one thing can—the nonrational inclination of the mind, the soul, the self.

Why not say that the "warrant" lies in the constant conjunction of impressions? Hume does speak in a manner which is very close to that, and seems to lend support for such an answer, but since necessity does not reside in things, that cannot be the case for Hume. Our natural tendency is to locate cause and effect in things, but Hume does not accept that conclusion, at least overtly and officially. To do so would put him in the traditional camp in epistemology.

The answer must be that, impressions can only affect minds or something very close to them like animal "souls." No minds (with their sensory "apparatus"), no impressions. Impressions do affect the mind (or self, or soul) to declare the presence of necessary connection. But without the inclination of the mind (or whatever else we want to call it), the constant conjunction of cause and effect would have as little meaning as they do to an inanimate object. The constant conjunction can be present, but without minds to notice, react, reflect, imagine, and suggest, the constant conjunctions amount to nothing. So minds are the indispensable condition for belief in causal relations, in necessary connection. If there are many necessary conditions for our belief in cause, the presence of a a mind like ours is the sufficient condition for our belief. In some sense or other, mental inclination is the cause of our belief in cause and effect.

Hume is aware of the paradoxical nature of his proposal. It runs against received opinion and the "inveterate prejudices of mankind." He views it as "the most violent" one of all the suggestions he will have occasion to advance in the course of the *Treatise* and hopes it may be admitted "merely by dint of solid proof and reasoning." (*Treatise*, p. 166) This is rather interesting, because it amounts to the use of reason to prove the efficacy or productive nature of the irrational (or the nonrational)! Then Hume repeats his claim that:
1. The simple view of any two objects or actions, however related, can never give us any idea of power or any connection between them.
2. The idea of necessary connection arises from repetition of their union.
3. The repetition neither uncovers nor causes anything in the union of two objects but influences the mind by the customary transition it produces.

4. This customary transition is, then, the same as power and necessity. (*Treatise*, p. 166)

Hume is afraid that the general run of his readers will carry a bias which will prejudice them against this doctrine. The realist conviction that causes operate independently of the mind will be too strong, and Hume's arguments will not prevail because this doctrine that mind determines necessity and therefore, cause, will be seen to be a reversal of the order of nature. To bestow what is clearly believed to be a part of the order of nature to the activity of the mind, on something that is in no way related to cause or effect is "a gross absurdity, and contrary to the most certain principles of human reason." (*Treatise*, p. 168)

Hume feels the force of this objection and feels compelled to answer, but he appeals to his reader's insight by the use of the illustration of the blind man who pretends that the difference between two qualities compared in a category mistake is absurd. In other words, Hume is saying that if a person can't see it, that is too bad. That will not change the situation, but "an efficacy is necessary in all operations." Hume admits that there may be many qualities and powers in objects with which we are completely unacquainted. We can call those "power" or "efficacy" if we want to but the whole thing will be of little consequence to the world. It is poor philosophy.

> But when, instead of meaning these unknown qualities, we make the terms of power and efficacy signify something, of which we have a clear idea, and which is incompatible with those objects, to which we apply it, obscurity and error begin then to take place, and we are led astray by a false philosophy. This is the case, when we transfer the determination of the thought to external objects, and suppose any real intelligible connexion betwixt them; that being a quality, which can only belong to the mind that considers them.
>
> As to what may be said, that the operations of nature are independent of our thought and reasoning, I allow it; and accordingly have observ'd, that objects bear to each other the relations of contiguity and succession; that like objects may be observ'd in several instances to have like relations; and that all this is independent of, and antecedent to the operations of the understanding. But if we go any farther and ascribe a power or necessary connexion to these objects; this is what we can never observe in them, but must draw the idea of it from what we feel internally in contemplating them ....
>
> When any object is presented to us, it immediately conveys to the mind a lively idea of that object, which is usually found to attend it; and this determination of the mind forms the necessary connexion of these objects. (*Treatise*, pp. 168-169)

"Thought and reasoning," the rational basis, will not give us the doctrine of cause. Only what we "feel internally," which is the nonrational, will do that.

Following this treatment in I, III, XIV of the *Treatise*, Hume gives us his two definitions of cause. These are given in the order in which he presents them. He says, we may define a cause as: (*Treatise*, p. 170)

> 'An object precedent and contiguous to another, and where all the objects resembling the former are plac'd in like relations of precedency and contiguity to those objects, that resemble the latter.'

> 'A CAUSE is an object precedent and contiguous to another, and so united with it, that the idea of the one determines the mind to form the idea of the other, and the impression of the one to form a more lively idea of the other.'

These definitions "are only different by their presenting a different view of the same object, and making us consider it either as a philosophical or as a natural relation; either as a comparison of two ideas, or as an association betwixt them." (*Treatise*, p. 170)

Hume gives a second statement of his two definitions of cause a couple pages later in the *Treatise*. The first definition has very small changes in verbiage, but the substance of the definition is the same. In the second definition, however, Hume makes a change which is completely consistent with the thesis I am arguing here. He defines a cause in this definition to be "*An object precedent and contiguous to another, and so united with it in the imagination, that the idea of the one determines the mind to form the idea of the other ....*" The relevant words are "in the imagination." This might be explained as a mere slip of Hume's pen. It, could be that, of course, but it doesn't appear likely when we notice the parallel idea in so many places. The imagination, for Hume, is a nonrational power or faculty. He contrasts it constantly to the reason. It appears, then, to be another instance where the rational content of our ideas rests on the nonrational, though active, powers of the mind.

When we compare Hume's two definitions of cause to each other it is possible to contrast still further the difference between the rational and the irrational approaches to cause in Hume's thought. The first definition is an ordered pair of objects, cause and effect, placed in the relations of temporal order (precedency) and closeness (contiguity). The ordered relation places cause first. This is an instance of general uniformity, and his definition does not require (so far as the first definition itself is concerned) that anyone has observed this ordering relation, or that if he observes it that he be aware that that is what he is observing. Furthermore, the first definition gives no indication that there is anything more involved in the ordering of this pair of objects than the presence of temporal precedency and contiguity.

The second definition, however, employs the same ordered pair of objects, cause and effect, in occurrences where the property ordering the pair is defined as a mental phenomenon. This ordering implies that human beings have observed both the objects, cause and effect, in various ways and at various times and because of their relationship now have the disposition to pass from the occurrence of the thing we have called the cause to an expectation of a thing we call the effect. This ordering tendency is a disposition because the presence of the one (cause) does not insure that the mind will always make the passage to the effect. But when temporal order and contiguity of the cause and effect occur, the idea of the one "determines" the mind to form the idea of the other.

Hume would be the first to admit that there can be (and are) many "secret" and "conceal'd" causes so that there are ordered pairs of "cause" and "effect" where no one suspects that there is the causal relation of necessary connection. If no one observes the two members of the ordered pair, then there can be no exercise of the disposition to pass from the one (cause) to the other (effect). And, conversely, there are cases where the first member of the ordered pair leads to a "determination of the mind" or a "propensity" to pass to the second, but where the second does not in fact take place. It is a regular part of human experience for us to expect an effect when we observed what we believe was the cause, but no effect occurs.

The first and the second definitions, then, differ in meaning whether or not they have the same extension. The first means that there is an order and connection between cause and effect even though that relation lacks the all-important element of necessary connection. The second means that the presence of the "cause" influences the mind to form the idea of the other.

Why do we have these different definitions? Isn't a cause what it is? Why then do we have two definitions with different meanings? The answer seems to be found in the words with which Hume introduces his two definitions. There are "two definitions given of this relation which are only different by their presenting a different view of the same object, and making us consider it either as a *philosophical* or as a *natural* relation; either as a comparison of ideas, or as an association betwixt them." (*Treatise*, pp. 169-170) Thus, the first definition is a definition of the cause-effect relation as a philosophical relation, and the second as a natural one.

Why did Hume make this distinction? What is to be gained by giving two definitions instead of one? Do the two definitions have the same meaning and refer to the same class of cases? How is a "philosophical" relation as Hume uses it here different from a "natural" relation? Robinson explains Hume's use of "philosophical relation" this way:

> To say that a relation R is "philosophical" is to make a factually empty statement; *all* relations are philosophical. The term is introduced by Hume simply in order to emphasize what a difference there is between the logical notion of a relation, as such, and the man-in-the-street's notion of "some sort of a connection" between things which leads one of them to recall the

other in our thoughts, from which he borrowed his own more technical concept of "natural" relations. It must not be thought that here we have a classification of all relations into two kinds, philosophical on the one hand and natural on the other. Thus the cause-effect relation, being a relation, is *ipso facto* a philosophical relation, and therefore to define it "as" a philosophical relation is, simply, to define it.[21]

Robinson, however, fails to do justice to one part of this definition. He hints at it when he talks about definition number one as a "logical notion," and we fail here to get all of Hume's meaning unless we get the part of the meaning that caused Hume to contrast this definition to number two as a "natural relation." Hume has the idea here as he does in other places of what logical analysis and empirical method can give us. All they can give us is contiguity and temporal precedence. Or to put it another way, Robinson stressed the metaphysical issue of the nature of cause when it appears obvious that Hume's main emphasis right here is epistemological.[22]

When Hume gives us the definitions, he uses the "is" of metaphysics but makes a subtle shift in the two definitions from what cause is to how we regard it. This is not as clear in the first definition as it is in the second. In the first definition, "plac'd" is the ambiguous word. If it means only that objects resembling the former (cause) are "in" the relations of "precedency and contiguity" to the latter, then we have the description of a metaphysical entity. If "plac'd" carries the idea that we, our minds, have anything to do with it, then we are on epistemological ground. That is, we are on epistemological ground unless Hume is an idealist of Berkeley's stamp and believes reality is somehow or other constituted by the mind, and no one so far has seriously argued that Hume carried Berkeley's position or even Kant's despite the similarity of Hume's and Kant's views on many particular doctrines.

If "plac'd" means that we by some kind of mental operation or instinctual reaction *regard* things that way, then this is an epistemological treatment of how our beliefs are formed.

This interpretation is favored by his second definition where the epistemological bent of Hume's discussion is clearer. When Hume says in the second definition that an "object precedent and contiguous to another, and so united with it, that the idea of the one determines the mind to form the idea of the other ...," our first response is that Hume sounds here like a regular old metaphysical realist. A little closer reading, however, shows that it is a matter of ideas and belief. The issue is epistemological or psychological. If the question is the justification for our ideas, it is epistemological; if it is how we actually do get them, it is psychological. But, the point is, it is not metaphysical.

We are used to having definitions be definitions of things and these are labeled definitions. Hume tips us off, however, a little farther down the page when he says, "I perceive, that such a relation can never be an object of reasoning, and can never operate upon the mind, but by means of custom, which determines the imagination to make a transition from the idea of one object to that of its usual attendant, and from the impression of one to a more lively idea of the other." (*Treatise*, p. 170) Hume here shows us that the issue is about our ideas, beliefs, and understanding. It is epistemological rather than metaphysical as the definitions first led us to believe.

Hume's last two sentences on p. 170 of the *Treatise* says,

> I perceive, that such a relation can never be an object of reasoning, and can never operate upon the mind, but by means of custom, which determines the imagination to make a transition from idea of one object to that of its usual attendant, and from the impression of one to a more lively idea of the other. However extraordinary these sentiments may appear, I think it fruitless to trouble myself with any farther enquiry or reasoning upon the subject, but shall repose myself on them as on establish'd maxims.

This quotation takes us back to the fideist thrust: It is not things but our customary tendencies which anchor for us our concept of cause, and so for Hume this is the end of the whole matter.

The next couple pages of the *Treatise* contains "some corrollaries" [sic] of this acceptance of cause, and then section xv gives us the "Rules by which to judge of causes and effects." His examination of cause is complete.

A little different approach will show us that Hume's regularity analysis in the first definition leaves us no reason to believe in the presence of necessary connection as an indispensable part of the notion of cause. The first definition is another way, then, of stressing the negative, skeptical conclusion of Hume's foregoing discussion. The absence of necessary connection and therefore the absence of a genuine case of cause in any situation is the best that the impression-analysis approach can yield.

Stroud's examination of Hume's two definitions leads him to say that "neither of them, strictly speaking, is a definition, or is intended by Hume to be an equivalence which expresses the full and precise *meaning* of 'X causes Y'."[23] Hume confesses in the *Enquiry* (p. 76) that *"it is impossible to give any just definition of cause, except what is drawn from something extraneous and foreign to it."* In spite of Hume's admission, this does not stop his giving what amounts to the same two definitions he gave before in the *Treatise*. (*Enquiry*, pp. 76-77) Stroud believes we can understand why Hume puts forward these two different accounts of cause:

> The relation between them is something like this. Any events or objects observed to fulfill the conditions of the first 'definition' are such that they will fulfil the conditions of the second 'definition' also. That is to say that an observed constant conjunction between As and Bs establishes a 'union

in the imagination' such that the thought of an A naturally leads the mind to the thought of a B. That is a fundamental, but contingent, principle of the the human mind.[24]

That is why the second definition is necessary. It rescues Hume from another reminder that his method has failed him, or has painted him into a corner, so to speak. The second definition follows these words about the first definition: "If this definition be esteem'd defective, because drawn from objects foreign to the cause, we may substitute this other definition in its place." (*Treatise*, p. 170) The antecedent of "this definition" is the first, the philosophical definition. Hume's acknowledgment that the first definition is defective and requires the second, is consistent with his practice in his philosophical analysis, so he gives us his definition of the "natural" relation.

The natural relation is the "determination" of the mind by which "an object precedent and contiguous to another" "determines the mind to form the idea of the other." Hume proceeds to explain how this is done:

> Shou'd this definition also be rejected for the same reason, [as was the first definition because the definition of cause was drawn from objects foreign to the cause] I know no other remedy, than that the persons, who express this delicacy, should substitute a juster definition in its place. But for my part I must own my incapacity for such an undertaking. When I examine with the utmost accuracy those objects, which are commonly denominated causes and effects, I find, in considering a single instance, that the one object is precedent and contiguous to the other; and in inlarging my view to consider several instances, I find only that like objects are constantly plac'd in like relations of succession and contiguity. Again, when I consider the influence of this constant conjunction, I perceive, that such a relation can never be an object of reasoning, and can never operate upon the mind, but by means of custom, which determines the imagination to make a transition from the idea of one object to that of its usual attendant, and from the impression of one to a more lively idea of the other. However extraordinary these sentiments may appear, I think it fruitless to trouble myself with any farther enquiry or reasoning upon the subject, but shall repose myself on them as on establish'd maxims. (*Treatise*, p. 170)

Once again we have a retreat to custom which "determines the imagination." The process, then is nonrational. It is a substitute for the failed philosophical one, that is, the logical or rational one, and in effect it is the same thing as if we were to call it irrational.

Robinson illustrates a continuing error in Humean scholarship when he takes the definition to be a metaphysical one rather than one which has a *primarily* epistemological thrust. He says that the second definition is now seen not to be a definition at all, but simply a restatement of the proposition that the (already defined) cause-effect relation is a *natural* relation, in a somewhat elliptical formulation. It is clearly an error on Hume's part to have offered it *as a definition*, and admittedly an extremely misleading error, leading to misinterpretations and confusions as to what he was trying to say about causation.[25]

If we understand the second definition, however, as an attempt to substitute a method for recovering or "saving" cause which the first definition had lost, then the definition can be seen to be perfectly meaningful. Definition two is necessary for Hume to preserve belief in the existence of cause as an abstract concept and its presence as a factor in human thought and experience because he had destroyed the real nature of cause in the first definition. Regularity of precedence and contiguity can never succeed in convincing us that this is the true nature of cause. Strawson is quite right that the regularity view is false, that Hume never held to it metaphysically though he admitted his inability to justify it epistemically.[26]

Since that was not convincing, Hume had to show how he could allow for its reality in another way. Hence the second definition. That is, if we allow the proper epistemological importance of the second definition, the "definition" is seen not as a philosophical definition of cause or the logical grounds for its acceptance by people but rather a psychological account of the genesis of the concept, of how in fact we do hold to the reality of cause. It is an account of our *belief* in cause not of its nature.

It has been remarked that for Hume the felt inclination of the mind is nonrational. This claim may seem curious, for why should our mental inclinations be nonrational? If our mental inclinations are a sort of disposition, and they help us in survival and other life functions aren't they "rational" at least in a certain sense? That is, an animal's natural instincts help it to survive. It is true that the animal does not engage in reasoning so if that is what "rational" means the animal's instincts are not rational. But, that makes perfectly good sense for a smaller animal to flee from a larger one, so, isn't that "rational"? If we talked about the animal's flight we would not be likely to say that it doesn't make sense, that it is not rational, because if we were in a situation like that of the animal then we would feel that it would be perfectly rational to flee from our enemy.

So, aren't the "felt inclinations of the mind" a part of reason, the *ratio*, or at least closely connected to the reason? If that is so, why present Hume's views as something less than rational? The answer has to be that Hume does it. He uses reason as the judge of truth and falsity, or theoretical adequacy and inadequacy. Earlier, this chapter presented a typical Humean case of analysis of some belief, concept, or doctrine which ends after all the *rational* tests with the conclusion, "we never therefore have any idea of power." (*Treatise*, p. 161)[27] When we subject the issue to the tests of reason, Hume concludes, we can find no justification for holding to the doctrine. Reason leaves us without basis for belief. Thus, when Hume comes with a reason for accepting the doctrine he has rationally abandoned, he does it with a basis which cannot bear rational examination. In not being able to stand the examination of reason, though nonrational it bears the mark of being irrational like many of our other tendencies.

In addition to the "inclination" or the "propensity" of the mind, Hume also uses "habit" and "custom". These are included as nonrational methods. Hume includes these two words along with the inclination of the mind as part of his explanation of our belief in cause. One term will occur in one place and the other in the next, so there is no regularity in usage. This seems to indicate that Hume saw no use in trying to separate them. Habit has the connotation of being more individual and personal while custom connotes the custom connotes the social and organizational, but for Hume they are the same. Custom designates actions that are regular and habitual, and habit refers to what is repetitive and customary.

Why are they irrational? Do habits and customs necessarily need to go against principles, canons, and methods? In the absolute sense, of course, they do not, because a rational way of thinking can be developed into a habit, and an evaluative approach to all questions can become a custom (and a virtue). The mere presence of a habit or a custom is no prima facie evidence that it is irrational, for it can be the result of careful decision, diligent practice, and disciplined reactions. There are, then, rational habits.

Most habits, though, cannot be so described. They have developed for no other reason than that some action has been repeated often enough that it approaches the nature of a reflex. Many habits do not appear to be very significant. They were not brought about deliberately but just grew up. They don't seem to have any "rhyme or reason" for their existence, that is, any intent, and they amount to little more than personal mannerisms. They just are facts of life for various people who find them eventually to be helpful, harmful, or neutral in quality. Customs are often little else than repeated actions which because of regular use have become traditions, and traditions are of all grades and kinds. There is a nonrational or irrational dimension to many habits, perhaps for most of them, so that a habit (or a custom) bears the expectation of having nothing to do with rational considerations. We ordinarily expect habits to be thus and would be surprised to find they are rational.

Lest it seem trivial to mention it, we need to remind ourself of the universal belief in cause in Hume's time as well as in our own, whether among philosophers or those innocent of philosophy. The habit of believing that an object which was followed by an effect and which was contiguous to it in place and time had a dimension called necessary connection to that effect is, to our minds, a perfectly rational idea. Hume was the first thinker who analyzed this idea, and he was convinced that on logical grounds the reality of cause cannot be sustained though he grants that habit and custom circumvent that. In Hume, "habit" and "custom" are words which denote the decisively nonrational and Hume almost always contrasts both habit and custom to the philosophical, rational analysis he had done.

Our thoughtful, reflective considerations leave us unable to defend our beliefs and force us to fall back on habit and custom. A few examples will suffice for us:

> We have already taken notice of certain relations, which make us pass from one object to another, even tho' there be no reason to determine us to that transition; and this we may establish for a general rule, that wherever the mind constantly and uniformly makes a transition without any reason, it is influenc'd by these relations. Now this is exactly the present case. Reason can never shew us the connexion of one object with another, tho' aided by experience, and the observation of their constant conjunction in all past instances. When the mind, therefore, passes from the idea of impression of one object to the idea or belief of another, it is not determin'd by reason, but by certain principles, which associate together the ideas of these objects, and unite them in the imagination. Had ideas no more union in the fancy than objects seem to have to the understanding, we cou'd never draw any inference from causes to effects, nor repose belief in any matter of fact. The inference, therefore, depends solely on the union of ideas. (*Treatise*, p. 92)

> Now let any philosopher make a trial, and endeavour to explain that act of the mind, which we call *belief*, and give an account of the principles, from which it is deriv'd, independent of the influence of custom on the imagination, and let his hypothesis be equally applicable to beasts as to the human species; and after he has done this, I promise to embrace his opinion. But at the same time I demand as an equitable condition, that if my system be the only one, which can answer to all these terms, it may be receiv'd as entirely satisfactory and convincing. And that 'tis the only one, is evident almost without any reasoning. Beasts certainly never perceive any real connexion among objects. 'Tis therefore by experience they infer one from another. They can never by any arguments form a general conclusion, that those objects, of which they have had no experience, resemble those of which they have. 'Tis therefore by means of custom alone, that experience operates upon them. All this was sufficiently evident with respect to man. But with respect to beasts there cannot be the least suspicion of mistake; which must be own'd to be a strong confirmation, or rather an invincible proof of my system.
>
> Nothing shews more the force of habit in reconciling us to any phænomenon, than this, that men are not astonish'd at the operations of their own reason, at the same time, that they admire the *instinct* of animals, and find a difficulty in explaining it, merely because it cannot be reduc'd to the very same principles. To consider the matter aright, reason is nothing but a wonderful and unintelligible instinct in our souls, which carries us along a certain train of ideas, and endows them with particular qualities, according to their particular situations and relations. This instinct, 'tis true, arises from past observation and experience; but can any one give the ulti-

mate reason, why past experience and observation produces such an effect, any more than why nature alone shou'd produce it? Nature may certainly produce whatever can arise from habit: Nay, habit is nothing but one of the principles of nature, and derives all its force from that origin. (*Treatise*, pp. 178-179)

Reason can never satisfy us that the existence of any one object does ever imply that of another; so that when we pass from the impression of one to the idea or belief of another, we are not determin'd by reason, but by custom or a principle of association. (*Treatise*, p. 97)

All our reasonings concerning causes and effects are deriv'd from nothing but custom; and that belief is more properly an act of the sensitive, than of the cogitative part of our natures. (*Treatise*, p. 183)

Lest it be concluded that this is Hume's position in the *Treatise* alone since these comments have all been taken from that work, it must be made clear that Hume takes exactly the same position in the *Enquiry*. Since the account in the *Enquiry* does not analyze contiguity, temporal precedence and constant conjunction of cause and effect there is a difference in tone between the two books. When Hume gets to his conclusions about our belief in necessary connection in the *Enquiry*, however, he says:

It appears, then, that this idea of a necessary connexion among events arises from a number of similar instances which occur of the constant conjunction of these events; nor can that idea ever be suggested by any one of these instances, surveyed in all possible lights and positions. But there is nothing in a number of instances, different from every single instance, which is supposed to be exactly similar; except only, that after a repetition of similar instances, the mind is carried by habit, upon the appearance of one event, to expect its usual attendant, and to believe that it will exist. This connexion, therefore, which we *feel* in the mind, this customary transition of the imagination from one object to its usual attndant, is the sentiment or impression from which we form the idea of power or necessary connexion. Nothing farther is in the case. Contemplate the subject on all sides; you will never find any other origin of that idea. This is the sole difference between one instance, from which we can never receive the idea of connexion, and a number of similar instances, by which it is suggested .... When we say, therefore, that one object is connected with another, we mean only that they have acquired a connexion in our thought, and give rise to this inference, by which they become proofs of each other's existence: A conclusion which is somewhat extraordinary, but which seems founded on sufficient evidence. Now will its evidence be weakened by any general diffidence of the understanding, or sceptical suspicion concerning every conclusion which is new and extraordinary. No conclusions can be more agreeable to scepticism than such as make discoveries concerning the weakness and narrow limits of human reason and capacity. (*Enquiry*, pp. 75-76)

These quotations have been given here with the risk of tiring the reader, but they have been included to punctuate the vigor and resoluteness of Hume's position. And one more case of repeating our claim: Let's not forget the issue here is epistemological. Hume is accounting for our *belief* in the existence of cause. Cause is "out there," so how can we justify our belief in it since we do not have any impression of the necessary connection of cause and effect? Our claim here is that Hume uses the fideist procedure of ignoring or abandoning the evidence of reason and of embracing the nonrational resources of custom, habit, propensity, imagination, association, human nature, etc.

Habit and custom are parts of the larger doctrine of association which Hume believed was adequate to explain all our complex ideas. Our mind has a propensity to accept certain ideas which reason is impotent to supply but which by its very nature mind uniformly supplies.

We may not be very impressed by Hume's theory of human nature and the innate principles of epistemological organization which they supply, but Hume was very proud of them and felt that they would serve to explain a wide variety of beliefs which he was neither able to supply nor to defend in any other way especially by the rational ways Hume was used to in philosophy.

THE REGULARITY THEORY OF CAUSATION

Several times we have spoken of the regularity theory of causal relations. This theory deserves some attention since it has been a prominent one in logical positivism, and it has been alleged by many commentators on Hume to be Hume's own position. Livingston's summary of that viewpoint has already been given, and Strawson's book has been listed as a forthright rejection of that whole position.

In the regularity view, something such as A can be said to be a cause of B provided that A is spatially and temporally contiguous to B and A is temporally prior to B, or, if A occurs at the same time as B it never follows B. There is no such thing as (empirical) necessary connection between A and B since there is no impression of that supposed relation. Thus, Hume's analysis of cause includes the first two conditions but does not involve necessary connection.

Doubt has been expressed as to whether even these first two conditions are genuine ingredients of all cases of cause and effect. Contiguity has been questioned because there seems to be action at a distance whether that distance is one of space or of time. Temporal priority has been questioned because some causes are claimed to be perfectly contemporaneous with the effect. There is no doubt, however, that we are unable to gain the impression of necessary connection just as Hume contends. Ayer illustrates Hume's denial of necessary connection by appealing to Hume's illustration of billiards:

> Hume's argument is simply that no such relations are observable. If we take his favourite example of a game of billiards, we do indeed speak in 'forceful' terms of the cue being used to 'strike' the ball and of one ball 'cannoning' off another. But all that we actually observe is a series of changes in spatio-temporal relations. First there is a movement of the player's arm, coinciding with a movement of the cue, then an instant at which the cue and the ball are in spatial contact, then a period during which the ball is in motion, relatively to the objects in its neighbourhood, then an instant at which it is in spatial contact with a second ball, then a period in which both balls are in motion, and then, if the player achieves his cannon, an instant at which the first ball is in spatial contact with a third. In the whole of such a process there is no observable relation for which terms like 'power' or 'force' or 'necessary connexion' could be needed to provide a name. And the same applies to any other example that one might have chosen, whether it be a sequence of physical events, or a conjunction of physcal properties. As Hume would put it, we are never furnished with an impression from which the idea of necessary connexion could be derived.
>
> If one is looking for such an impression, the most obvious place to seek it is in one's own experience of action. Do we not find it in the exercise of our wills? Hume considers this suggestion in the *Enquiry* and raises three objections to it. The first is that we do not understand the principle of 'the union of soul with body', which we should do if volition gave us the impression of power: the second is that we cannot explain why we move some of our bodily organs and not others, whereas we should not be embarrassed by this question if we were conscious of a force operating only in favoured instances: the third is that 'we learn from anatomy' that strictly speaking we have no power to move our limbs at all, but only to set in motion nerves, or 'animal spirits', from which the motion of our limbs eventually results; and certainly we are not conscious of any relation of force between the exercise of our wills and the movements of these 'animal spirits' or anything like them (E 64-7).[28]

Even if we did discover a relation r of necessary connection or a "communication of force" between the two billiard balls A and B when A strikes B (ArB) we would not be any further ahead according to Hume. Any right to make an inference from (ArB) is eliminated by the fact that r is a merely phenomenal relation, a relation such that accurate observation of the phenomena either is adequate to establish the connection r of A to B or it is not. Supposing that it is, the presence of relation r in this case says nothing whatever about what will happen at any other place or time. Supposing that r is not adequate to establish the relation, (ArB) can serve its intended purpose only if it comprises in its definition the clause that any terms which are related by it will always, under similar conditions, exhibit similar behaviour. But this makes the example just another case in which causal propositions are made true by fiat, and the same objections are fatal to it. Moreover, on this interpretation, what looked like the empirical proposition that necessary connexion is not detectable in any single instance of a conjunction of matters of fact, is promoted into a logical truth. For the relation is now defined in such a way that we have to examine every single instance of the phenomenon in question, in order to discover that it holds in any one of them.[29]

So, this is the positivist understanding of Hume, the "Humean" view of causation in contrast to Hume's own view in Strawson's words.[30]

All kinds of objections can be given to this position and in our preceding pages we have developed some of them. The biggest failure of the positivist position is to miss Hume's distinction between the nature of cause, the metaphysical question, and how much we can know about cause, the epistemological question. That Hume believed in the existence of cause appears unquestioned especially in light of his list of *Rules by which to judge of causes and effects*, (*Treatise*, p. 173f) and by the absence of any more questions about cause after that place in the *Treatise*, and the same point holds true for parallel portions in the *Enquiry*.

Hume did raise questions about our knowledge of cause and our ability to "penetrate" it, to discover its nature, but Hume's skepticism has been widely misunderstood as a positive doctrine, an affirmation that there is no cause present. It has generally been treated as a negative conclusion about causation, a "there is not ...," in contrast to a positive conclusion, "there is ..." or "it seems so-and-so." This is not the nature of Hume's kind of skepticism and Strawson reminds us that Hume's skepticism is a question-raising rather than a position-taking position:

> This point about Hume's strictly non-committal scepticism needs some further comment. The word 'sceptic' is often used loosely. It is often thought that to be a sceptic with respect to the existence of an external (or mind-independent) world is to hold that it does not exist. But this is not a strictly sceptical position, because it involves the positive claim that an external (or mind-independent) world does not exist. Genuine or strictly non-committal scepticism never makes such a claim. In general, it simply claims that we know far less than we think. In the case of the external world, it claims that we do not and cannot know whether or not there is such a thing. Strictly sceptical claims have the form 'We do not (and cannot) know that p (or that not p).' They never have the form 'It is definitely (knowably) not the case that p (or that not p).' Hume's scepticism is of this strictly non-committal kind.[31]

Since Strawson has written a thorough critique of the claim that Hume held the regularity view of causation, we will refer the reader to that work. He rightly concludes that while this position, the "standard view," of Hume's views on cause and effect, can claim textual support, it is "wildly implausible." It moves catastrophically from Hume's epistemological claim that all we can ever *know* of causation, in the objects, is regular succession to the positive ontological claim that all causation actually *is*, in the objects, is regular succession.[32]

HUME'S DOCTRINE OF SELF IDENTITY

A second example from the *Treatise* which will illustrate Hume's epistemological method is his discussion of personal identity. Hume left out of the first *Enquiry* any discussion of the mind or self except for the most cursory commnents excited by discussion on some other topic, but he did not make clear to us his motives for doing so. Here again in the *Treatise*, his rational analysis turns out stale, and Hume has to resort to another procedure to save his conclusion.

He starts his section on personal identity by describing the "received" opinion in philosophy. This is the view that we are continually ("every moment") conscious of our self, that we feel its existence and its continuance in existence. In addition, we are certain beyond the evidence of a deductive conclusion ("demonstration") of both the identity and simplicity of this self. The awareness of this, it is claimed, is of such compelling force that any evidence could only weaken the conclusion rather than strengthen it. If we are not certain of this, then nothing else could be certain.

Hume does not give over any section entirely to the discussion of the nature of the mind. The section immediately preceding *"Of personal identity"* (Section VI) discusses *"Of the immateriality of the soul."* He finds that doctrine filled with difficulties and contradictions; for example, Hume intimates that he doubts whether philosophers can give any meaning to "substance" or to "inhesion." When they can, Hume is willing to discuss the issue, but not till then. The difficulty of defining substance is impossible for the topics of mind and body, and Hume thinks that the mind presents not only the same kind of problems but a number of additional ones as well. And besides, every idea must be derived from an impression:

> As every idea is deriv'd from a precedent impression, had we any idea of the substance of our minds, we must also have an impression of it; which is very difficult, if not impossible, to be conceiv'd. For how can an impression represent a substance, otherwise than by resembling it? And how can an impression resemble a substance, since, according to this philosophy, it is not a substance, and has none of the peculiar qualities or characteristics of a substance?

> But leaving the question *of what may or may not be*, for that other *what actually is*, I desire those philosophers, who pretend that we have an idea of the substance of our minds, to point out the impression that produces it, and tell distinctly after what manner that impression operates, and from what object it is deriv'd. Is it an impression of sensation or of reflection? Is it pleasant, or painful, or indifferent? Does it attend us at all times, or does it only return at intervals? If at intervals, at what times principally does it return, and by what cause is it produc'd? (*Treatise*, pp. 232-233)

After further discussion and recitation of difficulties about this issue, Hume concludes two things: "We have, therefore, no idea of a substance" and "We have, therefore, no idea of inhesion." (*Treatise*, p. 234) Since we cannot form adequate and defensible ideas of these concepts, it is useless to try to determine whether perceptions inhere in a material or immaterial substance. Following such typical Humean stratagems and analysis calculated to show the contradictions and absurdities of reason, Hume concludes that the question concerning the substance of the soul is absolutely unintelligible. (*Treatise*, p. 250)

It is after that conclusion, then, that Hume begins his section "*Of personal identity.*" Hume cannot accept the traditional view which he sketches at the very beginning of section VI.

Hume interweaves two themes in this section, what constitutes personal identity and what is the nature of the mind. These themes emerge, disappear, and reemerge almost like the themes of a symphony. Just when the reader thinks that Hume is going to settle one of them, he finds that Hume has changed to a discussion of the other, so the conclusions we are looking for do not appear with the finality we could hope for.

The issue of personal identity is how person A can be A and not B or C or D with all the questions about how this is established, preserved, how time, physical and mental characteristics, experiences, and memories are related to a person's identity.

Hume's treatment of personal identity goes along with this customary way of dealing with it. He says, for example:

> We must distinguish betwixt personal identity, as it regards our thought or imagination, and as it regards our passions or the concern we take in ourselves. The first is our present subject; and to explain it perfectly we must take the matter pretty deep, and account for that identity, which we attribute to plants and animals; there being a great analogy betwixt it, and the identity of a self of person.
>
> We have a distinct idea of an object, that remains invariable and uninterrupted thro' a suppos'd variation of time; and this idea we call that of *identity* or *sameness*. (*Treatise*, p. 253)

This, then, is the metaphysical problem of identity, and specifically, of individual personal identity.

Questions about the mind are different from these in that they deal with the issues of the existence of mind, the nature of mental substance with its qualities, relations, and dispositions, the difference of mental from physical (material) substance, the relation of mental to physical substance, and in our case, the relation of mind and body. At this point Hume takes a position where it is hard to take him seriously and to believe that he means what he says. Hume says, "They are the successive perceptions only that constitute the mind; nor have we the most distant notion of the place, where these scenes are represented, or of the materials, of which it is composed." (*Treatise*, p. 253) Here when Hume deals with the metaphysical problem of mind, we find his initial offering to be surprising, shocking, skeptical, and even unbelievable. Our reaction to extreme statements and irresponsible positions is often to laugh and put them down as unworthy of our time. After perusing Hume's claims on space and time, cause and effect, skepticism with regard to the senses, and the existence of the mind, or even any one of these, it may have been that Hume's early readers concluded they were too short of time for the work of reading the volumes of this new, unknown figure. It may have been no wonder the *Treatise* did not fare very well. Hume's laments on how his book attracted little attention may be due to just some of these factors, for the readers who did take the time and trouble to "taste" the *Treatise* may have concluded they were much too busy for such things!

Back to Hume's specific doctrines on the mind: It is not hard to see that the two paragraphs just cited deal with essentially different things. But Hume combines them both in one section so that the issue of personal identity is interwoven with that of the nature of the mind. With his rationalist epistemological approach Hume rejects both of these two things and is forced finally to accept a nonrational method to explain how we have ideas of both of them. For that reason it will be useful (and harmless) to treat them together in much the same way that Hume does. The issue of personal identity will be distinguished from that of the nature of the mind when that is necessary and vice versa. Hume does this when he lists the "*soul*, and *self*, and *substance*" all on one line and all as the object of what we "feign" it be. (*Treatise*, p. 254) In addition to this, the almost universal habit of Hume scholars is to take section VI as Hume's discussion of the mind, a precedent which this study will follow.

In case of disagreement with this procedure, it should be noted that for the purposes of this argument the distinction does not have to be followed closely because with both of them we find the same pattern. Hume subjects personal identity and mind to a rational analysis which justifies skepticism and then recovers what he is loath to give up by appealing to an irrational or nonrational basis for his conclusion.

Let us follow, then, what Hume says in this example for evidence that Hume has fideistic elements in his metaphysical writings at a comparatively young age.

The procedure is prominent in the *Dialogues* as a product of the last period of Hume's life. It was not a late development, however, in his theory of knowledge. We can see one of the clearest and briefest treatments of the fideistic approach on the issue of the existence and nature of the mind very early in Hume's life. The *Enquiry*, the product of a self-conscious determined effort by Hume to make his thought palatable retains the resource of fideist nonrational grounds even though the *Enquiry* contains nothing more than the most cursory and accidental kinds of comments on the soul or self. In the later book, Hume says what he does about the mind only as he is stimulated to do so in discussion of other things.

His thought holds what he wants by the use of a method (or a stratagem) which cannot figure in his rational method. The rational method defeats him, strands him, disappoints him, and he is able to avoid the consequences of his *rational* method by abandoning it altogether. So, let us turn to the continuation of that argument.

The "received" opinion, that we are intimately aware of what we call our self, is not as sure as the advocates of that opinion claim, says Hume. These people make many positive assertions about the basis of our knowledge. For example, they claim that no sensation, no passion, or anything else can distract us from the view that we are intimately conscious of our self through every moment, etc., and that all the rest of our knowledge depends on our self-knowledge.

Unfortunately, Hume declares, the positive assertions made by these philosophers lacks the experience which is pleaded for them. Hume has enlarged his treatment of experience here since it is evident from the traditional Cartesian and Lockean understanding of the nature of mind that it cannot be apprehended by sense experience. Prior to this case, all (or almost all) of Hume's references to experience refer to sensory experience, but experience here refers to something inner rather than external, sensory experience, so this is a case of something more than just using our five senses. There is no way the self can be seen, smelled, or heard since it is not the sort of thing which powers of sensation can apprehend. Technically, then, Hume's reliance on impressions seems to be self-defeating, because impressions are supposed to be sensory, aren't they? And how could we have something sensory of something which by definition is not "sensible"? The problem is similar to the claim of having experience of God. So, then, Hume must be using impressions in a broader sense, an expanded use, of experience, to deal with what is intuitive and does not involve nerve endings. We get his point, but strictly speaking he has displayed to us a problem in any consistently-followed empirical program, especially in an atomistic one like Hume's.

But even with that proviso there are no impressions from which this idea could come. "It must be some one impression, that gives rise to every real idea." (*Treatise*, p. 251) Self or person, however, is not any one impression. It is rather, that very thing to which all our several and sundry impressions are supposed to have a reference. It follows, then, that there can be no justification for our belief in the self or soul.

Then Hume makes a blunder. He says that if any impression gives rise to the idea of self, then that impression must continue invariably the same through the whole course of our lives since the self is supposed to exist after that manner. It may be that impressions *give rise* to every idea (of reality), but it does not seem to follow that having a continuing idea means that we must have a uniform, invariable, continuing impression. That is what memory is for. Once we arrive at an idea on whatever kind of an impression, it does not seem necessary on Hume's principles to demand that the impression must continue the same. If that were the case, then we would be woefully short on ideas, because what can we think of in the empirical world that does not change?

Earlier in the *Treatise* Hume talked about complex ideas like the city of Paris. While he was writing the *Treatise* he certainly was not in Paris, and so was not having any current impressions of it, but he still indicated that he had an idea of it. Hume had said, "suppose I form at present an idea, of which I have forgot the correspondent impression, I am able to conclude from this idea, that such an impression did once exist." (*Treatise*, pp. 105-106) So epistemologically there seems to be an internal contradiction in Hume's work at this point, and the reader is led to ask whether Hume may not have been so intent on rejecting the doctrine of personal identity that he strained a little too hard here.

Hume enunciates another questionable doctrine when he says that it must be some one impression that gives rise to every real idea, that is, an idea of reality in contrast to the mere relations of ideas which do not have anything to do with "real" or actual existence. This is understandable only if the impression must be simple because mind is simple, but why should metaphysical and perceptual simplicity be linked? Hume does not mention or refer to any such doctrine, but since the received doctrine of the mind or soul was either the same (or close) to the Cartesian model, and since Clarke, Locke, Berkeley, and, in fact, practically everyone in the English philosophic tradition except Hobbes seems to have held such a view of the mind, he may have assumed that his reader would hold that view and so would understand that the idea of the mind or soul must itself be simple. Whatever the answer be to that, Hume uses this point to his personal advantage. He tells us: "It must be some one impression, that gives rise to every real idea. But self or person is not any one impression but that to which our several impressions and ideas are suppos'd to have a reference." (*Treatise*, p. 251)

This point can have force only if Hume was thinking of the mind being "simple," but even if it is simple there appears to be no reason why different impressions and ideas could not refer to it since it may appear in different ways and manners. The idea that something is simple, that is, that it does not have parts and hence is not capable of coming apart, does not seem to require that it appear only in one way or give us only one impression. The theistic conception of God will illustrate this point. Since God is a mind or "spirit," He has been understood to be (metaphysically) simple. This does not prevent God from being bafflingly complex in nature and beyond our understanding. Why could not the same thing be true of the mind? Does "simple" mean "elementary"? "Rudimentary"? "Primitive"? Hume seems to be relying on that point, however, and he regards that as a serious and formidable objection to the existence of the mind.

Further, in Hume's experience, pain and pleasure, grief and joy, passions and sensations succeed each other, and never all exist at the same time. "It cannot, therefore, be from any of these impressions, or from any other, that the idea of self is deriv'd; and consequently there is no such idea." (*Treatise*, p. 252)

Regardless of the objections we can raise against the inconsistency of Hume's analysis here as compared with his claim that he was bringing "the experimental method of reasoning into moral subjects," (*Treatise*, p. xi) Hume believed that he had made a telling point. In the Introduction to the *Treatise*, Hume claims that the science of human nature requires that our conclusions be "laid on experience and observation." (*Treatise*, p. xvi) Even though we must render our ideas as universal as possible, "'tis still certain we cannot go beyond experience." (*Treatise*, p. xvii) The science of man may possess the difficulty that it is very difficult to explain ultimate principles in that science (or in other sciences); still, "None of them can go beyond experience, or establish any principles which are not founded on that authority." (*Treatise*, p. xviii) Thus when Hume pontificates that "it cannot ... be from any of these impressions, or from any other that the idea of self is deriv'd," (*Treatise*, p. 252) it seems to Hume that he is keeping faith and is not departing from following the principles of the science of man.

After Hume concludes to his own satisfaction that there can be no *single* impression which gives rise to our convictions about the self or mind, he takes up the question about all the particular perceptions. His conclusion is that he can never catch himself, and so, there is no such thing as a self in him:

> But farther, what must become of all our particular perceptions upon this hypothesis? All these are different, and distinguishable, and separable from each other, and may be separately consider'd, and may exist separately, and have no need of any thing to support their existence. After what manner, therefore, do they belong to self; and how are they connected to it? For my part, when I enter most intimately into what I call *myself*, I always stumble on some particular perception or other, of heat or cold, light or shade, love or hatred, pain or pleasure. I never can catch *myself* at any time without a perception, and never can observe any thing but the perception. (*Treatise*, p. 252)

Hume proceeds to argue that when his perceptions are removed as they are in sleep, then for that length of time he is insensible of himself and may truly be said not to exist. And death further extends the same kind of thinking: If all his perceptions were removed by death, then there is nothing which could approach closer to being a non-entity. There is just no thing present because there is no impression of it, and there is no idea of self because ideas must come from impressions. The reason, he explains, is not hard to see because self or person is not any one impression but the very thing to which our various impressions and ideas are supposed to have a reference. So, since it is not the kind of thing which a single impression could give, naturally no single impression is going to give it to us.

It doesn't seem to have occurred to Hume that self or person might be a complex idea we could separate into its component simple ideas and hence simple impressions. That would seem to have been a reasonable view because the idea of a self seems to be unavoidable. If Hume couldn't "see" or "feel" it, why couldn't its existence be inferred from the effects something after the manner that Newton proposed gravitational attraction? That can't be seen or felt either, but surely Hume believed in it .... All this raises an interesting point. Even though Hume provides us a way by which we at least theoretically can trace all our complex ideas back to simple ideas and hence back to simple impressions, he in reality does very little of that. In fact, he may have had his doubts about the workability of this tracing, because Hume seems to rely only upon simple impressions. When any problematic conception arises and Hume asks what impression we have to support it, he seems to be looking for a simple impression. This conclusion seems justifiable because Hume asks, "from what impression is it derived?" or something similar and singular. Whether this pattern holds elsewhere, and it appears to me that it does, it seems clear that it is working here. A natural question to ask Hume, then, seems to be, "What if the self is a complex idea and hence stems (ultimately) from several simple impressions?" If that is a relevant question as it surely seems to be, then this would radically alter our estimate of the adequacy of Hume's analysis at this point. He seems to be looking for a single, simple impression. Perhaps this is one of the major things wrong with his conclusion here.

Hume allows that it may be different with other people. If anyone can say upon serious and unprejudiced reflection that he has a different notion of himself than the one Hume has just given, then it must be admitted that no further discussion can be carried along. The opponent may be as near right as Hume is, but "we are essentially different in this particular. He may, perhaps, perceive something simple and continu'd which he calls himself; tho' I am certain there is no such principle in me." (*Treatise*, p. 252)

Just what, then, is the mind? Hume ventures

> to affirm of the rest of mankind, that they are nothing but a bundle or collection of different perceptions, which succeed each other with an inconceivable rapidity, and are in a perpetual flux and movement .... They are the successive perceptions only, that constitute the mind; nor have we the most distant notion of the place, where these scenes are represented, or of the materials, of which it is compos'd. (*Treatise*, pp. 252-253)

Hume adds the analogy of the theater to his depiction of the mind as a place where movement and change constantly occur. On the stage of the theater actors and actresses appear, play their parts, and disappear. We must not be misled by the analogy, Hume warns, for there is nothing for the various passions, imaginations, or thoughts, in short, the internal activities, to appear in as the actors appear in the theater. We have nothing inside us comparable to the theater. To strain this analogy, if the theater is the same as our inner life, the actors and actresses would act without any stage to stand on at all. In other words, there is no mental "support"; the activities, sensations, and passions which Hume finds when he looks inside are just a collection.

This is Hume's "bundle" or "sand pile" theory of the mind. The self in this view is nothing more than the aggregate of what introspection reveals to be there. The only relation between the things he mentions is that they are there: they are perceptions of the kind that we get when we turn our attention inside, but there is no entity, substratum, substance, or stuff which unites any of these things. It seems surprising that Hume never asked what the "I ..." who enters "most intimately into what I call *myself*" could be. Surely something, the identity of which Hume was so sure, merited some notice! Of course, Hume passes up that possibility and in this way disposes of the claim that we can recognize the existence of the self empirically. Whatever other people may claim as their experience, Hume does not himself have any experience of his inner self.

This is not to say that Hume denies the existence of a mind, a mental substance. He is not a materialist. The issue for him is not the metaphysical one that the mind is matter in motion as with Hobbes or some of the French philosophes of Hume's time. His concern is to say that he cannot find it, that it never appears to him in any impression, and since there is no impression, there can be no idea that we may rightfully hold.

Hume's doctrine, "no impression ... no idea," carries over from other questions to his analysis of personal identity. The doctrine that no impression provides no *right*, no logical or epistemological justification, for his ideas, is true throughout. Why is it that Hume feels that he has no *right* to the idea and hence no one else does either—that is, unless the other person has a different "notion" of himself in which case Hume has no basis for disagreeing with him? Apparently Hume does not really think that anyone will claim to have a different notion of himself. He is convinced that the impressions he receives when he looks inside will be the case for others too. It is hard not to suspect that Hume had this thought conveniently tucked away. The problem of induction will preclude any defense of this, any argument from the impressions Hume has to the impressions others have. Hume is saddled with the metaphysical claim that in nature there is the possibility that things may be one way or another. We may suspect Hume doesn't believe that claim nor follow it, but at least epistemically he is bound by many claims of that kind he has made, and we are left to guessing as to what he might say. Hume's tendency to resort to custom, habit, feeling or some other noncognitive basis for his views probably would be his assurance that his experience is representative of other's experience too. That is, introspective, self-conscious experience, universal as Hume believes it to be, would impel another person to have his own view on that issue.

Nevertheless, Hume *does* have an idea of personal identity. He talks about it, describes its features, denies its existence as a perception and in the end accepts it by "faith." In his appendix to the *Treatise* Hume says: "Every idea is deriv'd from preceding impressions; and we have no impression of self or substance, as something simple and individual. We have, therefore, no idea of them in that sense." (*Treatise*, p. 633)

Let us turn now to Hume's "positive" doctrine of the mind. How did he hold what he believed? The claim throughout these chapters has been that Hume was not a skeptic, that is, Hume was not a skeptic at last. He was a preliminary skeptic as we described it in an earlier chapter, but he was not content to stay with the conclusions of his negative analysis. When Hume finished his philosophical reflections, he did not refuse to believe commonly-received doctrines, doctrines which to the bulk of modern people appear to be very difficult to avoid and even irresistible. Although the skeptical students of Hume claim that Hume did not believe these doctrines, it is claimed here that Hume did; thus, the manner in which Hume salvages his doctrine of the mind and of personal identity needs to be examined.

Hume says, "They are the successive perceptions only, that constitute the mind." (*Treatise*, p. 253) This is the closest Hume ever comes to denying the existence of the mind, but in the next sentence he asks why we believe in the existence of the mind: "What then gives us so great a propension to ascribe an identity to these successive perceptions, and to suppose ourselves possest of an invariable and uninterrupted existence thro' the whole course of our lives?" (*Treatise*, p. 253)

To answer his own question Hume responds that we must distinguish between personal identity as it regards our thought or imagination, and as it regards our passions or the concern we take in ourselves. He is concerned with the first of these questions, and to answer that one we must give an account, he believes, of that identity which we ascribe to plants and to animals since there is an analogy between these things and the identity of a self or person. Identity or sameness, he says, is that idea we have of an object which remains invariable and uninterrupted through a supposed variation of time, and he describes diversity as the idea of several different objects existing in succession and connected together by a close relation. But, says Hume, though these two ideas, identity and diversity, are perfectly distinct and are even contrary to each other, we commonly confound these ideas with each other.

This confusion is due to the imagination by which we consider the uninterrupted and invariable object on the one hand and the succession of related objects on the other. To the feeling, identity and difference, are almost the same.

Our feeling is the cause of our confusion and we make the mistake of substituting the notion of identity in place of that of related objects. At one time we consider the objects in one way (identity) and at another time we consider them in a different way (diversity), but the feeling "facilitates the transition of the mind from one object to another" and makes its passage as smooth as if it contemplated one continued object, the self or soul.

> However at one instant we may consider the related succession as variable or interrupted, we are sure the next to ascribe to it a perfect identity, and regard it as invariable and interrupted. Our propensity to this mistake is so great from the resemblance above-mention'd, that we fall into it before we are aware; and tho' we incessantly correct ourselves by reflexion, and return to a more accurate method of thinking, yet we cannot long sustain our philosophy, or take off this biass from the imagination. Our last resource is to yield to it, and boldly assert that these different related objects are in effect the same, however interrupted and variable. In order to justify to ourselves this absurdity, we often feign some new and unintelligible principle, that connects the objects together, and prevents their interruption or variation. Thus we feign the continu'd existence of the perceptions of our senses, to remove the interruption; and run into the notion of a *soul*, and *self*, and *substance*, to disguise the variation. (*Treatise*, p. 254)

This is another of Hume's psychological explanations to account for what his philosophical analysis had denied. He calls the conclusion an "absurdity" and contends that we "feign" the continued existence of the perceptions of our senses. Our propensity towards such a mistake (positing the continued existence of the discontinuous perceptions of our senses) causes us to "fall into it before we are aware." We need to correct ourselves of this mistake (by reflection) and return to a more accurate mode of thinking, but we just can't continue it. This propensity, Hume claims, is human nature. It's not like a vice which we have developed which we can no longer control such as a compulsive addition to alcohol or drugs. Instead of that, human nature is the normal and ever-present state of our thought, actions, and lives.

Let's go at Hume's whole discussion again with a different emphasis. On p. 252 Hume describes entering most intimately into himself and finding only some one or other of a group of perceptions. This leads him to conclude that we are nothing but a bundle of perceptions in a perpetual flux and movement succeeding each other with an inconceivable rapidity. Perceptions from our senses or from our mind are continually in movement, appearing, passing, and fading out.

On p. 253 he restates his bundle theory of the mind and confesses that we don't have the "most distant notion" of the place where our mental experiences take place or of the material of which the mind is composed. We are left, then, with a pretty thorough skepticism about this problem of the mind.

Hume's Metaphysical Doctrines

Then, in the middle of that page, he starts his departure from the skepticism we have outlined here: "What then gives us so great a propension to ascribe an identity to these successive perceptions, and to suppose ourself possest of an invariable and uninterrupted existence through the whole course of our lives?" (*Treatise*, p. 253) He had denied the existence of the mind; now he is going to account for his belief in it.

This is a dramatic shift in focus. A few lines before Hume was talking about perceptions, the ideas that could come from them, and differences in perception and in the understanding which could result from our perceptions. Then, Hume shifts to our human, natural propensities, and it will be on that, not on the ordinary, rationalist, philosophical tests that Hume will allow our natural ideas to be held and used.

On p. 253 he appeals to the kind of ideas we normally have about objects, succession, diversity, and identity. Although our ideas of identity and a succession of related objects may be perfectly distinct, Hume tells us, they are generally confounded with each other. The action of our imagination and our reflections on a succession of objects "are almost the same to the feeling." (*Treatise*, p. 254)

Hume then says "The relation facilitates the transition of the mind from one object to another, and renders its passage as smooth as if it contemplated one continu'd object." (*Treatise*, p. 254) Hume gains some advantages in his writings and especially in the *Treatise* from such ambiguity. What is "the relation"? Is it the feeling which unites ("relates") the imagination and reflection? Is it the action of the imagination which considers the uninterrupted object *and* by which we carry on our reflections? A rereading of this passage leaves us with the conviction that there is no way of deciding what Hume meant here.

But Hume continues: "This resemblance is the cause of the confusion and mistake, and makes us substitute the notion of identity, instead of that of related objects." (*Treatise*, p. 254) What resemblance? Surely identity cannot resemble diversity? Is the resemblance between the "transition of the mind" and "its passage"? These exegetical problems are presented here to illustrate the fact that we don't know precisely what Hume is doing here. This passage gets precious little attention from Hume scholars and in itself may illustrate why that is the case. But it leaves the reader baffled and frustrated.

We can get his general drift, however. Hume says our propensity to this mistake is great. Presumably, this is the mistake of confusing the "related succession" with a "perfect identity." The general idea here is clear enough. The "related succession" of thought refers to what we find then when we look inside: "some particular perceptions or other." This is confused with the perfect identity of something called a soul, or self, or person.

We fall into this mistake before we are aware, says Hume,

> and tho' we incessantly correct ourselves by reflexion, and return to a more accurate method of thinking, yet we cannot long sustain our philosophy, or

> take off this biass from the imagination. Our last resource is to yield to it, and boldly assert that these different related objects are ... the same .... Thus we feign the continu'd existence of the perceptions of our senses, to remove the interruption; and run into the notion of a *soul*, and *self*, and *substance* to disguise the variation. (*Treatise*, p. 254)

Here we have one of the shortest and most pungent displays of skepticism and fideism in the whole Humean corpus. In the space of four pages Hume takes the skeptic position on the mind or self, explains how the personal "mechanisms" of the imagination, feeling, personal propensity, etc. are involved and serve to justify our regular beliefs about our soul, mind, or self which we can hardly reject anyway. He rejects and recovers, analyzes away and adopts back the very doctrine in question. We could hardly ask for a more abbreviated treatment of a major issue than this one, and like Hume's essay, "On Immortality," this illustration of skepticism and fideism is so vivid as to leave us astounded.

In the pages which follow the statement just given, Hume attempts to explain more of his thinking. He maintains his claim that it is a mistake to regard the mind as an identity.

> For as such a succession answers evidently to our notion of diversity, it can only be by mistake we ascribe to it an identity; and as the relation of parts, which leads us into this mistake, is really nothing but a quality, which produces an association of ideas, and an easy transition of the imagination from one to another, it can only be from the resemblance, which this act of the mind bears to that, by which we contemplate one continu'd object, that the error arises. (*Treatise*, p. 255)

Hume then attempts to show that all the objects to which we ascribe identity are really just a succession of related "objects." He launches into a discussion of the identity of objects and how these things can change, and why we sometimes allow identity to continue (as in a ship whose planks have been replaced). Hume attributes this allowance to our habit of mind or customary way of looking at things. This is *human nature*, Hume's broadest category of nonrational inclination. Human nature collects together all those natural tendencies we display and all ordinary proclivities we follow, which things decide for us what we cannot determine intellectually.

Hume's explanation as to why we ascribe identity to things that consist of a succession of parts was carried out to explain personal identity. He says:

> We now proceed to explain the nature of *personal identity* .... And here 'tis evident, the same method of reasoning must be continu'd, which has so successfully explain'd the identity of plants, and animals, and ships, and houses, and of all the compounded and changeable productions either of art or of nature. The identity, which we ascribe to the mind of man, is

only a fictitious one, and of a like kind with that which we ascribe to vegetables and animal bodies. It cannot, therefore, have a different origin, but must proceed from a like operation of the imagination upon like objects. (*Treatise*, p. 259)

So, this is the pattern. Whether we talk about soul, self, and substance or personal identity, Hume's conclusion is the same: Intellectual, that is, philosophical and rational, analysis does not give the answer to us. What does give it to us is our nonrational inclinations, the habit, custom, propensity, inclination of the mind, association, imagination, feeling, or human nature.

Hume had committed himself to the view that our mind is a bundle of all the processes and states it experiences. Consequently, if he is going to claim any consistency he has to give a coherent account of mental processes. It still seems very difficult to see why there should be such a problem of identity and whether there "be something that really binds our several perceptions together." The bond is that they are *mine*, that I have them. They belong to me and are united by being a part of one consciousness. Whatever difficulties we might face in establishing the character of the owner, the self, to which we ascribe ownership, there is *something* separate and different from the manifold things we find when we "enter most intimately into what I call myself."

Such replies to Hume are somewhat tangential to our concerns here, but it is interesting that Hume uses the question of the nature of mental processes and the relation to the person who has them to reemphasize his fideistic bent. He had talked about this pattern and its relation to other topics, but he can apply the approach to mind as well:

The understanding never observes any real connexion among objects, and that even the union of cause and effect, when strictly examin'd, resolves itself into a customary association of ideas. For from thence it evidently follows, that identity is nothing really belonging to these different perceptions, and uniting them together; but is merely a quality, which we attribute to them, because of the union of their ideas in the imagination, when we reflect upon them. Now the only qualities, which can give ideas an union in the imagination, are these three relations above-mention'd. These are the uniting principles in the ideal world, and without them every distinct object is separable by the mind, and may be separately consider'd, and appears not to have any more connexion with any other object, than if disjoin'd by the greatest difference and remoteness. 'Tis, therefore, on some of these three relations of resemblance, contiguity and causation, that identity depends; and as the very essence of these relations consists in their producing an easy transition of ideas; it follows, that our notions of personal identity, proceed entirely from the smooth and uninterrupted progress of the thought along a train of connected ideas, according to the principles above-explain'd. (*Treatise*, pp. 259-260)

SUBSTANCE

Hume's treatment of substance occurs very near the beginning of Book I in the *Treatise*. (pp. 15-17) Part I, Section VI may not appear to be very significant because Hume's treatment there is very short. Nevertheless it contains a skeletal model of Hume's treatment of metaphysical issues and is important because the issue of substance appears again and again in the *Treatise*. The problem of substance was central in Hume's discussion of the mind, personal identity, and material objects. It is a source of frequent comments, questions, and various remarks which indicate its importance to Hume in his reflections on both the metaphysical and epistemological issues of Book I.

So, it is reasonable to ask what substance is according to Hume. He mentions that substance was commonly believed to be an unknown something in which the qualities which form a substance are supposed to inhere. (*Treatise*, p. 16) Such a view of substance seems to have been drawn from Locke. Locke conceived of substance as that which "stands under" the qualities, relations, dispositions, etc. and "supports" them. Such words are metaphorical, of course, but the main idea is that there has to be something which is colored, shaped, spatially located, impenetrable, etc. This something is substance, the substratum, what is left when all the properties are subtracted from it. We actually cannot "separate" the qualities and other descriptive features of the thing, but if we could, the remainder would be the substance. The accidents in this view can change, but the substance remains one and the same.

Substance can be material in the objects of our outer senses and impressions or immaterial in the supposed existence of the self. Neither exists, or more correctly, we have no justification for believing they exist in Hume's view, but if we could know that they are present in the world we would find substance divided into the two classes, material and mental.

Hume demonstrates in two paragraphs how he is able (at least to his satisfaction) to take away some article of metaphysical belief through raising problems about the origin of our belief in sensation or reflection. Neither one of these sources, he contends, is sufficient to give us the idea, and therefore we have no idea of substance.

In the second paragraph Hume retrieves what he had disposed of a paragraph before by attributing to the imagination the uniting force which is needed to restore to us the idea of substance.

This example of Hume's thinking is given here out of the order in which it occurs in the *Treatise* because of its extreme brevity and because its pattern of fideistic thinking can be seen more clearly after we have looked at some of the more elaborate examples in the *Treatise*. Nevertheless, it illustrates clearly for us what Hume does with his metaphysical doctrines.

THE EXISTENCE OF MATERIAL OBJECTS

In sharp contrast to Hume's treatment of substance which is so brief that it is likely to be overlooked, his treatment of external, material objects is long, tedious, and repetitive of what we have encountered before. Hume examines the issues on the reality and nature of material objects in much the same fashion as he did on the topics we have already discussed. *Consequently much of the issue is being assigned to the reader who may want to investigate the issue at length.*

This topic receives a slightly different treatment than do the other ones because Hume appears to be more interested in method in this section than he was in the preceding sections. The first words of I, IV, II affirms this: "Thus the sceptic still continues to reason and believe, even tho' he asserts, that he cannot defend his reason by reason; and by the same rule he must assent to the principle concerning the existence of body, tho' he cannot pretend by any arguments of philosophy to maintain its veracity." (*Treatise*, p. 187)

The subject of this present inquiry, he tells us, is concerning the causes which induce us to believe in the existence of body. We may ask what cause induce us to believe in the existence of body, but it would be vain and fruitless to ask "Whether there be body or not? That is a point which we must take for granted in all our reasonings." (*Treatise*, p. 187) Hume distinguishes two questions which he wants to discuss: Why we attribute a continued existence to objects, and why we suppose objects to have an existence distinct from the mind and perception.

The method for deciding on the answers will come from human nature, but Hume says we will have to find out whether it be the senses, reason, or the imagination which produces the opinion of a continued or distinct existence. Hume shows, he believes, that the answers cannot arise from the first two, so the imagination wins by default.

> Upon the whole our reason neither does, nor is it possible it ever shou'd, upon any supposition, give us an assurance of the continu'd and distinct existence of body. That opinion must be entirely owing to the IMAGINATION: which must now be the subject of enquiry. (*Treatise*, p. 193)

Hume's negative, rational, analytic, or reductive treatment of the existence of bodies or external objects starts on p. 187 of the *Treatise* (I, IV, II) and the positive, fideistic, reconstructive treatment occurs in several steps. His intermediate conclusion is about perception and the external objects of the world. Once again we get the familiar pattern of demolition and restoration, rejection and acceptance I have labeled as a fideism. We get the conclusion we need not on rational, philosophical grounds but upon "natural" ones.

> Objects have a certain coherence even as they appear to our senses; but this coherence is much greater and more uniform, if we suppose the objects to have a continu'd existence; and as the mind is once in the train of observing an uniformity among objects, it naturally continues, till it renders the uniformity as compleat as possible. The simple supposition of their continu'd existence suffices for this purpose, and gives us a notion of a much greater regularity among objects, than what they have when we look no farther than our senses. (*Treatise*, p. 198)

Hume's next step is to explain four points which play a large role in showing how for Hume our tendencies of human nature assure us of the answers about the external world which we cannot sanely deny but which Hume's philosophical examination gives us no reasons to accept. (*Treatise*, p. 199f)

The last reason Hume gives to account for the fruitfulness of human nature is the similarity of the answers derived by that irrational method to the answers of the vulgar. *Reason is not useful for giving us answers to our vexing questions about the external world but to follow the instincts, propensities, and inclinations of human nature is to take away the split between the doctrines of philosophers and the vulgar.* This enables philosophers to leave "their closets" and to "mingle with the rest of mankind." (*Treatise*, p. 216) To do that is to solve the struggles of reason and to continue to have the opinions about things which we naturally have anyway. That is as close to the pyrrhonist program as anyone could expect!

And so this section, as tedious, intricately reasoned, and even convoluted as any other in the *Treatise*, yields the same fideistic tendencies we have seen in the other examples of cause, personal identity, and substance. The split and inconsistency between philosophy and "vulgar" thinking are overcome by our natural tendency to return to a nonrational way of thinking.

CHAPTER 5

METHOD AND PYRRHONISM IN HUME'S PHILOSOPHY

So far our study of Hume has consisted of a sustained argument that Hume is a fideist, that he holds firmly to views he had eliminated rationally by appealing to nonrational means. This holds true for his metaphysics as well as for his philosophy of religion. It is our claim that Hume's philosophy bears broad fideistic tendencies in all the areas he examines, that when Hume is done with his work, he is not a skeptic but holds positive answers to all the questions he raised. By carrying through his rational analysis, by using the skeptic's approach, Hume comes to unacceptable conclusions, and he looks for ways of believing the doctrines he has discredited. So, he appeals to "human nature" as the catch-all term which provides for him the grounds upon which he *recovers* his views. Custom, habit, association of ideas, a felt inclination of the mind, propensity, human nature, the imagination, etc. are appealed to as ways or grounds upon which he can retain the conclusions he wants to believe and cannot deny except on pain of appearing trivial and silly. And cannot deny without feeling the distress of rejecting what is plain and clear to him.

Our argument started with the claim that Hume's philosophy of religion is a fideism. Philosophy of religion was taken first since fideism is a position and method traditionally associated with religion, and since fideisms most often appeal to faith, a basic and essential feature of religion. The next step in the argument dealt with Hume's metaphysical doctrines. The same pattern of analysis leading to skepticism is found there as was found in the area of religious doctrines. Doctrines are rejected on rational bases, on minute, piecemeal analysis based on reason or experience, and retained on nonrational ones.

This chapter, the third step in the argument, gives Hume's general remarks on method, beliefs, and conclusions. Previously, Hume's statements referred to one issue or another, and his comments on method were random and situational, given drop by drop as they "leaked" out in each discussion. The reader was left with the task of trying to see through what Hume was doing. That debate still continues on some issues, and that Hume is still being minutely studied shows that his method is not altogether clear and distinct.

Hume also thought reflectively and pensively about the very things he was doing and about his personal reactions to them. Our study of Hume in this chapter will focus on Hume's more general, deliberate, and self-conscious comments on the relation of reason and unreason. What before he gave in bits and pieces, Hume now discusses more methodically and consciously. We have here in Hume's comments on method, a sort of "metamethod." In I, IV, VII of the *Treatise* (p. 263f) Hume states some of the same things in his own words that I have argued in previous chapters from Hume's use and Hume's expressions.

In addition to the examination of Hume's general views in this chapter we have Richard Popkin's assessment of Hume as a Pyrrhonist thinker who followed in a long train of (French) skeptics. This different approach to Hume's conclusions which has not received enough recognition from Hume scholars, reinforces the arguments about Hume we have already given, and provides additional support for the fideist interpretation of Hume's philosophy.

At the end of his section "*Of scepticism with regard to the senses,*" where Hume deals with the questions about external bodies or objects, he gives this general conclusion:

> This sceptical doubt, both with respect to reason and the senses, is a malady, which can never be radically cur'd, but must return upon us every moment, however we may chace it away, and sometimes may seem entirely free from it. 'Tis impossible upon any system to defend either our understanding or senses; and we but expose them farther when we endeavour to justify them in that manner. As the sceptical doubt arises naturally from a profound and intense reflection on those subjects, it always encreases, the farther we carry our reflections, whether in opposition or conformity to it. Carelessness and in-attention alone can afford us any remedy. For this reason I rely entirely upon them; and take it for granted, whatever may be the reader's opinion at this present moment, that an hour hence he will be persuaded there is both an external and internal world. (*Treatise*, p. 218)

With such a forthright statement at the end of a chapter on a single topic it would not be surprising if Hume had some remarks on skepticism and belief in general, and so that topic will be an important concern of this chapter.

HUME SCHOLARSHIP AND THE FIDEIST CLAIM

Before we take up the issue of Hume's perspective on method, however, it is necessary to discuss another issue of concern in this debate. Running through all this discussion there has been an unexpressed question just under the surface about the fideist thesis for which I have argued. The question is this: If Hume is a fideist as you maintain, and there is as much evidence for this as you claim, then why haven't other commentators on Hume held what you are advocating? It is necessary at this point to answer that question, so we are inserting what amounts to a parenthesis before we go to the last step of the argument.

The answer to this question is not as quick or simple as we would like to have it, but very roughly, it is this: Philosophers have not paid enough attention to the Pyrrhonist skeptical movement in philosophy in the century which preceded that of David Hume. They have short changed that part of the intellectual environment of Hume's time. Philosophers have concluded that Locke's and Berkeley's influence were the major forces on Hume, combined, of course with British resistance to Cartesian, continental rationalism. Newton comes in a distant third in the list of influences on Hume with Bacon meriting some honorable mention. Modern Pyrrhonism was not known, and in recent years when our sources for this skepticism were expanded, too little attention was paid to that movement and its influence on Hume.

Later, this chapter will include a summary of the ideas and the program of this movement, but for the time being let's just review the prevailing situation among Hume scholars.

Up to the time of Norman Kemp Smith scholars generally regarded Hume as a skeptic and slanted their comments on him in that direction. Hume's *Dialogues concerning Natural Religion* were an exception and were sometimes given a fideistic interpretation. This began with Dugald Stewart, and since his time a persistent, though minority group has held to that interpretation. Richard Popkin, for example, is a current illustration. Although the *Dialogues* were so interpreted, the fideist interpreters were generally regarded as exceptions to the standard or majority position, that position being that Hume was a skeptic on all religious questions.

When we turn to the metaphysical problems Hume discusses, the unanimous or near-unanimous position has been that Hume was a skeptic, that he denied those beliefs and rejected those answers which ordinary, nonskeptical people hold. If it was recognized that Hume employed transcendental arguments or was quite like Kant in many ways, and was, in fact, a "Scottish Kant,"[1] that got buried in the preoccupation of Humean skepticism. Beck reminds us that forty to fifty years ago such a comparison was considered in bad taste.

The big change came in the work of Norman Kemp Smith. Although he introduced his naturalist thesis for understanding Hume's epistemology in 1905, the major impact on Hume scholarship came when his book, *The Philosophy of David Hume*, was published in 1941. John Hospers who was a graduate student at Columbia in the 1940s relates how the book created quite a sensation in philosophical circles, and it was concluded at Columbia that Kemp Smith regarded Hume as a common-sense philosopher along with some of his other Scotch peers. Kemp Smith's book still looms over Hume scholars as a classic, and his "naturalism" thesis for Hume's work is now the most widely-accepted understanding of what Hume does to escape a final skepticism. Perhaps the bulk of Hume scholars, though not all of them, have followed Kemp Smith's lead and the view that Hume appeals to the natural forces and tendencies of human personality and that we cannot ignore and escape these influences of our personality is very widely accepted. We might call this the new standard view of Hume, the majority view, the new Humean orthodoxy.

Not only Kemp Smith but Mossner and a broad group of Hume scholars have not seen the possibility that Hume is a fideist. These scholars had access to all of Hume's material, and surely Hume's intent and meaning is not that hard to extract. Well, then, why the claim that Hume is a fideist? And, if this claim is correct, why have so many Hume scholars missed it?

The first part of an answer to that question must be that scholarship, academic precedence, and tradition have their own weight. From Warburton, Stewart, Beattie, and Reid to our own day there has been a persistent tradition which labels Hume a skeptic. The weight of all those opinions has to be taken into account. For generations, too much as been written on the "skepticism of David Hume" for that view easily to be overcome.

There is another, more important reason why Hume scholars have not seen the possibility of a fideist understanding of Hume. It is due largely to the failure to pay attention to the history of Hume's times. There is still abroad the idea that Hume's writings can be interpreted completely and adequately from within Hume's text alone. We do not need to look around to see if there are any historical clues to assist us in dealing with some of the perplexing problems Hume hands us.

Hardly any attention is paid by many Hume scholars and commentators to modern French (Pyrrhonist) skepticism, to observe the influence on Hume of such figures as Pierre Bayle, and to gauge Hume's reactions to the highly self-confident figures in British natural theology and rationalistic continental metaphysics.

We now have historical resources in the work of Richard Popkin which were not available before 1950. Many other scholars have contributed articles and edited collections which illuminate the same group of problems and have enlarged our understanding of the Pyrrhonist movement and the people who belonged to it. Our treatment of Popkin's work is not meant to reflect on the worth of any other historical work. To all of it, to all the scholars who have added bits and pieces to the puzzle we owe our gratitude. Our emphasis on Popkin is due mainly to the breadth of his work and the wide availability of his writings. Kemp Smith with his naturalist hypothesis did not have the resources of current historical scholarship. If this had been available there is little doubt in my mind that he would have discussed the possibility of both a religious and a general fideism.

Kemp Smith's main book on Hume's philosophy contains three references to Pyrrho, but nothing in the context indicates that Smith views Pyrrhonism as anything but an ancient movement. He does not suggest why Hume would select that tradition when it belonged to centuries long gone by, and Smith may have regarded it as an accidental happenstance. Montaigne comes in with seven references, four of which are direct quotations at the top of chapters, one of them being repeated later in the book.[2] At one point he links Montaigne with Bayle's influence on Hume which he understands to be considerable.

Bayle gets extensive attention from Kemp Smith who was aware of the amount of material Hume drew from Bayle. He includes two appendices in his Hume book on Bayle's influence on Hume, and the particular issues where Hume's treatment reveals that he drew very heavily on Bayle without, however, giving any credit to Bayle. He attributes that to the difference between eighteenth century practice and ours in using work of an author. Hume gets linked to Montaigne as does Bayle and Kemp Smith remarks that Hume in most matters "was congenially minded with Bayle, as with their common master, Montaigne."[3]

Kemp Smith's edition of Hume's *Dialogues*, issued in 1947, does nothing to change our assessment of his lack of knowledge of the Pyrrhonist movement and of Montaigne's and Bayle's place in it nor the influence on Hume that the movement had. He identifies "a celebrated prelate ... of the Romish communion," given in Part I of the *Dialogues* as Peter Daniel Huet,[4] but without any indication of Huet's place in the group of modern Pyrrhonians. The uniform picture which seems to emerge is that Kemp Smith had no knowledge whatever of the modern Pyrrhonist movement. Historical research on the modern ("new") Pyrrhonians was simply not available to him as it is to us.

The main historical influence on Hume in Kemp Smith's view besides that of Locke and Berkeley was Francis Hutcheson. Locke and Berkeley each exercised considerable influence on Hume, and with this almost all Hume interpreters agree, but Kemp Smith has not been followed in his views on Hutcheson.

Philosophers are historic people who live during a particular time with its social, political, religious, economic, intellectual, cultural, and moral milieus. That may sound platitudinous, trivial, and banal, but it is often forgotten, and the treatments current philosophers give to those of the past seem to fall all too often into that very mistake. Past philosophers bear the effects of their times as do all the rest of us. So, *to fail to interpret a philosopher according to his own time is to doom ourselves to interpret that philosopher according to ours*. We need only look at some extremes like logical positivism in our own age to see how this works. We are not free of the influences, pressures, preoccupations, prejudices, biases, hopes, and fears of our own time. If we make no consistent and disciplined attempt to surmount these, we face little prospect of being able to escape them, but present they are and we fool ourselves if we refuse to acknowledge them. The ahistorical approach to interpreting David Hume falls into that trap.

The mistake, then, of failing to pay enough attention to Hume's age is a major mistake made by many, though not all, Hume scholars. We do pretty well in understanding that Hume's excision of his treatment on miracles from the *Treatise* had to do with Hume's respect for and fear of Joseph Butler, that he saw the need for "experiments" from his respect for Galilean-Newtonian science, that his rejection of innate ideas is traceable to Locke and Berkeley. But contemporary

Hume studies have sometimes been short on viewing Hume in "context," and of asking how Hume related to those who preceded him and how he related to his contemporaries such as the French philosophes.

The pervasive influence on Hume of Pyrrhonism, especially as this was worked out and put forward by Bayle, has seldom been properly recognized. To put it another way, when it comes to making a difference in the way Hume is interpreted, the presence and nature of Pyrrhonism has generally been overlooked by philosophers. So, it seems evident that the absence of attention to and work on the external influences on Hume has been a major shortcoming of a considerable portion of studies devoted to Hume. The historical influences involves not only the Pyrrhonians, but Malebranche, Leibniz, and orthodox apologists like Clarke.

Most Hume scholars of the past quarter century have failed to realize the potential of their work by failing to see how deeply Hume was affected by this tradition, how he tried to escape its defeating influence, and how the outcome of his work bears its unmistakable stamp. Hume scholars have tended to look only within Hume's writings for the keys to understanding him and have failed to see how the outside, the historical movement affected Hume. One group of Hume scholars largely ignore the linkage Hume had to the Pyrrhonists, especially Bayle, some give some time and attention to Pyrrhonism since Hume mentions it, and all examine Hume's "skepticism." This is not the situation in all the cases, of course. A scholar such as Penelhum[5] sees the connection between Hume and Pyrrhonism quite clearly and does an outstanding job in illuminating the connection, and Popkin has already been mentioned.

So far our comments on Hume scholarship and the failure to take historical connections to Hume seriously enough has been entirely *general*. To make this *particular* I have chosen a couple examples of recent Hume scholarship to illustrate this point. They are presented in the chronological order of their publication.

The first is David Pears' *Hume's System*.[6] His book illustrates an interesting phenomenon: commentary on Hume's doctrines from the first book of the *Treatise* alone is still being done. Recent Hume scholarship has tended to study Hume as a unit, including his historical and political writings. Pears' approach is in sharp contrast to the unified corpus approach of trying to account for all of Hume's writings so that we can form a properly synthetic understanding of his philosophy in all its completeness.

From the treatment in Pears' book we would have no reason ever for thinking that skepticism, and, hence, skeptics, had any historical antecedents, any consensus, or common viewpoint on philosophy, any agreed-upon procedure in facing questions, any justification or defense for their negative, skeptical answers, or any sense of group cohesion. From what we could get from Pears, the skeptic might be nothing more than an occasional intellectual curiosity who would turn up in a university, might be discovered in an academic society, or possibly could become conspicuous in some literary circle. We get no inkling from Pears that there ever was a thing like the modern Pyrrhonist movement or even an ancient one. There are no entries in his index on Pyrrhonism or the Pyrrhonists, no reference to any figures like Montaigne or Bayle, and no intimation that Bayle had had any influence whatever on Hume. The skeptic, for all that Pears' book would give to us is an individual, autonomous as philosophers like to imagine that they are, a solitary intellect standing alone against the world, owing no intellectual or cultural debt to anyone, to any institution, to any tradition.

Naturalism emerges as an important issue consistent with this philosophic orthodoxy in circles of Hume scholarship and discussion and it is repeated by Pears as the assured results of Humean criticism. He sums up the doctrine nicely by saying, "Where reason fails us, nature supports us. That is the message of Hume's naturalism."[7] If Pears had paid more attention to the Pyrrhonist position, he might have recognized this as the fideist pattern.

Pears' treatment of the *Treatise* is another case where Hume is viewed from the standpoint of twentieth-century analytic philosophy, especially linguistic philosophy. Russell's problems of logical atomism, his principle of acquaintance, the task of logical analysis, and the theory of meaning all are treated by Pears as problems anticipated by Hume in the *Treatise*. Pears warns us that

> "It is important not to be over-impressed by this similarity [between Russell's principle of acquaintance and Hume's impressions]. For when we look back at Book I of the *Treatise*, we shall miss the richness of its philosophy if we interpret it entirely from a later linguistic point of view."[8]

A brief perusal of Pears' book, however, shows that he still talks about Hume as if he were a twentieth-century figure: "He [Hume] too is not abandoning his empiricist theory of meaning, and he too regards physical objects as theoretically inaccessible."[9] Pears' disclaimer didn't seem to have much effect.

Wittgenstein is the second analytic philosopher Pears links to Hume, and Pears sees Hume as anticipating Wittgenstein's arguments against intrinsic powers, that the meaning of an image is the use we make of it,[10] and that Humean naturalism is the same as Wittgenstein's appeal to and how a mathematician finds it natural to go on in his mathematical series.

Pears remarks that Hume drew no distinction between philosophy and science (after our current manner) and that this explains Hume's inability to take the matter any "deeper" in his exploration of what he was doing.[11]

Pears is a current philosopher who reads twentieth-century concerns back into Hume, due, apparently, to his failure to plumb the history of Hume's times. He does not mention the modern Pyrrhonist movement, Bayle, Montaigne, Leibniz, or Malebranche. Outside of Spinoza and Kant all the figures Pears mentions are English. Sextus Empiricus is mentioned in a footnote because Hume's claim made in the *Treatise* (p. 103) that in philosophy we must follow taste and sentiment was supported by a quotation previously found in Sextus' writings. On this passage from the *Treatise*, Pears remarks:

So we must conclude that he was carried away by his own rhetoric in the provocative passage that has just been quoted. [*Treatise*, p. 103] He ought not to have implied that causal inference is ever a response to autonomous feeling. That is an excess which spoils his real point, that, though it is a response to evidence, it is mediated by the non-rational part of our nature.[12]

All in all, Pears' treatment illustrates the tendency to interpret a philosopher in current fashion when we lose sight of the historical influences of that person's time. Quite disappointing.

Our second illustration is a very recent work by Annette Baier.[13] Her book is a sensitive and perspicuous treatment of Hume's *Treatise* and catches every nuance and shift in the book. The book is right on the trail of Hume's negative and skeptical treatment of topics like causation and the resolution of the dialectical tension on that topic through Hume's doctrine of sentiment.

When we look for connections Hume may have had to other historical groups or movements, or to historic figures like Bayle, Malebranche, or Leibniz, we find these to be conspicuously lacking. She mentions the Pyrrhonian and academic skeptics[14] but only as ancient specimens not as possible influences on Hume from his time. Some of the notes contain good comments on the work of Myles Burnyeat, James Allen, and C. L. Stough, but the reader is left with the impression that no connection was made between Hume and Pyrrhonian skeptics of the century before him. Thus, she says in a note that "Hume's *Enquiry* treatment of varieties of scepticism is different from that of the *Treatise* (and perhaps truer to ancient scepticism and its varieties)."[15]

Such comments leave the impression that Hume was thinking of ancient skepticism, and no connection is made between Hume and modern Pyrrhonic skepticism. Baier's discussion of skepticism and the skeptics is done without an apparent awareness of who the skeptics are or where they get their inspiration. The skeptical tendencies of modern philosophy have been very puzzling to philosophers in the past who seemed to see no reasons for its presence and blight on modern philosophy. Historical research in the past fifty years hs cleared this up and helped us to understand why such figures as Descartes relied on a method of skepticism to establish his starting point, etc. So, an omission of the skeptical movement in the account of an historical figure like Hume is a mistake which affects far more than just our understanding of Hume.

Pyrrhonism comes in for explicit mention and evaluation by Hume in the *Enquiry*, but since Baier's book concentrates on the *Treatise* alone, any help the *Enquiry* might give in providing any insight into our understanding of the *Treatise* is not available. Even here, however, if we view the movement only an ancient phenomenon we cannot account for Bayle, Montaigne, or the lesser-known French clerics described for us by Popkin. The lack of historical material in Baier's book is a considerable shortcoming. The book is very suggestive on many issues, but it is a distinct disappointment in the historical "department," and it is a pity that this area of influence on Hume was not examined.

When we look for mention of philosophers of Hume's time we find a like paucity of references. Locke merits considerable attention, Berkeley gets a couple references, Leibniz is mentioned once in the text, Malebranche is referred to a couple times, but there is no mention of Bayle. If Bayle is the influence on Hume that Popkin claims, then the omission is bound to affect our (and Baier's) understanding of Hume. The most shocking omission of all is the work of Richard Popkin. No reference whatever to his work occurs in the book. This affects Baier's treatment of the new (modern) Pyrrhonists, the skeptical group which so exercised Hume and stimulated his thinking, his responses, and his recommendations. All told, this part of Baier's work is very disappointing.

HUME'S REFLECTIONS ON HIS PHILOSOPHY

David Hume is quite open with his readers. When he is distressed or perplexed, he is not afraid to communicate this, and when he feels strongly about some issue this is usually made clear as well. Perhaps Hume does have the tendency to "play to the gallery." Since he seeks to attract attention and to provoke his readers in other places and about other issues, what is there to prevent the same thing here? Hume's penchant for the dramatic raises our doubts when we come to the last section of Book I of the *Treatise*. But though Hume loved notoriety and the effect of shocking others, there appears to be good reasons why we should take him seriously when he voices distress about his atomistic empiricism, minute analysis, skeptical bent, and the sterile conclusions to which this led him. It is hard to see what he might gain from such utterances. These expressions were not likely to provoke public outcry during Hume's lifetime, to attract attention, or to establish his fame. There doesn't seem to be any good reason to feel that such expressions could be due to ulterior motives, consequently it seems reasonable to take him seriously and at face value. What would Hume have stood to gain by articulating his feelings, expressing his distress, and confessing his misgivings about his conclusions, method, and his overall success?

Section VII of Book I, Part IV, of the *Treatise* appears to serve that purpose. It is the conclusion of the first third of the *Treatise*, the first volume, published in 1739. This first book contains Hume's discussion of all the metaphysical issues and the majority of the (conscious) epistemological issues in the *Treatise*. As the final portion of that part, section VII acts as a kind of sounding board for everything that has gone before.

After expressing some doubts about the size of the job which lies before him and his misgivings about his ability to meet them, he tells us about his feelings of isolation and distress. (*Treatise*, p. 264) His remarks are puzzling because the first volume of the *Treatise* had not yet been published, and so, it would seem, no one outside the acquaintance of some of his intimate friends had a basis for knowing what were Hume's ideas. Our understanding of Hume's life is that he was not a socialite and stayed quite generally to himself. Writing is a lonely activity so this way have been due to necessity, but Hume does not seem to have been an antisocial person. He does not describe himself that way, and his friends seem to agree on his capacity for enjoying company and having a good time. But, surely, Hume's circle of associations at the end of his twenties was not very broad. The educated class in eighteenth Scotland comprised a very small group in that society. It is possible that he penned these remarks while he was still living and writing in France and left the comments in the book. This feeling of isolation he had before the publication of the *Treatise* had added to it the absence of any recognition when it did hit the market, for he complains that when the *Treatise* was published, "It fell *dead-born from the Press*; without reaching such distinction as even to excite a Murmur among the Zealots."[16] His friends who knew and understood his views would have had little inclination to cause him trouble and those who later did seek to cause trouble did not yet know his views. It would not seem, then, that there was anything external in Hume's social circles, among his academic acquaintances, or in the Scottish clergy to cause such feelings of isolation and distress. His expressions of distress appear to us to be quite extreme:

> I am first affrighted and confounded with that forelorn solitude, in which I am plac'd in my philosophy, and fancy myself some strange uncouth monster, who not being able to mingle and unite in society, has been expell'd all human commerce, and left utterly abandon'd and disconsolate. Fain wou'd I run into the crowd for shelter and warmth; but cannot prevail with myself to mix with such deformity. I call upon others to join me, in order to make a company apart; but no one will hearken to me. Every one keeps at a distance, and dreads that storm which beats upon me from every side. I have expos'd myself to the enmity of all metaphysicians, logicians, mathematicians, and even theologians; and can I wonder at the insults I must suffer? I have declar'd my disapprobation of their systems; and can I be surpriz'd, if they shou'd express a hatred of mine and of my person? When I look abroad, I foresee on every side, dispute, contradiction, anger, calumny and detraction. When I turn my eye inward, I find nothing but doubt and ignorance. All the world conspires to oppose and contradict me; tho' such is my weakness, that I feel all my opinions loosen and fall of themselves, when unsupported by the approbation of others. Every step I take is with hesitation, and every new reflection makes me dread an error and absurdity in my reasoning. (*Treatise, pp. 264-265)*

Mossner attributes Hume's remarks to "philosophical melancholy" and finds its relief in "nature" which cures him of "philosophical melancholy and delirium" by relaxation, some change in vocation, dining, conversation, or backgammon!

No doubt the isolation and loneliness of writing bore heavily on a personality who, according to the reports of his friends, was quite social. He keenly felt the lack of people and the absence of recreation and leisure. Hume, also, may have had clearer foresight than he dared admit to himself of the criticism, opposition, and enmity which his system of philosophy was bound to bring.

So, with all the misgivings Hume harbors about the *Treatise* he turns to the question of validation: how can he establish his philosophy and why should he (and others) assent to it? "Can I be sure, that in leaving all established opinions I am following truth; and by what criterion shall I distinguish her, even if fortune shou'd at last guide me on her foot-steps?" (*Treatise*, p. 265) Hume's concludes that he has no reason which could be adequate to that need:

> After the most accurate and exact of my reasonings, I can give no reason why I shou'd assent to it; and feel nothing but a *strong* propensity to consider objects *strongly* in that view, under which they appear to me. Experience is a principle, which instructs me in the several conjunctions of objects for the past. Habit is another principle, which determines me to expect the same for the future; and both of them conspiring to operate upon the imagination, make me form certain ideas in a more intense and lively manner, than others, which are not attended with the same advantages. Without this quality, by which the mind enlivens some ideas beyond others (which seemingly is so trivial, and so little founded on reason) we cou'd never assent to any argument, nor carry our view beyond those few objects, which are present to our senses. (*Treatise*, p. 265)

The demands of logic have been contrasted to the inclinations of the mind already in this argument and need not be reviewed here, but it is clear that this belief of Hume's, this method of procedure, applies to his philosophy *in toto*. Although this study has been restricted to Hume's metaphysics, epistemology, and philosophy of religion, this method can be claimed for all matters throughout the first volume of the *Treatise*. Not only is it argued for cause and effect, personal identity, substance, and physical objects, the issues covered in this study, but it also can be argued equally well for other issues such as abstract ideas (*Treatise*, pp. 17-23) or the immateriality of the soul. (*Treatise*, p. 232f) It is Hume's reasoned conclusion that "the memory, senses, and understanding are therefore, all of them founded on the imagination, or the vivacity of our ideas." (*Treatise*, p. 265)

In the next paragraph Hume remarks that it is no wonder that a principle so inconstant and fallacious should lead us into errors when it is followed implicitly. And it must be followed in all its variations because it is this principle which makes us reason from causes and effects and convinces us of the continued existence of external objects when they are absent from our senses. The choice of "makes" does not appear to be accidental to Hume. He implies in many places that these nonrational forces are more than merely influential. "These two operations [are] equally natural and necessary in the human mind." (Treatise, p. 266) They are irresistible with a sort of physical or biological necessity:

> Nature, by an absolute and uncontroulable necessity has determin'd us to judge as well as to breathe and feel; nor can we any more forbear viewing certain objects in a stronger and fuller light, upon account of their customary connexion with a present impression, than we can hinder ourselves from thinking as long as we are awake, or seeing the surrounding bodies, when we turn our eyes towards them in broad sunshine. (*Treatise*, p. 183)

In some circumstances our rational and nonrational operations run directly counter to each other. In fact, because the second one runs "counter" to our rational ones, we could call it *irrational*. This theme appears in many different places in the *Treatise*; for example, he says: "Thus there is a direct and total opposition betwixt our reason and our senses; or more properly speaking, betwixt those conclusions we form from cause and effect, and those that persuade us of the continu'd and independent existence of body." (*Treatise*, p. 231)

Cause is one of the basic issues in the *Treatise* since causation alone "informs us of existences and objects, which we do not see or feel." (*Treatise*, p. 74) But, from the last section of Book I he says:

> How must we be disappointed, when we learn, that this connexion, tie, or energy lies merely in ourselves, and is nothing but that determination of the mind, which is acquir'd by custom, and causes us to make a transition from an object to its usual attendant, and from the impression of one to the lively idea of the other? (*Treatise*, p. 266)

Hume sees the problems with this approach since it prevents our ever (rationally) knowing what is the case. He recognizes that when we say we desire to know the ultimate principle of something, we are talking about something which resides in the external object, unless, of course, we contradict ourselves or use meaningless talk. In ordinary life we do not perceive this, nor are we aware that we are as ignorant of the usual, regular, and common causes and the principle which binds them together as we are of the causal bond in the most unusual and extraordinary cases. We simply don't know what the ultimate principle is which binds things together in the world, and with regard to that, we are faced with the question of how far we ought to yield to the illusions of our imagination.

So we are faced with a dangerous dilemma. We can choose to follow the "fancy" or the understanding. If we follow the fancy, we are in trouble:

> If we assent to every trivial suggestion of the fancy; besides that these suggestions are often contrary to each other; they lead us into such errors, absurdities, and obscurities, that we must at last become asham'd of our

credulity. Nothing is more dangerous to reason than the flights of the imagination, and nothing has been the occasion of more mistakes among philosophers. (*Treatise*, p. 267)

But if we follow the understanding we are in deeper trouble and must revert to the fancy as the lesser of evils:

> But on the other hand, if the consideration of these instances makes us take a resolution to reject all the trivial suggestions of the fancy, and adhere to the understanding, that is to the general and more establish'd properties of the imagination; even this resolution, if steadily executed, wou'd be dangerous, and attended with the most fatal consequences. For I have already shewn, that the understanding, when it acts alone, and according to its most general principles, entirely subverts itself, and leaves not the lowest degree of evidence in any proposition, either in philosophy or in common life. We save ourselves from this total scepticism only by means of that singular and seemingly trivial property of the fancy, by which we enter with difficulty into remote views of things, and are not able to accompany them with so sensible an impression, as we do those, which are more easy and natural. (*Treatise*, pp. 267-268)

Here then is Hume's forthright statement of the difficulty faced by his approach with a confession that that reverting to fancy is about all he can do. And then he goes back to questioning whether his rejection of ("refin'd or elaborate") reasoning is productive and wise in light of the consequences: (*Treatise*, p. 268)

1. By this means we cut off entirely all science and philosophy. (Apparently he means that the most careful thinking, rigorous deduction, and diligent reflection are needed in those areas. Any other approach leaves us out.)
2. We proceed upon one singular quality of the imagination. (Hume doesn't tell us what it is, but he generally pits the imagination against the reason, so it would seem that the use of "imagination" here would signify the use of natural inclinations, common sense, or whatever nonrational tendency he was thinking of, and on the basis of which Hume made the final acceptance of his doctrines.) But if we take some conclusions, on its basis we must take all of its conclusions. (Stated a different way, he is asking how if we use the principle we can limit its application.)
3. We contradict ourselves because the principle of not using reason is a decision of reason, built upon our preceding use of reason refined and metaphysical as it is.

Hume confesses that he is distressed over the choice of following a false reason (which subverts the human understanding) or none at all, and he doesn't know which to choose. Most of the time philosophers simply do not think of these difficulties, he thinks, or if they do they quickly forget them. "Refined" (technical?) reflections influence us very little and yet we cannot argue that they ought not to have any influence—which Hume believes implies a "manifest contradiction," but reason is self defeating.

So Hume finds himself in a difficult, even upsetting, position. What are the answers to our pressing intellectual problems? Where do we get answers to the issues we face? How do we tell what answers we should adopt? How can we view one opinion or answer as more probable than another? It is all very depressing, Hume asserts, and only "nature herself" rescues us from this impasse:

> Most fortunately it happens, that since reason is incapable of dispelling these clouds, nature herself suffices to that purpose, and cures me of this philosophical melancholy and delirium, either by relaxing this bent of mind, or by some avocation, and lively impression of my senses, which obliterate all these chimeras. I dine, I play a game of back-gammon, I converse, and am merry with my friends; and when after three or four hour's amusement, I wou'd return to these speculations, they appear so cold, and strain'd, and ridiculous, that I cannot find in my heart to enter into them any farther. (*Treatise*, p. 269)

This may be merely a playful confession, but consistent with Hume's other fideistic comments it appears that he means to be taken seriously. His skeptical approach has provided for him a dead end, and no escape can be found for it outside of some nonrational influence such as human nature. Even escaping from philosophical analysis into the entertainments and diversions of our common world is a sort of recreational equivalent to the escape from intellectual rigor and skepticism he repeatedly gives us through habit, custom, association, inclination, propensity, or human nature. These are the opposite of reason. They restore what reason had destroyed. They enliven what reason had deadened. They contribute belief for what reason had denied.

This, then, is the sort of intellectual tension Hume reveals. He is "absolutely and necessarily determin'd to live, and talk, and act like other people in the common affairs of life." (*Treatise*, p. 269) Once more Hume reminds us of the necessitarian dimension of human nature. He is *not* free to avoid the nonrational, the nonphilosophical, the popular or "vulgar." His natural propensity impels him into that position. Along with this, however, Hume still clings to his belief that we should not give up our philosophical skepticism. This together with the forces of human nature causes him to have "that splenetic humour" which he now expresses. The whole enterprise is very distressing since the analysis philosophy provides shuts us off from the natural beliefs and natural attitudes which we so desire. Hume feels that he is ready to throw all his books and papers into the fire! The entire thing is out of Hume's hands and involves forces he cannot control: "I may, nay I must yield to the current of nature, in submitting to my senses and understanding; and in this blind submission I shew most perfectly my sceptical disposition and principles." (*Treatise*, p. 269)

Method and Pyrrhonism in Hume's Philosophy 155

The fideistic nature of Hume's approach is often captured in his sharp, little contrasts. In a paragraph or two he will spell out the frustration and the solution in bold terms. We have some of those little snippets on pp. 266-269 (I, IV, VII) of the *Treatise* where he gives his more systematic attention to the problem of skepticism. He claims that we can never get any intellectual or philosophic satisfaction out of an examination of the world itself, or of something particular from the world. That cannot satisfy our need for answers.

Let us contrast the two poles of Hume's philosophy by putting his labored responses on this tension side by side. In the space of three pages Hume again and again demolishes and repairs, denies and recovers, rejects and replaces, excludes and reinstates, explains why skepticism comes and responds as to why it won't work, expresses frustration and relief in several parallel statements.

When we say we desire to know the ultimate and operating principle, as something, which resides in the external object, we either contradict ourselves, or talk without a meaning. (*Treatise*, p. 267)	And how must we be disappointed, when we learn, that this connexion, tie, or energy lies merely in ourselves, and is nothing but that determination of the mind, which is acquir'd by custom, and causes us to make a transition from an object to its usual attendant, and from the impression of one to the lively idea of the other? (*Treatise*, p. 266)
I have already shewn, that the understanding, when it acts alone, and according to its most general principles, entirely subverts itself, and leaves not the lowest degree of evidence in any proposition, either in philosophy or common life. (*Treatise*, pp. 267-268)	We save ourselves from this total scepticism only by means of that singular and seemingly trivial property of the fancy, by which we enter with difficulty into remote views of things, and are not able to accompany them with so sensible an impression, as we do those, which are more easy and natural. (*Treatise*, pp. 268)
Since reason is incapable of dispelling these clouds .... (*Treatise*, p. 269)	Most fortunately it happens, that ... nature herself suffices to that purpose, and cures me of this philosophical melancholy and delirium, either by relaxing this bent of mind, or by some avocation, and lively impression of my senses, which obliterate these chimeras. (*Treatise*, p. 269)
I still feel such remains of my former disposition, that I am ready to throw all my books and papers into the fire, and resolve never more to renounce the plea-	My natural propensity, and the course of my animal spirits and passions reduce me to this indolent belief in the general maxims of the world. (*Treatise*, p. 269)

sures of life for the sake of reasoning
and philosophy. (*Treatise*, p. 269)

Hume goes on through the next few pages alternating between his skeptical proclivities and the unavoidable, necessary action of opposing them in thought and life. He has both intellectual and emotional problems with this solution. Intellectually, that is, philosophically, he can believe nothing with assurance: "If I must be a fool, as all those who reason or believe any thing *certainly* are, my follies shall at least be natural and agreeable." (*Treatise*, p. 270) On the other side, he again expresses his conviction that the replacement or irrational side is the only one which can provide us with any solution: "These are the sentiments of my spleen and indolence; and indeed I must confess, that philosophy has nothing to oppose to them, and expects a victory more from the returns of a good-humor'd disposition, than from the force of reason and conviction." (*Treatise*, p. 270) Another word for non-rational inclinations is inserted here, "disposition," and it is a variation on the continual theme around which Hume has "orchestrated" his *Treatise*. When reason and rational procedures fail we can fall back on some irrational or nonrational tendency which can salvage what we lost because of reason. This does not mean that Hume is willing to abandon his sterile method. He advises us to continue to do what has been unproductive so far.

> In all the incidents of life we ought still to preserve our scepticism. If we believe, that fire warms, or water refreshes, 'tis only because it costs us too much pains to think otherwise. Nay if we are philosophers, it ought only to be upon sceptical principles, and from an inclination, which we feel to the employing ourselves after that manner. (*Treatise*, p. 270)

Thus we find the continual seesaw in Hume's philosophy. Although this study has focused predominently on the *Treatise* (in order to argue that these principles in Hume's philosophy are present from his earliest publications), the same views are found in the first *Enquiry*. His *Dialogues* demonstrates that this fideistic approach was still his refuge to the very end of his life. Since Hume did not discuss personal identity nor the existence of external objects in the *Enquiry* we do not have any parallels there to those discussed in the *Treatise*. There is, however, a discussion on cause and effect which follows the same pattern of reasoning seen in the *Treatise*. *Enquiry* §§ 35-38 (pp. 42-47) give us the same conclusions.

Hume's treatment in the *Enquiry* runs parallel to his treatment in the *Treatise*, although it is much shorter and more tightly written. The sum and substance of it, however, hasn't changed from the *Treatise*, and it would be a waste of time to go over it again. His summary conclusions, however have not changed from *Treatise* to *Enquiry*: (*Enquiry*, pp. 44-45, 46-47)

Custom, then, is the great guide of human life. It is that principle alone which renders our experience useful to us, and makes us expect, for the future, a similar train of events with those which have appeared in the past. Without the influence of custom, we should be entirely ignorant of every matter of fact beyond what is immediately present to the memory and senses. We should never know how to adjust means to ends, or to employ our natural powers in the production of any effect. There would be an end at once of all action, as well as of the chief part of speculation ....

What, then, is the conclusion of the whole matter? A simple one, though, it must be confessed, pretty remote from the common theories of philosophy. All belief of matter of fact or real existence is derived merely from some object, present to the memory or senses, and a customary conjunction between that and some other object. Or in other words; having found, in many instances, that any two kinds of objects—flame and heat, snow and cold—have always been conjoined together; if flame or snow be presented anew to the senses, the mind is carried by custom to expect heat or cold, and to *believe* that such a quality does exist, and will discover itself upon a nearer approach. This belief is the necessary result of placing the mind in such circumstances. It is an operation of the soul, when we are so situated, as unavoidable as to feel the passion of love, when we receive benefits; or hatred, when we meet with injuries. All these operations are a species of natural instincts, which no reasoning or process of the thought and understanding is able either to produce or to prevent.

In addition to this Hume has an important section in the *Enquiry* (Section XII) where he discusses scepticism of all varieties which we shall refer to in the discussion on Hume's Pyrrhonism to which we now turn.

THE SKEPTICAL TRADITION PRIOR TO HUME

David Hume has been regarded as one of the greatest skeptics in philosophy, but very little attention has been given to this skepticism, to Hume's treatment of it, or to his attempts to escape it. The skeptics who receive Hume's attention and whom Hume tries to answer were the Pyrrhonists. He could not bring himself to accept Pyrrhonist conclusions, but he followed Bayle's style of Pyrrhonist analysis. Hume refers to them as "that fantastical sect," but in spite of such comments Hume maintained a reasonably consistent Pyrrhonian point of view.

The best writing on Hume's Pyrrhonism has been done by Richard Popkin in a series of articles on Pyrrhonic skepticism since the renaissance.[17] Popkin shows that Hume's skepticism did not appear suddenly without historical precedent and precursors. Rather it is a part of a long tradition beginning with Sextus Empiricus' *Outlines of Pyrrhonism*, updated for modern times by many figures.[18]

Descartes attempted to resolve the skeptical crisis of the renaissance and reformation in Europe brought about the *"nouveaux Pyrrhoniens."* These new skeptics who constituted the avant-garde of the French intellectual world had revitalized the Pyrrhonic skepticism of ancient Greece to attack renaissance Platonism, scholasticism, Calvinism, astrology, alchemy, and almost anything which attracted their attention. Descartes' method outdoubted his skeptical opponents even to the point of challenging them with his evil-demon hypothesis, and then claimed that on the basis of doubt he had found certainty.

Cartesianism was attacked by empirically-minded people like Pierre Gassendi, Samuel Sorbiere, Gassendi's disciple, Bishop Pierre-Daniel Huet, and Simon Foucher. Huet and Foucher used all the epistemological weapons of classical skepticism. The story with its necessary details is too long to tell here and the reader must be referrred to Popkin's account and list of sources.[19]

The most important person in this broad attack was Pierre Bayle, who was not concerned solely with Descartes but mounted a broad attack on the entire rational endeavor. Whatever the answer or theory, whether of knowledge, science, metaphysics, or theology, all came under his scrutiny and skeptical onslaught. Bayle's predecessors had been concerned mainly with epistemology. With Bayle every intellectual concern was fair game for his dialectical analysis, and his effort was directed towards any and all attempts to understand our world and ourselves.

Bayle's importance as a figure in this history of skepticism and as an influence on Hume was contributed to by his background. The Pyrrhonists were French almost to a man, and those who were not French were influenced directly by French thinkers. Bayle was French, but he does not fit exactly into the skepticism of Montaigne and the tradition stemming from him. Montaigne and almost all those who followed him were Roman Catholics. Bayle was not Catholic, but coming as he did from a staunch Calvinist protestant family, and having been affected by the controversies between the hounded Huguenots and the triumphant Catholics, he regarded himself as a Protestant "in the full sense of the word, one who is against everything that is said and everything that is done."[20]

Further, Bayle was not reared in the skeptical court circles and he did not come from the Cartesian and anti-Cartesian controversy. He studied in a Jesuit college in Toulouse, became a Catholic because he was convinced that the Protestant arguments provided no basis for their position. Having argued himself into Catholicism, he argued his way out of that and back into Protestantism. He studied in Geneva, taught philosophy in Sedan and at Rotterdam, and spent the last period of his life there devoting himself to scholarship and controversy. This culminated in his *Historical and Critical Dictionary* of 1697 which he revised and expanded into the edition of 1702 before his death in 1706. Few have read this seven or eight million word work, and fewer have read it through. Popkin tells us he has read the entire work and claims that intellectually it is all of a piece and aims at a central message.

Bayle is one of the chief influences on Hume. When Hume went to France in 1734 to write his *Treatise of Human Nature*, he carried with him the folio volumes of Bayle's *Dictionary* and *Oeuvres diverse*.[21] When it comes to the texture of Hume's *Treatise* and the individual articles, Popkin writes:

> Hume, like many of his contemporaries, was immersed in various skeptical themes raised by Bayle. Also, for Hume, as for many others of the time, the *Dictionary* was a major reference source. Hume's *Treatise* reveals all sorts of gleanings from Bayle's interminable erudition and argumentation, especially in Parts II and IV of Book I, where Hume leans heavily on the articles *Zeno of Elea*, *Pyrrho*, *Rorarius*, and *Spinoza*.
>
> The strange Part II on mathematics is mostly a commentary and attempted answer to Bayle's discussion of the Zeno paradoxes, and of the nature of space and time.[22]

Popkin goes on to describe the care with which Bayle handled these themes so as to make sure there are no loopholes his opponents could slip through. He brilliantly states Zeno's paradoxes and uses this to show that everything, every theory of the nature of extension, matter, time, space, and motion is "big with contradiction and absurdity." Popkin calls him a "philosopher's philosopher." He is prolix, precise and careful beyond measure, explores problems minutely and brilliantly, etc. He peels off the "layers" of theories as if they were an onion until there is nothing left. Hume does not compare very well with Bayle's thoroughness and care, according to Popkin:

> In contrast to the precision and detail in Bayle, Hume's text in Part II and in Part IV on Spinoza is exceedingly sloppy. Hume takes various phrases out of Bayle, mixes them together, confuses various layers of the problem, and rushes exuberantly [sic] to a conclusion. Bayle used all the source material while Hume used only Bayle. Hume was indifferent about whether Spinoza, Zeno, or X or Y said or meant what he attributed to them. Hume's discussion of Spinoza is a scandalous treatment, if intended as a serious comment on what Spinoza actually said, whereas Bayle's is a really serious analysis of certain aspects of Spinozistic metaphysics.[23]

Bayle tackles problems in the style of the "subtle" Arriaga, one of the last of the great Spanish scholastics who died in 1667. In this approach, every possibility, every theory is of interest. Every theory is inspected, questioned, and dissected until in the process it disintegrates into contradictions and paradoxes. Leibniz tells us in his *Theodicy* what it was like to have an argument with his friend Bayle. If he asserted anything, Bayle would proceed to analyze the assertion and to question it until he was ready to give up and assert the opposite. Bayle would then proceed to analyze the second assertion and so on.[24] Nothing was exempt from this approach; everything and everyone was fair game.

Descartes, Spinoza, Malebranche, Aristotle, Epicurus, Gassendi—all came under Bayle's dialectical knife. When Isaac Newton turned up, Bayle attacked him. When John Locke, Bayle's friend, published his works, Bayle started in on them, and so on interminably.

Bayle, says Popkin, is not solely or merely concerned to challenge a theory, but to use the occasion to generalize the attack to all theories and to show the hopeless abysses to which all human intellectual endeavors lead. This is what Popkin calls the "high road to Pyrrhonism."

> This high road to Pyrrhonism is the utter and total *reductio ad absurdum* (quite literally) of all our intellectual pretensions. Thus, the *Dictionary* is really two guides—one for becoming completely perplexed, by trying to make sense of any aspect of our universe, and the other for overcoming complete perplexity, by turning to faith and Revelation.[25]

Bayle takes the role of a new Maimonides and keeps urging faith and revelation as the only way of solving any problems. The rational man can start off with the best of intentions to comprehend an aspect of man's philosophical, scientific, moral, or theological cosmos. As long as he remains within the bounds of rationality and employs the tools of reason with its basic maxims, etc., he can only construct theories that are pregnant with contradiction and absurdity. When he gives up in complete perplexity and turns to faith and revelation, he finds out the explanation for this sad state of affairs. It is that God has created and governs a totally and radically different world from that which the rational man starts with and reasons in. For Bayle, skepticism about any matter is always a preparation for the faith. This was his defense to his church colleagues in Rotterdam who were unsure about his *Dictionary* after reading some of the articles.

Bayle viewed three men as heroes, the "subtle" Arriaga, Moses Maimonides, and Pierre Bunel.[26] These men and Bayle did not stand with other seventeenth-century skeptics such as Gassendi, Sorbiere, Foucher, and Huet. This latter group of men may have supplied the rationale for a science without metaphysics which was to answer all of man's problems by destroying Descartes' enterprise of a science based on metaphysical knowledge. Bayle's program was not a substitute intellectual one, bent on the destruction of Descartes' system. It was, instead, an attack on *any* and *all* uses of reason, for he had no illusions himself about what man's reason could accomplish.

Students of modern philosophy have continued to find it strange that David Hume, a figure of the age of reason, should aim his arrows at reason, at intellectualism. Enlightenment figures were reasonably close to agreeing that the twin foci of authority, the monarchy and the church, were the chief obstacles to good, but reason itself, presumably mechanical science, held the promise of all good. Hume, however, does not fit into this pattern. For him reason can produce only absurdities and contradictions. If we look at Hume's relationship to the approach of Bayle (and Leibniz) this can be better understood. Bayle, in particular, is the forgotten and little-understood influence on David Hume.

Hume had several links to Bayle: Mandeville and Shaftesbury were both personally influenced by Bayle, and both were major precursors of Hume. The first had studied under Bayle at Rotterdam and the latter had lived under the same roof with Bayle arguing with him about all sorts of topics day by day. Pierre Desmaizeaux, Bayle's official biographer, knew Hume in London where they lived together in the same house when Hume came back from France. According to the stories given to us, Hume gave Desmaizeaux a copy of the *Treatise* and solicited his comments as to whether it appeared sufficiently intelligible to him and true. Desmaizeaux wrote one of the first reviews of it. Many of the philosophical entries entered in Hume's early memoranda are items dealing with Bayle.

HUME'S OWN PYRRHONISM

The historical forces operative upon David Hume are very important, and Popkin has shown that the English response to the French enlightenment skepticism was one of calmness and contented living:

> While the French world was struggling throughout the seventeenth century with the skeptical crisis engendered by the Reformation and the Renaissance, the English world was taking the matter rather calmly. They were in fact accepting a kind of semi-skepticism and stating it as if it were an answer to skepticism. They were conceding without a fight the basic epistemological issues, and insisting on the merits of what were found to be basic beliefs of mankind, regardless of their lack of philosophical support. The depths of the skeptical challenge were ignored, and the Anglican divines and their scientific friends placidly and contentedly lived through the century hoping to hang onto man's commonsense beliefs and the core of his religious ones in the face of the colossal upheavals going on around them. Their reasonable religion, which they thought was being buttressed and confirmed by modern science, the voyages of discovery, ancient learning, etc., seems to have provided a sufficient shield.[27]

Popkin thinks that Hume's writings were, and were intended to be, a decimation of this kind of optimism and then cites Hume's essay on miracles, "Hume's earliest philosophical writing,"[28] as a kind of *reductio ad absurdum* of Stillingfleet's principles of empirical and common sense standards as a basis for reasonable religion. Hume stressed that it would take a miracle for the reasonable man to believe in the Judeo-Christian religion, a miracle that would subvert all understanding and make one believe something contrary to all custom and experience.[29]

Popkin believes that the key to Hume's entire skeptical outlook is found in Hume's recurrent criticisms of "that fantastical sect," the Pyrrhonian skeptics. We have already summarized, albeit all too briefly, some of the historical antecedents and influences on Hume. Our summarization is as brief as it is since the reader can consult the writings of Popkin for himself.

> In every one of his discussions of the extreme skeptical view of the Pyrrhonians, Hume contended that such a position could not be refuted by reason, and yet, at the same time, could not be believed. The Pyrrhonian point of view is the logical outcome of philosophical analysis, and yet, there is something in the nature of human beings that prevents one from accepting it. "Philosophy would render us entirely Pyrrhonian, were not nature too strong for it."[30]

"Pyrrhonism," typified in Bayle and illustrated in Hume in the examples taken of Hume's skeptical conclusions, was the intellectual dead end calculated to drive a person to seek some solution to the problem outside of an intellectual, rational one. Bayle forthrightly presented faith for the disoriented. According to Bayle, God setup and runs a different universe from that presented in the misleading theories proposed by self-sufficient philosophers. Bayle had no hesitation whatever about recommending faith for the intellectually distressed, no matter what the topic and issue. Following the Pyrrhonist pattern, Hume arrived at his skeptical conclusions by way of the negative, rational analysis, and then recovered his beliefs by means of a nonrational, fideistic-type of procedure. Bayle considered it an art, but Hume considers it not an art, but as a sort of relief, a substitute procedure for solving all sorts of intellectual and practical problems. No problem, he maintains, can be given a rational basis for determining what the solution may be. In Pyrrhonism, if two possible judgments conflict, there is no rational way for preferring one or the other of them. In no area of theoretical or practical concern can anyone attain certain and indisputable knowledge. Therefore, dogmatic acceptance of any proposition or set of propositions is without adequate rational foundation. Such skeptics "hold that all is uncertain, and that our judgment is not in *any* thing possest of *any* measures of truth and falshood." (*Treatise*, p. 183) Since we cannot discover adequate grounds for any opinion, Pyrrhonian skeptics propose that we should suspend judgment with regard to all questions. We must cultivate an attitude of mind in which we will have no opinion or principle concerning any subject, either of action or of speculation.

Hume himself declares in the *Treatise*, I, IV, I, "Of scepticism with regard to reason," that "all knowledge resolves itself into probability." (*Treatise*, p. 181) Then this probability is successively and systematically diminished:

> Having thus found in every probability, beside the original uncertainty inherent in the subject, a new uncertainty deriv'd from the

weakness of that faculty, which judges, and having adjusted these two together, we are oblig'd by our reason to add a new doubt deriv'd from the possibility of error in the estimation we make of the truth and fidelity of our faculties. This is a doubt, which immediately occurs to us, and of which, if we wou'd closely pursue our reason, we cannot avoid giving a decision. But this decision, tho' it shou'd be favourable to our preceeding judgment, being founded only probability, must weaken still further our first evidence, and must itself be weaken'd by a fourth doubt of the same kind, and so on *in infinitum*; and even the vastest quantity, which can enter into human imagination, must in this manner be reduc'd to nothing. Let our first belief be never so strong, it must infallibly perish by passing thro' so many new examinations, of which each diminishes somewhat of its force and vigour. (*Treatise*, pp. 182-183)

In the next paragraph Hume saves himself from absurdity by falling back on human nature, *his equivalent of Bayle's faith*:

Shou'd it here be ask'd me, whether I sincerely assent to this argument, which I seem to take such pains to inculcate, and whether I be really one of those sceptics, who hold that all is uncertain, and that our judgment is not in *any* thing possest of *any* measures of truth and falshood; I shou'd reply, that this question is entirely superfluous, and that neither I, nor any other person was ever sincerely and constantly of that opinion. Nature, by an absolute and uncontroulable necessity has determin'd us to judge as well as to breathe and feel; nor can we any more forbear viewing certain objects in a stronger and fuller light, upon account of their customary connexion with a present impression, than we can hinder ourselves from thinking as long as we are awake, or seeing the surrounding bodies, when we turn our eyes towards them in broad sunshine. Whoever has taken the pains to refute the cavils of this *total* scepticism, has really disputed without an antagonist, and endeavor'd by arguments to establish a faculty, which nature has antecedently implanted in the mind, and render'd unavoidable. (*Treatise*, p. 183)

Popkin notes two ways in which Hume's conception of Pyrrhonian skepticism differs from its standard formulation in Sextus Empiricus:

First of all, Hume's version is more dogmatic than that of Sextus. The latter attempted to list a series of arguments, pro and con, on many questions, and then suspended judgment on them, instead of dogmatically holding that all questions are unanswerable. Secondly, Hume's rendering of Pyrrhonism omits any reference to the basis that Pyrrhonian offers for deciding practical questions once the suspensive attitude has been adopted. Sextus maintained that the skeptic could accept appearances undogmatically, and live naturally. The former means that one can assent to, or recognize, or have opinions about what appears to be the case, without giving up one's suspensive attitude as to what really is the case. The latter doctrine states that one can live "naturally," without having to make any judgments, by obeying one's natural compulsions unconsciously, or by habit, and by accepting, without judging their worth, the customs and regulations of one's social and cultural environment.[31]

Philosophical analysis was the source of some of these Pyrrhonic tendencies. When we examine our grounds for judgments concerning matters of fact, matters of value, or even mathematical values, Hume claimed, we can see that the basis for these values is neither rational nor certain. No judgment can be considered more firmly based than another. The corrosive effect of Hume's rational analysis has been stressed throughout this examination of his work. This effect, of course, distressed Hume and caused him to admit that "The *intense* view of the manifold contradictions and imperfections in human reason has so wrought upon me, and heated my brain, that I am ready to reject all belief and reasoning, and can look upon no opinion even as more probable or likely than another." (*Treatise*, pp. 268-269) And this malady is not one which can be cured. (*Treatise*, p. 218)

In the *Enquiry* Hume distinguishes between two different kinds of skeptical arguments that the Pyrrhonians present. The first is a popular type consisting of arguments about and illustrations of the fallaciousness or contradictoriness of sense information, the natural weakness of the human understanding, the long and tedious disagreement of people on every conceivable subject, and the influence on our conclusions of internal and external circumstances. Hume did not put much stock in these arguments because the difficulties with sense prove only that the senses alone cannot be depended upon and must be corrected by other sources of information such as the memory or reason. Second, Hume believed these popular arguments were directed against the sort of judgments made in everyday life which Hume was not about to give up: "For as, in common life, we reason every moment concerning fact and existence, and cannot possibly subsist, without continually employing this species of argument, any popular objections, derived from thence, must be insufficient to destroy that evidence." (*Enquiry*, p. 158)

The philosophical types of argument show that, at bottom, there is no rational or certain basis either for our factual and moral judgments or for the rational and mathematical judgments we make. These arguments hold the basic strength of Pyrrhonism, the claim that our rational and factual judgments sometimes conflict, and that there is no basis whatever for choosing the one judgment in place of the other. That is a radical conclusion, but Hume believes the reasoning leading to it is irrefutable and epistemologically completely devastating to any attempt to discover certain knowledge. Hume states that "these arguments might be displayed at greater length, if any durable good or benefit to society could ever be expected to result from them." (*Enquiry*, p. 159) Popkin's summarizes: "The basis for all factual and probable reasoning is ... irrational, determined by certain natural instinctive forces resulting in certain emotional effects."[32] And Popkin draws our attention to a statement of Hume found not in this final section of the *Treatise*, but in an earlier section of that book:

> Thus all probable reasoning is nothing but a species of sensation. 'Tis not solely in poetry and music, we must follow our taste and sentiment, but likewise in philosophy. When I am convinc'd of any principle, 'tis only an idea, which strikes more strongly upon me. When I give the preference to one set of arguments above another, I do nothing but decide from my feeling concerning the superiority of their influence. Objects have no discoverable connexion together; nor is it from any other principle but custom operating upon the imagination, that we can draw any inference from the appearance of one to the existence of another. (*Treatise*, p. 103)

Hume waivers somewhat on the issue of demonstrative knowledge, of relations of ideas. In I, III of the *Treatise*, Hume contends that though geometry excels the loose judgments of the senses and the imagination, it never attains a perfect precision because its first principles are still drawn from appearance, and appearances can never afford us complete assurance. It is different, however, with arithmetic and algebra. In these two sciences, we can carry on a chain of intricate reasoning while still preserving exactness and certainty, so perfect demonstrative knowledge concerning quantity and number are possible. (*Treatise*, pp. 70-72) This is at variance with Pyrrhonism found in both the second book of Sextus Empiricus' *Outlines of Pyrrhonism* and in Montaigne's *Apology for Raimond Sebond*. These books contend that no genuine proof can ever be given for anything no matter what its nature.

In the *Treatise*, I, IV, however, Hume argues that the supposed demonstrative knowledge can at best be but probable or as the heading of Section I has it, we must adopt a "Scepticism with regard to reason." (*Treatise*, p. 180) He maintains that we know from experience that our ability to carry out a chain of reasoning is not perfect. A survey of our past mistakes leads us to see that all knowledge "degenerates" into probability which is, of course, less than certainty or 1. Furthermore, we may not have properly evaluated our ability to judge our conclusions about the accuracy of our reasonings, etc. Each introduction of new probabilities can go on indefinitely, thus reducing to almost nil the possibility of ever recognizing a correct piece of reasoning: "When I proceed still farther, to turn the scrutiny against every successive estimation I make of my faculties, all the rules of logic require a continual diminution, and at last a total extinction of belief and evidence." (*Treatise*, p. 183)

The next section contains an analysis of Hume's doctrine "Of scepticism with regard to the senses." (*Treatise*, p. 187f) Hume's views in that section of the *Treatise* add to the general Pyrrhonian skepticism: we cannot question whether there is body or not. We must take that point for granted in all our reasonings.

(*Treatise*, p. 187) This is a universal tendency, Hume admits, "but this universal and primary opinion of all men is soon destroyed by the slightest philosophy, which teaches us, that nothing can ever be present to the mind but an image or perception." (*Enquiry*, p. 152)

Hume employs another major argument based on the then-current distinction between primary and secondary qualities with the first being objective, "out there," in nature, and the second being subjective, "in here," in the mind. Hume used Berkeley's arguments to show that there is no justification for distinguishing the one kind of quality from the other. In addition, our knowledge of primary qualities is actually knowledge of certain arrangements of secondary qualities.

> If colours, sounds, tastes, and smells be merely perceptions, nothing we can conceive is possest of a real, continu'd, and independent existence; not even motion, extension and solidity, which are the primary qualities chiefly insisted on ... 'tis impossible to conceive extension, but as compos'd of parts, endow'd with colour or solidity .... These simple and indivisible parts, not being ideas of extension, must be non-entities, unless conceiv'd as colour'd or solid .... We may make the same observation concerning mobility and figure; and upon the whole must conclude, that after the exclusion of colours, sounds, heat and cold from the rank of external existences, there remains nothing, which can afford us a just and consistent idea of body. (*Treatise*, pp. 228-229)

Once again natural belief in an external world turns out to be contrary to rational principles, and the latter appears to be indefensible. So, Hume's Pyrrhonic principles of criticism and analysis have driven him to the only conclusion He could come to from such conflicting views: "Thus there is a direct and total opposition betwixt our reason and our senses; or more properly speaking, betwixt those conclusions we form from cause and effect, and those that persuade us of the continu'd and independent existence of body." (*Treatise*, p. 231)

HUME'S CRITIQUE OF PYRRHONISM

Hume did not believe that the extreme skepticism of the Pyrrhonians can be refuted. It is the logical result of an epistemological analysis of the bases of our beliefs in factual, demonstrative, and metaphysical matters. Just as Hume expressed personal distress about his skepticism, so he felt distressed over the implications of his Pyrrhonism for all intellectual endeavors. Hume held those areas of investigation and thought in high esteem and was not reserved in his expressions of distress. He had been deeply influenced by the Pyrrhonians, and now, whatever his reaction, the effects of that influence was still with him.

Distressed as Hume was over the skeptical implications of all this reasoning, and over the struggles it gave him, he nowhere asked if his epistemological analysis was wrong, misdirected, or perverse. Let us not forget that Hume followed its analytical techniques. Pyrrhonism, he claimed on the one hand, cannot be refuted, but on the other, neither can it be believed. Hume felt that Berkeley's writings illustrate this and indeed provide some of the best lessons of skepticism. They upset our intellectual equilibrium, but they don't convince us:

> Most of the writings of that very ingenious author [Berkeley] form the best lessons of scepticism, which are to be found either among the ancient or modern philosophers, Bayle not excepted. He professes, however, in his title-page (and undoubtedly with great truth) to have composed his book against the sceptics as well as against the atheists and free-thinkers. But that all his arguments, though otherwise intended, are, in reality, merely sceptical, appears from this, *that they admit of no answer and produce no conviction*. Their only effect is to cause that momentary amazement and irresolution and confusion, which is the result of scepticism. (*Enquiry*, p. 155, note)

What is the solution to the dilemma? It is that "nature breaks the force of all skeptical arguments in time, and keeps them from having any considerable influence on the understanding." (*Treatise*, p. 187) Hume believes that we do not dare take the approach some have taken with the skeptic of rejecting at once all their arguments without enquiry or examination. (*Treatise*, p. 186) The skeptic is to be taken seriously, that is, his arguments and analysis are to be taken seriously, but nevertheless that is not the end of the matter. The skeptic continues to reason and believe even though he asserts that he cannot defend his reasons by reason. (*Treatise*, p. 187) The skeptical view that we cannot, ought not, and do not hold any opinions is false because nature forces us to hold these opinions. It is not a question of what we should do, but rather it is a question what we have to do.[33] There is an ambiguity of "nature" here. One use of the word is to refere to the world around us. The other is our own nature, i.e. our tendencies, bent, dispositions to think a certain way. Hume seems to mean the second, but he does not make it clear for us.

We are required to judge about factual, moral, and rational matters regardless of the lack of rational support we have available. Though the moral matters are omitted in this discussion, we have seen Hume argue at length that our belief in matters of fact is not due to rational evidence but is the result of custom or habit. These nonrational influences produce in us a strong feeling regarding certain ideas usually conjoined with an impression now present to the senses or memory. Our mental constitution so works that an association of ideas according to the principles Hume listed suffices to give us nonrationally what we are shut out of rationally.

The skeptical arguments indicating that we can never acquire certain demonstrative knowledge likewise conflict with what nature compels us to believe. Hume felt his claim was right that we are never able to be sure that any demonstrative reasoning is correct. It is in fact unanswerable, he believes, but it does not prevent people from being sure on this topic. Our assurance is not rationally grounded, but is due to natural factors. Our minds are unable to carry doubts about their ability *ad infinitum* because it is distressing. When such an approach is tried, "The attention is on the stretch: The posture of the mind is uneasy; and the spirits being diverted from their natural course, are not govern'd in their movements by the same laws, at least not to the same degree, as when they flow in their usual channel." (*Treatise*, p. 185) We reason by nature, and by a very fortunate inclination of mind we are unaffected by doubts cast on our reasoning abilities.

Nature has other effects. It not only compels everybody, including the skeptic, to reason and to belief about factual and demonstrative matters even though there is no rational defense for doing so, but nature also *compels* us to believe in the existence of certain types of metaphysical objects, though there is no proof that they exist, and though a belief in their existence leads to paradoxes. Body, mind, and God, the three substances of Descartes, are such even though rational arguments cannot support their existence. For Hume, all of the three are believed in on nonrational grounds, due either to the irresistible force of human nature or the propensity we have, another name for the same thing. Rationally we simply cannot support belief in these three things, argue for their alleged qualities and relations, or settle any speculative questions about them. If we will but relax, however, and let nature take its course, everything will be alright, and we will be able to bring our beliefs into line with commonly accepted opinions.

Not only does nature require us to make judgments on all such matters, even though we cannot support them, but we are moved to philosophize. We may not be able to settle our questions, but it does not follow that we are free to quit thinking. There are pleasures and satisfactions to philosophizing which are often sufficient to entice the skeptic, and which even compel him to "do" philosophy:

> To whatever length anyone may push his speculative principles of skepticism, he must act, I own, and live, and converse like other men; and for this conduct he is not obliged to give any other reason than the absolute necessity he lies under of so doing. If he ever carries his speculations farther than this necessity constrains him, and philosophizes either on natural or moral subjects, he is allured by a certain pleasure and satisfaction which he finds in employing himself after that manner. (*Dialogues*, p. 134)

> At the time, therefore, that I am tir'd with amusement and company, and have indulg'd a *reverie* in my chamber, or in a solitary walk by a riverside, I feel my mind all collected within itself, and am naturally *inclin'd* to carry my view into all those subjects, about which I have met with so many

disputes in the course of my reading and conversation. I cannot forbear having a curiosity to be acquainted with the principles of moral good and evil, the nature and foundation of government, and the cause of those several passions and inclinations, which actuate and govern me. I am uneasy to think I approve of one object and disapprove of another; call one thing beautiful, and another deform'd; decide concerning truth and falshood, reason and folly, without knowing upon what principles I proceed. I am concern'd for the condition of the learned world, which lies under such a deplorable ignorance in all these particulars. I feel an ambition to arise in me of contributing to the instruction of mankind, and of acquiring a name by my inventions and discoveries. These sentiments spring up naturally in my present disposition; and shou'd I endeavour to banish them, by attaching myself to any other business or diversion, I *feel* I shou'd be a loser in point of pleasure; and this is the origin of my philosophy. (*Treatise*, pp. 270-271)

Such remarks from two publications as diverse as the Book I of the *Treatise* and the *Dialogues* and from the two extremes of his life appear to be adequate evidence of the uniformity of Hume's thought on this matter. This may be just the confession of Hume's reasons for philosophizing, but it indicates at least one way nature leads us into speculative activity.

It is a good thing in Hume's view that there is such a thing as human nature. He apparently believes that nature does amazing things to us and with us in order to protect us and to permit us to live in the world. The skeptics from Montaigne to Bayle and avowedly nonskeptical philosophers like Descartes had so stressed the weakness of our reasoning faculties and the manifold possibility of error that our safety and survival just cannot be trusted to reason. The beliefs we are compelled to accept are not dependent upon any arguments of philosophy. "Nature has not left this to his choice, and has doubtless esteem'd it an affair of too great importance to be trusted to our uncertain reasonings and speculations." (*Treatise*, p. 187) Such judgments and inferences nature has made instinctive.

This leads to the last and perhaps most important reason why Pyrrhonism is incredible: it is incompatible with the actions necessary to support human life.[34] The Pyrrhonians encouraged us to carry a "suspensive" attitude towards life, but this would destroy life if it were followed consistently.

> A Pyrrhonian cannot expect, that his philosophy will have any constant influence on the mind: or if it had, that its influence would be beneficial to society. On the contrary, he must acknowledge, if he will acknowledge anything, that all human life must perish, were his principles universally and steadily to prevail. All discourse, all action would immediately cease; and men remain in a total lethargy, till the necessities of nature, unsatisfied, put an end to their miserable existence. (*Enquiry*, p. 160)

In order to exist in the world we have to act and to hold to some opinions. Our actions are not based upon reason but on irrational instincts and natural mechanisms which allow us to survive. This is as true of the Pyrrhonian skeptic as it is of the rest of us: "To whatever length anyone may push his speculative principles of scepticism, he must act, I own, and live, and converse like other men; and for this conduct he is not obliged to give any other reason than the absolute necessity he lies under of so doing." (*Dialogues*, p. 134)

So, apart from any pleasure he may find in doing philosophy, he is not free to avoid living and acting. If the Pyrrhonian skeptic were sincere and consistent in his skepticism, there would be no reason for doing one thing rather than another. He might go out of the room through the window rather than the door and have doubts as to whether his body has weight ("gravity") and can be injured by a fall. (*Dialogues*, p. 132)[35] The skeptic, however, shows by his conduct that in practical matters he is like other people: "Your own conduct in every circumstance, refutes your principles, and shows the firmest reliance on all the received maxims of science, morals, prudence, and behavior." (*Dialogues*, p. 137) He may engage in the ivory-tower practice of suspending judgment on the validity of such maxims, but in practice he accepts them just the same. The skeptic may undermine the reasons for what we do, but since he can undermine theory only and not nature, he cannot prevent us from doing what we do. "Nature will always maintain her rights, and prevail in the end over any abstract reasoning whatsoever." (*Enquiry*, p. 41) The skeptic may question, but there is nature; he may dispute, but there is common practice; he may feel separate from life around him, but society quickly restores him to common life.

> These principles may flourish and triumph in the schools; where it is, indeed, difficult, if not impossible, to refute them. But as soon as they leave the shade, and by the presence of the real objects, which actuate our passions and sentiments, are put in opposition to the more powerful principles of our nature, they vanish like smoke, and leave the most determined sceptic in the same condition as other mortals. (*Enquiry*, p. 159)

> And though a Pyrrhonian may throw himself or others into a momentary amazement and confusion by his profound reasonings; the first and most trivial event in life will put to flight all his doubts and scruples, and leave him the same, in every point of action and speculation, with the philosophers of every other sect, or with those who never concerned themselves in any philosophical researches. When he awakes from his dream, he will be the first to join in the laugh against himself, and to confess, that all his objections are mere amusement, and can have no other tendency than to show the whimsical condition of mankind, who must act and reason and believe; though they are not able, by their most diligent enquiry, to satisfy themselves concerning the foundation of these operations, or to remove the objections, which may be raised against them. (*Enquiry*, p. 160)

In introductory logic books such comments might be dismissed as a fallacy or irrelevancy, of *argumentum ad hominem*, but here we have Hume doing what any sophomore logic student is warned not to do. It is necessary to notice here that Hume is not making a minute analysis of logical difficulties the Pyrrhonian theory may have. His criticism is mainly psychological and practical and seems to explain what we do even if it is the case, as Hume appears to believe, that Pyrrhonism is logically unassailable. What people believe or do not believe is no comment on the truth or falsity of Pyrrhonic claims. His analysis, he believes, has disposed of that possibility, so if we are going to be able to believe in anything it has to be on another basis than that.

> The reasons why people believe or do not believe a given doctrine are not necessarily comments on its truth or falsity. If people do not believe Pyrrhonism, as Hume portrayed it, because of certain natural attitudes that they have, this is no philosophical reflection on Pyrrhonism. However, pointing out the incredibility of a doctrine, and the unfortunate consequences of believing it, has often sufficed, historically for leading people to give up a doctrine. E.g., consider Hume's criticism of popular religion, or Voltaire's of optimism. Neither of these proves the doctrines at issue to be incorrect logically, but are sufficient to raise great doubts as to their merits.[36]

Hume tries to show how we must live in such a Pyrrhonic universe. He does not offer any of our naturally-acquired beliefs as truths or knowledge with which to refute the Pyrrhonist. These "truths" and beliefs are irrational though necessary to our existence. We judge because we have to, and we act because we have to, but neither our judgments nor our actions show that we have any rational basis for what we do.

Popkin argues that Hume's criticisms of Pyrrhonism has philosophical significance as the only "consistent" version of the old skeptical theory, more consistent even than the formulation in Sextus Empiricus. Other Pyrrhonians have been either too skeptical or too dogmatic to hold the position consistently. Popkin believes Hume found the proper mixture of dogmatism and skepticism, of belief and suspense, for Pyrrhonism.[37]

It has been disputed whether Hume is a naturalist or a Pyrrhonist, and as an example, Popkin refers us to the dispute between John Laird and Norman Kemp Smith. Hume is both, Popkin declares, depending on how we look at him. These two things are really one and the same: "Hume, the naturalist who subverts all reason to emotion was just Hume the Pyrrhonist in his dogmatic mood. Hume the reasoner was Hume the Pyrrhonist in his skeptical mood."[38]

Popkin's account of Hume's Pyrrhonism is inclined to notice those passages and to quote those places where Hume uses "human nature" as the irrational basis for preserving his beliefs. The treatment of Hume's doctrines in this book has been more inclined to stress such things as custom, habit, association of ideas, a felt inclination of the mind, propensity, and the like, because those are the terms which Hume tends to use in specific places in response to specific problems. Noticing this difference is not mean to contrast the claims of Popkin to those made in this chapter. They are two different ways of expressing the thesis that Hume's rational approach results in skepticism, distress, and absurdity. Hume's desired, positive conclusions are recovered by means of nonrational means, by personal, psychic, deep-rooted "mechanisms" (a good word for Hume's era) which are fideistic in nature. These things work in the same way to overcome skepticism as faith does in matters of religion.

Popkin's historical analysis argues strongly for the one in this book. Popkin generalizes all the various nonrational means Hume resorts to in order to make sense of things by calling them "human nature," and indeed, Hume's own usage is consistent with this by naming his largest work, *A Treatise of Human Nature*. Popkin approaches Hume from a different direction than I have and with different vocabulary but the results are those I have argued for. My thesis is strengthened by the plausibility of Popkin's work on skepticism. The precise wording used here and by Popkin have varied to a small degree; the conclusions, however, appear to be the same: nonrational resources are the central strategy and tactic Hume uses to uphold his conclusions, to preserve his sanity, and to commend his philosophy. *That is precisely the thesis that Hume is a fideist.*

CONCLUSION

Our examination of Hume recognizes that He is one of the most important philosophers of modern times. His influence on Kant brought about Kant's famous "Copernican" revolution in philosophy, the turning point in Kant's career, and Hume's influence in the English-speaking world has been enormous in this century. Through Kant fideism has become a prominent modern position. It was Hume, however, who was the first important proponent of that position in the English-speaking world, and to understand the contemporary breadth of fideistic thinking we must mention David Hume along with Pascal, Kant, and Kierkegaard. Though Hume was not the first fideist of modern times, Bayle and others of that tradition had little influence on English philosophy. It is to Hume, then, that we must attribute a good portion of such influence.

The examination of Hume's writings in this book has borne out the claim that Hume is a fideist. His fideism is a *general* fideism, however, not a narrow, specialized, religious one. It is a self-conscious, deliberate epistemological position. That such a fideism is found in all his discussions of religious topics seems clear. But *it belongs not only to his* **Dialogues concerning Natural Religion** *and his lesser essays on religion, but to his views on metaphysics* as well.

This is in keeping with the practices of Hume's time, which we see so clearly in Bayle and the other members of the modern Pyrrhonist tradition. Popkin's research on early modern Pyrrhonism has provided us with a coherent and comprehensive understanding of skepticism, fideism, and their interrelations.

I have used "nonrational" to describe the mechanisms by which Hume attempts to fix the beliefs he cannot hold fast in his philosophy by analysis and reason. Popkin describes these mechanisms as irrational. I have avoided "irrational" since that word seems to mean "against reason" and to imply the "violation" of reason and rationality. It seems better to describe the mechanisms of human nature as nonrational since they simply are not related to reason at all except as replacements. A pretty good case can be made for using "irrational," however. It's this: If reason cannot establish our beliefs, as Hume says, then the things which supplant reason (such as human nature, etc.) and are not reasonable at all, *go against reason*. They work against reason and are antithetical to reason in their nature. So, properly, they could be called *ir*rational as long as we keep that specialized meaning for the term.

Whether we call them nonrational or irrational, the mechanism is essentially a fideism. It is the *general fideism* I have advocated and not just a fideism of a religious kind. Hume orchestrates this theme with every kind of variety and nuance. A diverse group of topics and emphases causes his work to have many subtleties, gradations, tensions, and puzzles. In spite of the detail Hume's philosophical writings contain, and the bewilderment this often brings to the reader, Hume invariably resolves the tension and relieves the "dissonance" in his account. Human nature, association of ideas, a felt propensity of the mind, habit, custom, inclination, imagination, animal spirits, passions, disposition, or fancy always comes through for him to save or recover the ideas he had banished rationally.

The case for this conclusion about Hume's philosophy can be tabulated thus:
1. Hume's philosophy of religion in all its parts follows the fideist model. Initial skepticism based on rational examination of a particular issue is resolved by Hume's appeal to faith as the way out of his negative, skeptical malaise.
2. Hume's philosophical examination ends with skepticism as well in his metaphysical doctrines. He finds this skepticism burdensome, distasteful, and distressing. His way out is to appeal to the nonrational mechanisms loosely lumped together under "human nature." We find a *general fideism*, therefore, in his metaphysical conclusions which are not religious or at best have only the most distant relationship and tenuous connection to religion. Since they are not religious matters, "faith" is not used. Nevertheless, the nonrational mechanisms we have continually mentioned serve the purpose which faith did on matters of religion. The rational-nonrational relationship for metaphysical doctrines is precisely parallel to reason-faith for religious issues and doctrines.

3. Hume's reflective statements on method throughout his works, but especially in the *Treatise*, continually state the claim that conventional, traditional positions or answers in metaphysics depend in some sense or other on the mind rather than on reality. This is another way he has of affirming the claim that somehow we don't discover but create or constitute the realities or the answers in question.
4. Historical research in the Pyrrhonist skepticism of early modern thinkers shows that David Hume belongs in that tradition. Such skepticism, unsatisfying as it was, almost invariably led to a fideism applying both to religious and to nonreligious issues. Bayle, the chief influence on Hume in this respect, is the best example of the practice of applying faith to nonreligious issues as well as to religious ones. Richard Popkin is the chief authority for these conclusions but his work is reinforced by recent work from Terence Penelhum.

With all things considered, I propose the fideist interpretation as the only coherent account of Hume's philosophy as a whole. This interpretation recognizes the skeptical elements that Hume students have discussed endlessly, and it explains more completely than the naturalist thesis of Hume's work just how Hume escaped his skeptical dilemmas. Our interpretation is reinforced by historical scholarship like that of Richard Popkin which was unavailable to earlier Hume scholars like Kemp Smith. It is, then, proposed as the only understanding which ties the strands of Hume's writings together in a self-consistent account.

NOTES

For abbreviations of Hume's works, and the editions used, see p. xi.

CHAPTER 2

[1] William Kelley Wright, *A History of Modern Philosophy* (New York: The Macmillan Co., 1941), 208.

[2] W. T. Jones, *Hobbes to Hume: A History of Western Philosophy*, 2d ed. (New York: Harcourt, Brace & World, Inc., 1969), p. 347.

[3] Ernest Campbell Mossner, *The Life of David Hume*, 2d ed. (Oxford: Clarendon Press, 1980), see esp. pp. 64, 128, 130, 291, 486, 545. Some of these pages include comments by others which Mossner receives with full acceptance.

[4] Barry Stroud, *Hume* (London: Routledge & Kegan Paul, 1977), p. 1. Many other comments could be added, but Livingston assembles a good collection of comments on the view of Hume as a destructive skeptic from Warburton to Randall. See Donald Livingston, *Hume's Philosophy of Common Life* (Chicago and London: University of Chicago Press, 1984), pp. 25-26.

[5] Robert J. Fogelin, *Hume's Skepticism in the Treatise of Human Nature*, International Library of Philosophy (London, Boston, Melbourne and Henley: Routledge & Kegan Paul, 1985), p. xi.

[6] *The Encyclopedia of Philosophy*, 1967, s. v. "Hume, David."

[7] Skeptical expressions are numerous in Hume, so it would hardly be useful to assemble a large collection of them. Allusions to most of them can be found in the following chapters. Hume includes some larger, deliberate discussions of

his skeptical emphases in the *Treatise*, Book I, Sections I, II, and VII of Part IV, in Section XII of the first *Enquiry*, in the *Abstract*, p. 24, and in many smaller remarks in the *Dialogues*.

[8]D. C. Stove, "The Nature of Hume's Skepticism," in *McGill Hume Studies* ed. David Fate Norton, Nicholas Capaldi, and Wade L. Robison (San Diego: Austin Hill Press, Inc., 1979), p. 203.

[9]Sextus Empiricus, *Outlines of Pyrrhonism*, trans. R. G. Bury, 4 vols. (New York: G. P. Putnam & Sons, 1933), 1:139f.

[10]John Immerwahr, "A Skeptic's Progress: Hume's Preference for the First Enquiry," in *McGill Hume Studies*, p. 228.

[11]Ibid., p. 227.

[12]Richard Popkin, "David Hume: His Pyrrhonism and His Critique of Pyrrhonism," *The Philosophical Quarterly* 1 (October, 1951): 385-407; reprinted in Richard H. Popkin, *The High Road to Pyrrhonism*, ed. Richard A. Watson and James E. Force (Studies in Hume and Scottish Philosophy; San Diego: Austin Hill Press, Inc., 1980), pp. 103-132.

[13]Paul Edwards, "The Existence of God: Introduction," in Paul Edwards and Arthur Pap, eds., *A Modern Introduction to Philosophy*, 3d ed. (New York: The Free Press, 1973), p. 391.

[14]John Hick, ed., *Classical and Contemporary Readings in the Philosophy of Religion*, 2d ed. (Englewood Cliffs, N. J.: Prentice-Hall, Inc., 1970), p. 533.

[15]John Hick, "Theology and Verification," *Theology Today* 17 (April, 1960): 18.

[16]John Hick, *Faith and Knowledge*, 2d ed. (Ithaca, N.Y.: Cornell University Press, 1966), p. 159.

[17]Terence Penelhum, *God and Skepticism* (Dordrecht, Boston, Lancaster: D. Reidel Publishing Co., 1983), p. 1.

[18]Ibid., p. 2.

[19]Ibid., p. 19.

[20]Ibid., p. 26.

[21]F. H. Bradley, *Appearance and Reality*, 2d ed. (Oxford: The Clarendon Press, 1897), p. x.

[22]Bertrand Russell, *A History of Western Philosophy* (New York: Simon and Schuster, 1945), p. 659.

[23]Terence Penelhum, "Hume's Skepticism and the Dialogues," in *McGill Hume Studies*, p. 253.

[24]Terence Penelhum, *Hume* (New York: St. Martin's Press, 1975), p. 17. Professor Penelhum has just published a new book on Hume which came too late for me to use: *David Hume: An Introduction to His Philosophical System* (West Lafayette, Ind.: Purdue University Press, 1992). It is written with characteristic breadth, sagacity, and polish. It will no doubt become an indispensable standard work on Hume for which we can all be grateful. The work includes a very valuable appendix giving notes on Hume studies literature.

[25]Norman Kemp Smith, *The Philosophy of David Hume: A Critical Study of Its Origins and Central Doctrines* (London: Macmillan and Co., Ltd., 1941), p. v.

[26]From a conversation with Professor John Hospers.

[27]M. Jamie Ferreira, *Scepticism and Reasonable Doubt: The British Naturalist Tradition in Wilkins, Hume, Reid, and Newman* (Oxford: Clarendon Press, 1986), p. 234.

[28]In addition to the books by Kemp Smith and Penelhum, there are other recent treatments of the naturalist position: Robert Connon, "The Naturalism of Hume Revisited," and Terence Penelhum, "Hume's Skepticism and the Dialogues", both in *McGill Hume Studies*; Wade L. Robison, "David Hume: Naturalist and Meta-sceptic," in *Hume: A Re-evaluation*, eds. Donald W. Livingston and James T. King (New York: Fordham University Press, 1976); Stroud, *Hume*. These treatments vary widely.

[29]Penelhum, "Hume's Skepticism and the Dialogues," p. 254.

[30]Robison, "David Hume: Naturalist and Meta-sceptic," pp. 26-27.

[31]Kemp Smith, *The Philosophy of David Hume*, p. vi.

[32]Donald W. Livingston, *Hume's Philosophy of Common Life* (Chicago and London: University of Chicago Press, 1984), p. 27.

[33]Penelhum, "Hume's Skepticism and the Dialogues," p. 255.

[34]Nicholas Capaldi, "The Problem of Hume and Hume's Problem," in *McGill Hume Studies*, p. 10f.

[35]For literature discussing the nature of faith, the use of the word, its relations to belief, etc. the following can be suggested: Martin D'Arcy, *The Nature of Belief* (New York: Sheed and Ward, 1945); John Hick, "Faith" in Paul Edwards, ed., *The Encyclopedia of Philosophy*; John Hick, ed., *Faith and the Philosophers* (New York: St. Martin's Press, 1966); Anthony Kenny, *Faith and Reason* (New York: Columbia University Press, 1983); Terence Penelhum, ed., *Faith* (New York: Macmillan Publishing Company, 1989) and *God and Skepticism* (Dordrecht, Boston, Lancaster: D. Reidel Publishing Co., 1983); Richard H. Popkin, "Fideism" in Paul Edwards, ed., *The Encyclopedia of Philosophy*; Richard Swinburne, *Faith and Reason* (Oxford: Clarendon Press, 1981).

[36]Psalms 37:23.

[37]William of Occam, *Sentences*, 2.

[38]Frederick Copleston, *A History of Philosophy, vol. 2: Ockham to Suarez* (Westminster, Md.: The Newman Press), p. 84.

[39]E. M. Plass, *What Luther Says*, I, Sec. 1400, cited in Brand Blanshard, *Reason and Belief* (London: George Allen & Unwin, Ltd., 1974), p. 177 and in many other works.

[40]Penelhum, *God and Skepticism*, p. 180.

[41]Some exceptions to this are: Jonathan Bennett, *Rationality: An Essay Towards an Analysis* (London: Routledge & Kegan Paul, 1964); Max Black, *The Prevalence of Humbug and Other Essays* (Ithaca, N.Y. and London: Cornell University Press, 1983); Harold I. Brown, *Rationality* (London and New York: Routledge, 1988); Christopher Cherniak, "Minimal Rationality," *Mind* 90 (April 1981): 161-183; C. F. Delaney, ed., *Rationality and Religious Belief* (Notre Dame, Ind.: University of Notre Dame Press, 1979); Roy Edgley, *Reason in Theory and Practice* (London: Hutchinson University Library, 1969); Theodore F. Geraets, ed., *Rationality Today/La Rationalite Aujourd'hui* (Ottawa: The University of Ottawa Press, 1979); John Kekes, *A Justification of Rationality* (Albany: State University of New York Press, l976). John Kekes' volume is the outcome of thirteen articles published in various journals between 1969 and 1975. Most of them are listed on p. xiv of his book.; Haig Khatchadourian, "What is Rationality?," *Theoria* 24 (1958): 172-187; R. Kirk, "Rationality Without

Language," *Mind* 76 (July, 1967): 369-386; Robert Leet Patterson, *Irrationalism and Rationalism in Religion* (Westport, Conn.: Greenwood Press, Publishers, 1954); Hilary Putnam, "The Impact of Science on Modern Conceptions of Rationality," *Synthese* 46 (1981): 359-381; Henryk Skolimowski, "Evolutionary Rationality" in R. S. Cohen, C. A. Hooker, A. C. Michalos, and J. W. Van Evra, eds. *Proceedings of the 1974 Biennial Meeting, Philosophy of Science Association, Boston Studies in the Philosophy of Science*, eds. Robert S. Cohen and Marx W. Wartofsky, vol. 32 (Dordrecht, Holland: D. Reidel Publishing Co., 1976): 191-213; Richard Swinburne, *Faith and Reason* (Oxford: Clarendon Press, 1981); Bryan R. Wilson, ed., *Rationality: Key Concepts in the Social Sciences* (Evanston,Ill. and New York: Harper and Row, Publishers, 1970). Wilson's book is listed as an example of the wide range of articles on rationality in the social sciences. In addition to these listings Kai Nielsen has contributed a large number of essays, parts to discussions, etc., so he deserves mention as a major contributor to the topic.

[42]Bernard Gert, *The Moral Rules*, quoted in Kekes, *A Justification of Rationality*, p.111.

[43]Patrick Burke, "Rationality in Religion" in Geraets, ed. *Rationality Today*, p. 464.

[44]Ibid.

[45]Swinburne, *Faith and Reason,* pp. 45-54.

[46]Interview with Bill Durbin: "A Scientist Caught between Two Faiths," *Christianity Today*, August 6, 1982, pp. 15-16.

[47]Hilary Putnam, "Science and Rationality," *Synthese* 46 (1981): 378.

[48]Ibid.

[49]See John Hospers, *An Introduction to Philosophical Analysis*, 2d ed. (Englewood Cliffs, N. J.: Prentice-Hall, Inc., 1967), p. 149f.

CHAPTER 3

[1] See list of abbreviations.

[2] David Hume to Henry Home, London, 2 December, 1737, *The Letters of David Hume*, ed. J. Y. T. Greig (Oxford: Clarendon Press, 1932), I:24-25; *New Letters of David Hume*, eds. Raymond Klibansky and Ernest C. Mossner (Oxford: Clarendon Press, 1954), pp. 2-3.

[3] A. E. Taylor, *David Hume and the Miraculous* (Cambridge: The University Press, 1927), p. 3.

[4] David Hume, *My Own Life* in Mossner, *The Life of David Hume*, 2d ed., p. 615.

[5] John Herman Randall, *The Career of Philosophy, Vol. 1: From the Middle Ages to the Enlightenment* (New York: Columbia University Press, 1962), p. 634.

[6] Hume, *My Own Life* in Mossner, *Life of Hume*, 2d ed., p. 612.

[7] Mossner, *Life of Hume*, 2d ed., p. 553.

[8] Taylor, *David Hume and the Miraculous*, pp. 2-3.

[9] David Wootton, "Hume's 'Of Miracles': Probability and Irreligion," in *Studies of the Philosophy of the Scottish Enlightenment*, ed. M.A. Stewart (Oxford: Clarendon Press, 1990), p. 199. See p. 223 for suggestions on why probability is not linked to miracles in the *Enquiry*.

[10] Hume, *My Own Life* in Mossner, *Life of Hume*, 2d ed., p. 612.

[11] Taylor, *David Hume and the Miraculous*, pp. 2-3. See also Gary Colwell, "On Defining Away the Miraculous," *Philosophy* 57 (1982): 327-337. Whether miracles are impossible on apriori grounds or whether the rejection of miracles is based on Hume's inductive approach is still a debated issue. An instance of this can be found in *Hume Studies* where Fogelin and Flew debate this point and Keith Ferguson provides a discussion which he believes will accommodate both parties.

The presumption of all participants in this debate is that Hume rejects any and all miracles. The issue is on what grounds. See Robert Fogelin, "What Hume Actually Said About Miracles," *Hume Studies* 16 (Apr., 1990): 81-86. Anthony Flew replies to this in "Fogelin on Hume on Miracles," *Hume Studies* 16 (Nov., 1990): 141-144. The attempt to adjudicate this debate is given by Kenneth G. Ferguson, "An Intervention into the Flew/Fogelin Debate," *Hume Studies* 17 (Apr., 1992): 105-112.

[12]Ibid.

[13]Samuel Clarke, *A Defence of Natural and Revealed Religion*, eds. Letsome and Nicholl (London: 1739), quoted in Mossner, *Life of Hume*, 2d ed., p. 287.

[14]John Calvin, *An Admonition Showing the Advantages Which Christendom Might Derive from an Inventory of Relics* in John Calvin, *Tracts and Treatises of the Reformation of The Church*, Trans. Henry Beveridge, ed. Thomas F. Torrance. (Grand Rapids, Mich.: William B. Eerdmans Publishing Co., 1958), I, 287-341. Reprinted from the Calvin Society edition, Edinburgh, 1844.

[15]Mossner, *Life of Hume*, 2d ed., p. 174.

[16]James Noxon, *Hume's Philosophical Development* (Oxford: Clarendon Press, 1973), p. 26.

[17]J. C. A. Gaskin, *Hume's Philosophy of Religion*, 2d ed. (Atlantic Highlands, N.J.: Humanities Press International, Inc., 1988), p. 165.

[18]Ibid.

[19]Norman Kemp Smith, "Introduction" to David Hume, *Dialogues concerning Natural Religion*, ed. Norman Kemp Smith (New York: Thomas Nelson & Sons Ltd., 1947; reprint ed.: Library of Liberal Arts; Indianapolis, Ind.: The Bobbs-Merrill Company, 1979), p. 1.

[20]Ibid., p. 60.

[21]Ibid., p. 58.

[22]Gaskin, *Hume's Philosophy of Religion*, 2d. ed., p. 16.

[23]Kemp Smith lists these philosophers who agree with Dugald Stewart: A. S. Pringle-Pattison, *Idea of God in the Light of Recent Philosophy* (New York: Oxford University Press, 1920); Friedrich Jodl, *Leben und Philosophie David*

Humes (Halle: C. E. M. Pfeffer, 1872), p. 175; Wilhelm Windelband, *A History of Philosophy*, trans. James H. Tufts, rev. ed. (New York: The Macmillan Company, 1901; reprint ed. Harper Torchbooks; New York: Harper & Row, Publishers, 1958), pp. 494, 498; James Hastings, *Encyclopedia of Religion and Ethics*, 1921, s.v. "Theism" by A. E. Taylor; C. W. Hendel, *Studies in the Philosophy of David Hume* (Princeton: Princeton University Press, 1925), pp. 306-307; B. M. Laing, *David Hume* (London: Ernest Benn Ltd., 1932), p. 179; André Leroy, *La Critique et la Religion chez David Hume* (Paris: F. Alcan, 1934), pp. 289-293, 369; Rudolf Metz, *David Hume, Leben und Philosophie (Stuttgart: F. Frommann, 1929), pp. 345f.* Listed in Hume, *Dialogues concerning Natural Religion*, ed. Norman Kemp Smith, p. 59, notes.

[24] Richard H. Popkin, "Introduction" to David Hume, *Dialogues concerning Natural Religion and the posthumous essays Of the Immortality of the Soul and Of Suicide*, ed. Richard Popkin (Indianapolis, Ind.: Hackett Publishing Co., 1980), pp. xiv-xv.

[25] Kemp Smith, ed., Hume, *Dialogues*, p. 59.

[26] Gaskin, *Hume's Philosophy of Religion*, 2d ed., p. 209f.

[27] Ibid. Gaskin lists two pieces which complement Kemp Smith's thesis: Ernest C. Mossner, "The Enigma of Hume," *Mind* n.s. 45 (July, 1936): 334- 349 and John Valdimir Price, "Scepticism in Cicero and Hume," *Journal of the History of Ideas* 25 (Jan., 1964): 97-106.

[28] James Noxon, "Hume's Agnosticism," *The Philosophical Review* 73 (1964). Reprinted in V.C. Chappell, ed., *Hume* (Notre Dame, Ind.: University of Notre Dame Press, 1968), p. 361f.

[29] Gaskin, *Hume's Philosophy of Religion*, 2d ed., p. 218.

[30] Ibid., p. 220. The references Gaskin is referring to are assembled in order on pp. 219-220.

[31] Ibid., p. 221.

[32] I am following Kemp Smith, ed., Hume, *Dialogues*, pp. 15-19, quite closely for the three points of Hume's list of evils. These points are from *The Natural History of Religion*. Gaskin gives a quite full summary of Hume's charges in *The Natural History of Religion* in his *Hume's Philosophy of Religion*, 2d ed., pp. 184-187.

Notes

³³John Calvin, *The Ordinances for the Supervision of Churches in the Country* in Calvin, *Theological Treatises*, ed. and trans. J. K. S. Reid (Philadelphia: The Westminster Press, 1954), 22.

³⁴Kemp Smith, ed., Hume, *Dialogues*, pp. 12-13.

³⁵Geddes MacGregor, *Introduction to Religious Philosophy* (Boston: Houghton Mifflin Company, 1959), pp. 327-328.

³⁶David Hume to Gilbert Elliot of Minto, Ninewells, 10 Mar., 1751, *Letters of David Hume*, ed. Greig, I, 153.

³⁷Kemp Smith, ed., Hume, *Dialogues*, pp. 61-62.

³⁸Ibid., p. 68.

³⁹Ibid., p. 69.

⁴⁰Ibid.

⁴¹Ibid., p. 70.

⁴²Ibid.

⁴³Ibid.

⁴⁴Ibid., note.

⁴⁵David Hume, *The Natural History of Religion*, ed. A. Wayne Colver and *Dialogues concerning Natural Religion*, ed. John Valdimir Price (Oxford: Clarendon Press, 1976), pp. 250-251, note.

⁴⁶Gaskin, *Hume's Philosophy of Religion*, 2d ed., pp. 16, 209.

⁴⁷Ibid., p. 211.

⁴⁸David Hume to Gilbert Elliot of Minto, Ninewells, 10 Mar., 1751, *Letters of David Hume*, ed. Greig, I, 154.

⁴⁹Gaskin, *Hume's Philosophy of Religion*, 2d ed., p. 211.

⁵⁰Ibid., pp. 211-212.

[51] Noxon, "Hume's Agnosticism," p. 372.

[52] Gaskin, *Hume's Philosophy of Religion*, 2d ed., p. 215.

[53] Ibid., p. 212.

[54] Ernest Campbell Mossner, "The Enigma of Hume," *Mind* n.s. 45 (July, 1936): 334-349.

[55] Price, "Scepticism in Cicero and Hume," *Journal of the History of Ideas*.

[56] Gaskin, *Hume's Philosophy of Religion*, 2d ed., p. 212.

[57] Ibid.

[58] Noxon, "Hume's Agnosticism," pp. 361-383.

[59] Gaskin, *Hume's Philosophy of Religion*, 2d ed., p. 217.

[60] T. E. Jessop in A. E. Taylor, John Laird, and T. E. Jessop, Symposium: "The Present-Day Relevance of Hume's Dialogues concerning Natural Religion," *Aristotelian Society Supplementary Volume*, 18 (1939), p. 220.

[61] Noxon, "Hume's Agnosticism," p. 367.

[62] Gaskin, *Hume's Philosophy of Religion*, 2d ed., p. 72.

[63] Mossner, *The Life of David Hume*, 2d ed., p. 298. Quoted from *Stewart, Smith, Robertson, and Reid*, p. 417. The letter is no longer extant.

[64] Livingston, *Hume's Philosophy of Common Life*, pp. 296-297.

[65] Mossner, *Life of David Hume*, 2d ed., p. 173.

[66] Ibid., pp. 173-174, quoted from *The Autobiography of Alexander Carlyle of Inveresk*, ed. John Hill Burton (London and Edinburgh, 1910), p. 287.

[67] Hume, "Of the Immortality of the Soul," in Popkin, ed., Hume, *Dialogues*, et. al., p. 91.

[68] Ibid., pp. 96-97.

[69] Gaskin, *Hume's Philosophy of Religion*, 2d ed., p. 166.

[70]Ibid., p. 181.

[71]Ibid.

[72]Hume, "Of the Immortality of the Soul,", p. 92.

[73]Ibid.

[74]Ibid.

[75]Ibid.

[76]Hume, "Of Suicide," in Popkin, ed., Hume, *Dialogues*, et. al, pp. 104-105, note.

[77]Popkin, "Introduction," in Popkin, ed., Hume, *Dialogues*, et. al., p. viii.

[78]James Boswell, "An Account of My Last Interview with David Hume, Esq." from Geoffrey Scott and Frederick A. Pottle, eds., *Private Papers of James Boswell* 12 (1932), pp. 227-228, reprinted in Kemp Smith, ed., *Dialogues*, pp. 76-77.

[79]David Hume to Gilbert Elliot of Minto, Ninewells, 10 Mar., 1751, *Letters of David Hume*, ed. Greig, I, 155.

[80]Livingston, *Hume's Philosophy of Common Life*, p. 172.

[81]Ibid.

[82]Ibid.

[83]David Hume, *An Enquiry concerning Human Understanding* and *A Letter from a Gentleman to His Friend in Edinburgh*, ed. Eric Steinberg (Indianapolis: Hackett Publishing Company, 1977), p. 117. We must allow for some exaggeration here, but Hume is hardly in a mood to tone down the truth.

[84]Ibid., pp. 117-118.

[85]The story is given in Gaskin, *Hume's Philosophy of Religion*, 2d ed., p. 245 and Mossner, *Life of David Hume*, 2d ed., p. 395.

[86]R. J. Butler, "Natural Belief and the Enigma of Hume," *Archiv für Geschichte der Philosophie* 42 (1960): 87, cited in William H. Capitan, "Part X

of Hume's Dialogues," *American Philosophical Quarterly* 3 (Jan., 1966); reprinted in Chappell, ed., *Hume*, p. 388, note.

CHAPTER 4

[1] This is a portion of paragraph which Hume used as an advertisement of the *Enquiry concerning Human Understanding*.

[2] *Treatise*, pp. 16, 58, 65, 155, 161-162, 165, 234, 251-252. Also, Enquiry, pp. 74, 77. The general idea occurs often in the first book of the *Treatise* but without the precise word formula.

[3] Livingston, *Hume's Philosophy of Common Life*, p. 155.

[4] Annette C. Baier, *A Progress of Sentiments: Reflections on Hume's Treatise* (Cambridge and London: Harvard University Press, 1991), p. 56.

[5] Galen Strawson, *The Secret Connexion: Causation, Realism, and David Hume* (Oxford: Clarendon Press, 1989). The closest Strawson comes to dealing with this locution is Hume's reference to having "really no *distinct* meaning" of causation. (*Treatise*, p. 162) Strawson understands this to mean that we really have no "distinct" idea or meaning "because there is no impression-source for the idea in objects." See Strawson, p. 106.

[6] Ibid., pp. vii, 8, 9, note, 10, 20-31, 43-46, 275, etc.

[7] Stroud, *Hume*, p. 45.

[8] Hume starts with the role that cause and effect have with our ideas before he gets to situations like the collisions of billiard balls. His first mention of cause and effect in the *Treatise* (p. 11) concerns the connection which makes one idea recall another. A similar discussion occurs in the *Enquiry*, p. 26.

[9] Anthony Flew, *Hume's Philosophy of Belief: A Study of His First Inquiry* (London: Routledge & Kegan Paul, 1961), p. 123.

[10] Stroud, *Hume*, p. 245. For the synonymous terms, see *Treatise*, p. 157.

[11] The discussion on cause and effect begins seriously on p. 73 of the *Treatise* and finishes on p. 176 with many parentheses between such as pp. 94-130 and 143-154. These "parenthetical" pages range over various issues such as the

nature of belief, its causes, probability, etc. So with these lacunae in the dicussion of cause, it is reasonable to say that the problem of induction occurs "right in the middle" of the discussion on cause.

[12]Kemp Smith, *The Philosophy of David Hume,* p. 99, note.

[13]Stroud, *Hume*, p. 55.

[14]*Treatise*, pp. 92, 94, 95, 140, 193, 463, 468, 469, 626, etc.

[15]Livingston, *Hume's Philosophy of Common Life,* p. 150.

[16]David Hume to John Stewart, February, 1754, in *The Letters of David Hume*, ed. Greig, I:187. The letter is reprinted also by Kemp Smith, *The Philosophy of David Hume*, pp. 412-413. This letter was Hume's response to a note written by John Stewart in a volume published by the Philosophical Society of Edinburgh. The portion of the second article penned by John Stewart is given to us by Kemp Smith, p. 411.

[17]Strawson, *The Secret Connexion*, pp. 2, note, and 146f.

[18]Ibid., p. 146.

[19]Written note to me from Professor John Hospers.

[20]*Treatise*, p. 165. Illustrated here but repeated in many other places.

[21]J. A. Robinson, "Hume's Two Definitions of 'Cause'," *The Philosophical Quarterly* 12 (April, 1962), reprinted in V. C. Chappell, ed., *Hume* (Notre Dame, Ind. and London: University of Notre Dame Press, 1968), p. 138.

[22]See Strawson, *The Secret Connexion*, p. 10f.

[23]Stroud, *Hume*, p. 89.

[24]Ibid., p. 90. Stroud says: "Furthermore, things could fulfil the conditions of the first 'definition' even if there were no minds at all, or if minds were very different from the way they actually are. The existence and precise nature of minds is irrelevant to the question whether members of one class of things are regularly followed by members of another class. But it is only because there are minds that any things at all fulfil the conditions of the second 'definition', and it is only because those minds are the way they are that things fulfil the conditions of the second 'definition' whenever they are observed to fulfil the conditions of the

first. Only if there are minds will there be ideas of those things, and only if those minds are like ours will the idea of a member of one of those classes naturally give rise to an idea of a member of the other. And Hume thinks he has shown that it is only because things fulfil the conditions of the second 'definition' that any things in the world are thought to be related *causally* or *necessarily* at all. We get the idea of necessary connection only because of the passage of the mind from the thought of something to the thought of its 'usual attendant.' That is perhaps why he feels constrained to include something like the second 'definition' in any attempt to characterize our idea of causality. It is only because causality is in fact a 'natural' relation that we ever manage to get the idea at all. And that is a very important part of Hume's theory.

[25] Robinson, "Hume's Two Definitions of 'Cause'," p. 139.

[26] Strawson, *The Secret Connexion*, p. 2, note, and other places.

[27] See also pp. 155, 158 for parallel expressions.

[28] A. J. Ayer, *Hume* (New York: Hill and Wang, 1980), pp. 63-64.

[29] Ibid., pp. 65-66.

[30] Strawson, *The Secret Connexion*, p. 7f and throughout the book.

[31] Ibid., pp. 11-12.

[32] Ibid., p. 11.

CHAPTER 5

[1] Lewis White Beck, "A Prussian Hume and a Scottish Kant" in Norton, Capaldi, and Robison, eds. *McGill Hume Studies* (San Diego: Austin Hill Press, Inc., 1976), pp. 63-78; reprinted in Lewis W. Beck, *Essays on Kant and Hume* (New Haven: Yale University Press, 1978), pp. 111-129.

[2] Kemp Smith, *The Philosophy of David Hume*, pp. 272, 542.

[3] Ibid., p. 285.

[4] Kemp Smith, ed., Hume, *Dialogues*, p. 138.

Notes

⁵Penelhum, *God and Skepticism*.

⁶David Pears, *Hume's System: An Examination of the First Book of his Treatise* (Oxford and New York: Oxford University Press, 1990).

⁷Ibid., p. 79.

⁸Ibid., p. 4.

⁹Ibid., p. 195.

¹⁰Ibid., p.25.

¹¹Ibid., p. 98.

¹²Ibid., p. 97.

¹³Baier, *A Progress of Sentiments*.

¹⁴Ibid., p. 58.

¹⁵Ibid., p. 301, note 3.

¹⁶Hume, *My Own Life*, reprinted in Mossner, *The Life of David Hume*, 2d ed., p. 612.

¹⁷Most of Richard Popkin's work has appeared in a series of journal articles. Among many he has written is one we are using extensively here: "David Hume: His Pyrrhonism and His Critique of Pyrrhonism," *The Philosophical Quarterly* 1 (October, 1951): 385-407. It is reprinted in V. C. Chappell, ed., *Hume* (Garden City, N.Y.: Doubleday & Co., Inc., Anchor Books, 1966; Notre Dave, Ind. and London: University of Notre Dame Press, 1968), and also in Richard H. Popkin, *The High Road to Pyrrhonism*, ed. Richard A. Watson and James E. Force (San Diego: Austin Hill Press, Inc., 1980), pp. 103-132. The references given here will be from Popkin's reprints in *The High Road to Pyrrhonism*. In addition to this article, Popkin also has "The High Road to Pyrrhonism," "David Hume and the Pyrrhonian Controversy," "Bayle and Hume," and other highly significant contributions. Popkin's work is almost alone in both historical insight and critical acumen in assessing Hume's skepticism and attempts to escape it, and much of what is included in this section has been taken with gratitude from Richard Popkin.

¹⁸Sextus Empiricus *Outlines of Pyrrhonism*, Loeb Classical Library.

¹⁹Popkin, *The High Road to Pyrrhonism*, p. 13f.

²⁰Ibid., p. 26.

²¹Ibid., p. 56.

²²Ibid., p. 152.

²³Ibid., p. 153.

²⁴Gottfried W. von Leibniz, *Essais de Theodicée sur la bonité de Dieu, la liberté de l'homme et l'origine du mal* (Amsterdam, 1710), p. 547. Listed in Popkin, *The High Road to Pyrrhonism*, p. 28. I have not been able to find this in the editions of the *Theodicy* available to me.

²⁵Ibid., p. 29.

²⁶Ibid., p. 27.

²⁷Ibid., pp. 63-64.

²⁸Ibid., p. 64. Popkin's remark refers to Hume's intention to include a section on miracles in the *Treatise*. He included the section in his early manuscript, but deemed it wise to secure the advice of his friends on the matter. He confided his plan for the *Treatise* to Henry Home, his uncle, and sent him a copy of the essay. He wanted to show the essay to Joseph Butler but cut it out at the last minute. He felt that "this is a piece of cowardice" but persisted with his plans. Home is reported to have advised total suppression and that is what was done. The letter can be found in Greig, ed., *The Letters of David Hume*, I:23-25 and in Klibansky and Mossner, eds., *New Letters of David Hume*, pp. 1-3. The letters are the same except that Klibansky and Mossner publish the letter in Hume's form with capitalized nouns, abbreviations, and one crudely suggestive sentence which Greig excised from his edition.

²⁹See pp. 28-37 of this book for Hume's fideistic views on the subject of miracles.

³⁰Popkin, *The High Road to Pyrrhonism*, p. 104. The quotation from Hume is found in his *Abstract* included in the *Treatise*, p. 657.

³¹Ibid., pp. 104-105. References to Sextus Empiricus are being omitted here since Popkin includes them in his notes.

[32]Ibid., p. 107.

[33]Hume, *Treatise*, p. 183. A portion of the first paragraph and the entirety of the second paragraph have already been quoted at length, so to avoid redundancy the reader is referred to p. 160.

[34]This section follows Popkin quite closely.

[35]See also Myles F. Burnyeat, "Can the Skeptic Live His Skepticism?" reprinted in Myles Burnyeat (ed.), *The Skeptical Tradition* (Berkeley, Los Angeles, London: University of California Press, 1983), p. 117f. Published earlier in Malcolm Schofield, Myles Burnyeat, and Jonathan Barnes (eds.), *Doubt and Dogmatism: Studies in Hellenistic Epistemology* (Oxford: Clarendon Press, 1980).

[36]Popkin, *High Road to Pyrrhonism*, p. 126.

[37]Ibid., pp. 126-132.

[38]Ibid., p. 132, note.

BIBLIOGRAPHY OF WORKS CITED

Ayer, A. J. *Hume*. New York: Hill and Wang, 1980

Baier, Annette C. *A Progress of Sentiments: Reflections on Hume's Treatise*. Cambridge and London: Harvard University Press, 1991.

Beck, Lewis White. *Essays on Kant and Hume*. New Haven: Yale University Press, 1978.

——. "A Prussian Hume and a Scottish Kant." In *McGill Hume Studies*. Edited by Norton, Capaldi, and Robison. Reprinted in Beck. *Essays on Kant and Hume*.

Bennett, Jonathan. *Rationality: An Essay Towards an Analysis*. London: Routledge & Kegan Paul, 1964.

Black, Max. *The Prevalence of Humbug and Other Essays*. Ithaca, N.Y. and London: Cornell University Press, 1983.

Blanshard, Brand. *Reason and Belief*. London: George Allen & Unwin, Ltd., 1974.

Boswell, James. "An Account of My Last Interview with David Hume, Esq." In *Private Papers of James Boswell*, 12. Edited by Geoffrey Scott and Frederick A. Pottle. Reprinted in David Hume. *Dialogues concerning Natural Religion*. Edited, with an Introduction by Norman Kemp Smith.

Bradley, F. H. *Appearance and Reality*. 2d ed. Oxford: The Clarendon Press, 1897.

Brown, Harold I. *Rationality*. London and New York: Routledge, 1988.

Burke, Patrick. "Rationality in Religion." In *Rationality To-Day/La Rationalité Aujourd'hui*. Edited by Theodore F. Geraets.

Burnyeat, Myles, ed. *The Skeptical Tradition*. Berkeley, Los Angeles, London: University of California Press, 1983.

Burton, John Hill, ed. *The Autobiography of Alexander Carlyle of Inveresk*. London and Edinburgh, 1910. Quoted in Mossner. *The Life of David Hume*. 2d ed.

Butler, R. J. "*Natural Belief and the Enigma of Hume*." *Archiv für Geschichte der Philosophie* 41 (1960). Cited in William H. Capitan. "Part X of Hume's Dialogues." *American Philosophical Quarterly* 3 (Jan. 1966). Reprinted in Chappell, ed. *Hume*.

Calvin, John. *An Admonition Showing the Advantages Which Chistendom Might Derive from an Inventory of Relics*. Vol. 1, *Tracts and Treatises on the Reformation of the Church*. Trans. by Henry Beveridge. Edited by Thomas F. Torrance. Grand Rapids: William B. Eerdmans Publishing Co., 1958.

———. *The Ordinances for the Supervision of Churches in the Country*. In John Calvin. *Theological Treatises*, 22. Edited and translated by J. K. S. Reid. Philadelphia: The Westminster Press, 1954.

Capaldi, Nicholas. "The Problem of Hume and Hume's Problem." In *McGill Hume Studies*. Edited by Norton, Capaldi, and Robison.

Capitan, William H. See Butler, R. J.

Chappell, V. C., ed. *Hume*. Notre Dame, Ind. and London: University of Notre Dame Press, 1968.

Cherniak, Christopher. "Minimal Rationality." *Mind* 90 (Apr. 1981): 161-183.

Clarke, Samuel. *A Defence of Natural and Revealed Religion*. Edited by Letsom and Nicholl. London, 1739. Quoted in Mossner. *The Life of David Hume*. 2d ed.

Colwell, Gary. "On Defining Away the Miraculous." *Philosophy* 57 (1982): 327-337.

Connon, Robert. "The Naturalism of Hume Revisited." In *McGill Hume Studies*. Edited by Norton, Capaldi, and Robison.

Copleston, Frederick. *A History of Philosophy. Vol. 3: Ockham to Suárez*. Westminster, Mar.: The Newman Press, 1953.

D'Arcy, Martin. *The Nature of Belief*. New York: Sheed and Ward, 1945.

Delaney, C. F., ed. *Rationality and Religious Belief*. Notre Dame, Ind.: University of Notre Dame Press, 1979.

Durbin, Bill. A Scientist Caught Between Two Faiths." *Christianity Today*, 6 August 1982, 15-16.

Edgley, Roy. *Reason in Theory and Practice*. London: Hutchinson University Library, 1969.

Edwards, Paul. "The Existence of God: Introduction." In *A Modern Introduction to Philosophy*. Edited by Paul Edwards and Arthur Pap. 3d ed. New York: The Free Press, 1973. Pp. 374-402.

──────, ed. *The Encyclopedia of Philosophy*. S.v. "Faith," by John Hick; "Fideism," by Richard H. Popkin; "Hume, David," by D. G. C. MacNabb.

Ferguson, Kenneth G. "An Intervention into the Flew/Fogelin Debate." *Hume Studies* 17 (Apr. 1992): 105-112.

Ferreira, M. Jamie. *Scepticism and Reasonable Doubt: The British Naturalist Tradition in Wilkins, Hume, Reid, and Newman*. Oxford: Clarendon Press, 1986.

Flew, Anthony. *Hume's Philosophy of Belief: A Study of His First Enquiry*. London: Routledge & Kegan Paul, 1961.

Fogelin, Robert J. *Hume's Skepticism in the Treatise of Human Nature*. International Library of Philosophy. London, Boston, Melbourne, and Henley: Routledge & Kegan Paul, 1985.

──────. "What Hume Actually Said About Miracles." *Hume Studies* 16 (Apr. 1990): 81-86.

Gaskin, J. C. A. *Hume's Philosophy of Religion*. 2d ed. Atlantic Highlands, N. J.: Humanities Press International, Inc. 1988.

Geraets, Theodore F., ed. *Rationality Today/La Rationalité Aujourd'hui*. Ottawa: The University of Ottawa Press, 1979.

Gert, Bernard. *The Moral Rules*. Quoted in John Kekes. *A Justification of Rationality*. Albany: State University of New York Press, 1976.

Greig, J. Y. T., ed. *The Letters of David Hume*. 2 vols. Oxford: Clarendon Press, 1932.

Hastings, James, ed. *The Encyclopedia of Religion and Ethics*. 1921. S.v. "Theism" by A. E. Taylor.

Hendel, C. W. *Studies in the Philosophy of David Hume*. Princeton: Princeton University Press, 1925.

Hick, John, ed. *Classical and Contemporary Readings in the Philosophy of Religion*. 2d ed. Englewood Cliffs, N.J.: Prentice-Hall, Inc., 1970.

—————. *Faith and Knowledge*. 2d ed. Ithaca, N.Y.: Cornell University Press, 1966.

—————, ed. *Faith and the Philosophers*. New York: St. Martin's Press, 1966.

—————. "Theology and Verification." *Theology Today* 17 (Apr. 1960): 12-31.

Hospers, John. *An Introduction to Philosophical Analysis*. 2d ed. Englewood Cliffs, N.J.: Prentice-Hall, Inc., 1967.

Hume, David. *An Abstract of a Treatise of Human Nature*. Introduction by J. M. Keynes and P. Sraffa. London: Cambridge University Press, 1938; reprint, Hamden, Conn.: Archon Books, 1965.

—————. *Dialogues concerning Natural Religion*. Edited with an introduction by Norman Kemp Smith. Indianapolis, Ind.: The Bobbs-Merrill Co., Inc., 1947.

—————. *Dialogues concerning Natural Religion and the posthumous essays Of the Immortality of the Soul and Of Suicide*. Edited with an introduction by Richard H. Popkin. Indianapolis, Ind.: Hackett Publishing Co., 1980.

—————. *Enquiries concerning Human Understanding and concerning the Principles of Morals*. Edited by L. A. Selby-Bigge. 3d ed. revised by P. H. Nidditch. Oxford: Clarendon Press, 1975.

Bibliography

―――. *An Enquiry concerning Human Understanding and A Letter from a Gentleman to His Friend in Edinburgh.* Edited by Eric Steinberg. Indianapolis, Ind.: Hackett Publishing Co., 1977.

―――. *My Own Life.* Reprinted in Mossner, *The Life of David Hume.* 2d ed. Oxford: Clarendon Press, 1980.

―――. *The Natural History of Religion.* Edited by A. Wayne Colver. And: *Dialogues concerning Natural Religion.* Edited by John Valdimir Price. Oxford: Clarendon Press, 1976.

―――. *Of the Immortality of the Soul.* In Richard H. Popkin, ed. *Dialogues concerning Natural Religion and the posthumous essays Of the Immortality of the Soul and Of Suicide.*

―――. *Of Suicide.* In Richard H. Popkin, ed. *Dialogues concerning Natural Religion and the posthumous essays Of the Immortality of the Soul and Of Suicide.*

―――. *A Treatise of Human Nature.* Edited by L. A. Selby-Bigge. 2d ed. revised by P. H. Nidditch. Oxford: Clarendon Press, 1978.

Immerwahr, John. "A Skeptic's Progress: Hume Preference for the First Enquiry." In *McGill Hume Studies.* Edited by Norton, Capaldi, and Robison.

Jessop, T. E. In A. E. Taylor, John Laird, and T. E. Jessop. Symposium: "The Present-Day Relevance of Hume's Dialogues concerning Natural Religion." *Aristotelian Society Supplementary Volume* 18 (1939).

Jodl, Friedrich. *Leben und Philosophie David Humes.* Halle: C. E. M. Pfeffer, 1872.

Jones, W. T. *A History of Modern Philosophy.* New York: The Macmillan Co., 1941.

Kekes, John. *A Justification of Rationality.* Albany: State University of New York Press, 1976.

―――. "Logic and Rationality." *Rationality Today.* Edited by Geraets.

Kenny, Anthony. *Faith and Reason.* New York: Columbia University Press, 1983.

Khatchadourian, Haig. "What is Rationality?" *Theoria* 24 (1958): 172-187.

Kirk, R. "Rationality Without Language." *Mind* (July 1967): 369-386.

Klibansky, Raymond and Ernest C. Mossner, eds. *New Letters of David Hume*. Oxford: Clarendon Press, 1954.

Laing, B. M. *David Hume*. London: Ernest Benn Ltd., 1932.

Leibniz, Gottfried W. von. *Essais de Theodicée sur la bonité de Dieu, la liberté de l'homme et l'origine du mal*. Amsterdam, 1710.

Leroy, André. *La Critique et la Religion chez David Hume*. Paris: F. Alcan, 1934.

Livingston, Donald W. *Hume's Philosophy of Common Life*. Chicago and London: University of Chicago Press, 1984.

Livingston, Donald W. and James T. King, eds. *Hume: A Re-evaluation*. New York: Fordham University Press, 1976.

MacGregor, Geddes. *Introduction to Religious Philosophy*. Boston: Houghton Mifflin Co., 1959.

Metz, Rudolf. *David Hume, Leben und Philosophie*. Stuttgart: F. Frommann, 1929.

Mossner, Ernest Campbell. *The Life of David Hume*. 2d ed. Oxford: Clarendon Press, 1980.

―――. "The Enigma of Hume." *Mind* n.s.45 (July 1936): 334-349.

Norton, David Fate. *David Hume: Common Sense Moralist, Sceptical Metaphysician*. Princeton: Princeton University Press, 1982.

Norton, David Fate, Nicholas Capaldi, and Wade L. Robison. *McGill Hume Studies*. San Diego: Austin Hill Press, Inc., 1979.

Noxon, James. "Hume's Agnosticism." *The Philosophical Review* 73 (1964). Reprinted in Chappell, ed. *Hume*.

―――. *Hume's Philosophical Development*. Oxford: Clarendon Press, 1973.

Pears, David. *Hume's System: An Examination of the First Book of his Treatise.* Oxford and New York: Oxford University Press, 1990.

Penelhum, Terence. *Faith.* New York: Macmillan Publishing Co., 1989.

———. *God and Skepticism: A Study in Skepticism.* Dordrecht, Boston, Lancaster: D. Reidel Publishing Co., 1983.

———. *Hume.* New York: St. Martin's Press, 1975.

———. "Hume's Skepticism and the Dialogues." In *McGill Hume Studies.* Edited by Norton, Capaldi, and Robison.

Plass, E. M. *What Luther Says.* Cited in Blanshard, *Reason and Belief.*

Popkin, Richard H. "Bayle and Hume." "David Hume and the Pyrrhonian Controversy." "David Hume: His Pyrrhonism and His Critique of Pyrrhonism." "The High Road to Pyrrhonism." "Skepticism and Anti-Skepticism in the Latter Part of the Eighteenth Century." In *The High Road to Pyrrhonism*, pp. 149-159, 133-147, 103-132, 11-37, 55-77. Edited by Richard A. Watson and James E. Force. San Diego: Austin Hill Press, Inc., 1980.

———. "Fideism." In *The Encyclopedia of Philosophy.* Edited by Edwards.

Price, John Valdimir. "Scepticism in Cicero and Hume." *Journal of the History of Ideas* 25 (Jan. 1964): 97-106.

Pringle-Pattison, A. S. *Idea of God in the Light of Recent Philosophy.* New York: Oxford University Press, 1920.

Putnam, Hilary. "The Impact of Science on Modern Conceptions of Rationality." *Synthese* 46 (Mar. 1981): 359-382.

Randall, John Herman. *The Career of Philosophy. Vol. 1: From the Middle Ages to the Enlightenment.* New York: Columbia University Press, 1962.

Robinson, J. A. "Hume's Two Definitions of 'Cause'." *The Philosophical Quarterly* 12 (Apr. 1962): 162-171. Reprinted in *Hume.* Edited by Chappell.

Robison, Wade L. "David Hume: Naturalist and Meta-sceptic." In *Hume: A Re-evaluation.* Edited by Livingston and King.

Russell, Bertrand. *A History of Western Philosophy*. New York: Simon and Schuster, 1945.

Schofield, Malcolm, Myles Burnyeat, and Jonathan Barnes, eds. *Doubt and Dogmatism: Studies in Hellenistic Epistemology*. Oxford: Clarendon Press, 1980.

Sextus Empiricus. *Outlines of Pyrrhonism*. Vol. 1. Loeb Classical Library, 1933.

Skolimowski, Henryk. "Evolutionary Rationality." In R. S. Cohen, C. A. Hooker, A. C. Michalos, and J. W. Van Evra, eds. *Proceedings of the 1974 Biennial Meeting, Philosophy of Science Association, Boston Studies in the Philosophy of Science*. Edited by Robert S. Cohen and Marx W. Wartofsky. Vol. 32. Dordrecht: D. Reidel Publishing Co., 1976.

Smith, Norman Kemp. *The Philosophy of David Hume: A Critical Study of Its Origin and Central Doctrines*. London: Macmillan and Co. Ltd.; New York: St. Martin's Press, Inc., 1941.

Stewart, M. A., ed. *Studies of the Philosophy of the Scottish Enlightenment*. Oxford: Clarendon Press, 1990.

Stove, D. C. "The Nature of Hume's Skepticism." In *McGill Hume Studies*. Edited by Norton, Capaldi, and Robison.

Strawson, Galen. *The Secret Connexion: Causation, Realism, and David Hume*. Oxford: Clarendon Press, 1989.

Stroud, Barry. *Hume*. London, Henley, and Boston: Routledge & Kegan Paul, 1977.

Swinburne, Richard. *Faith and Reason*. Oxford: Clarendon Press, 1981.

Taylor, A. E. *David Hume and the Miraculous*. Cambridge: The University Press, 1927.

———. "Theism." *The Encyclopedia of Religion and Ethics*. Edited by Hastings.

Taylor, A. E., John Laird, and T. E. Jessop. "The Present-Day Relevance of Hume's Dialogues concerning Natural Religion." *Aristotelian Society Supplementary Volume*, 18 (1939).

William of Occam. *Sentences*.

Wilson, Bryan R., ed. *Rationality: Key Concepts in the Social Sciences*. Evanston, Ill. and New York: Harper and Row, Publishers, 1970.

Windelband, Wilhelm. *A History of Philosophy*. Translated by James H. Tufts. Rev. ed. New York: The Macmillan Co., 1901; reprint ed. Harper Torchbooks; New York: Harper & Row, Publishers, 1958.

Wootton, David. "Hume's 'Of Miracles': Probability and Irreligion." In *Studies of the Philosophy of the Scottish Enlightenment*. Edited by Stewart.

Wright, William Kelley. *A History of Modern Philosophy*. New York: The Macmillan Co., 1941.

INDEX OF NAMES

Allen, James, 148

Arriaga, Rodrigo de, 159, 160

Ayer, A. J., 122, 188, 193

Bacon, Francis, 2, 143

Baier, Annette C., 88, 148, 186, 189, 193

Barnes, Jonathan, 191, 200

Bayle, Pierre, 2, 3, 11, 12, 15, 79, 81, 84, 144-149, 157-163, 167, 169, 172-174, 189, 199

Beattie, James, 13, 144

Beck, Lewis White, 70, 143, 188, 193

Bennett, Jonathan, 178, 193

Berkeley, George, 2, 5, 12, 115, 129, 143, 145, 149, 166, 167, 191, 194

Beveridge, Henry, 181, 194

Black, Max, 178, 193

Blair, Hugh, 65

Blanshard, Brand, 193, 199

Boswell, James, 76, 185, 193

Boyle, Patrick, 70, 71, 77

Bradley, F. H., 11, 177, 193

Brown, Harold I., 178, 194

Brown, John, 46

Bunel, Pierre, 160

Burke, Patrick, 23, 24, 179, 194

Burnyeat, Myles, 148, 191, 194, 200

Burton, John Hill, 184, 194

Bury, R. G., 176

Butler, Joseph, 28, 30, 37, 46, 50, 59, 145, 190

Butler, R. J., 82, 185, 194

Calvin, John, 34, 38, 47, 48, 181, 183, 194

Capaldi, Nicholas, 17, 70, 176, 178, 188, 193-195, 197-200

Capitan, William H., 185, 194

Carlyle, Alexander, 70, 71, 184, 194

Chappell, V. C., 182, 186, 187, 189, 194, 198, 199

Charlemont, James C. (Lord), 81

Cherniak, Christopher, 178, 194

Cicero, 38, 39, 59, 183, 184, 199

Clarke, Samuel, 34, 37, 59, 129, 146, 181, 194

Cohen, Robert S., 179, 200

Colver, A. Wayne, xi, 183, 197

Colwell, Gary, 181, 194

Connon, Robert, 177, 194

Copleston, Frederick, 20, 178, 195

D'Arcy, Martin, 178, 195

Delaney, C. F., 178, 195

Descartes, René, 1-3, 23, 148, 158, 160, 168, 169

Desmaizeaux, Pierre, 161

Durbin, Bill, 179, 195

Edgley, Roy, 178, 195

Edwards, Paul, 9, 176, 178, 195, 199

Elliot, Gilbert, 50, 57, 183, 185

Erasmus, Desiderius, 11

Fackenheim, Emil, 9

Ferguson, Kenneth G., 180, 181, 195

Ferreira, M. Jamie, 13, 177, 195

Flew, Anthony, 59, 70, 97, 180, 181, 195

Fogelin, Robert J., 6, 175, 180, 181, 195

Force, James E., 176, 189, 199

Foucher, Simon, 158, 160

Galen, 55, 56

Gaskin, J. C. A., 36, 39-42, 57-60, 70, 72, 73, 181-185, 195

Gassendi, Pierre, 158, 160

Geraets, Theodore F., 178 179, 194, 196, 197

Gert, Bernard, 22, 179, 196

Gibbon, Edward, 43

Green, T. H., 13

Greig, J. Y. T., 180, 183, 184, 186, 188, 190, 196

Grose, T. H., 13

Hastings, James, 182, 196, 200

Hendel, C. W., 70, 182, 196

Hick, John, 9, 10, 176, 178, 195, 196

Hobbes, Thomas, 129

Home, John (David Hume's brother), 58

Index of Names

Home, Joseph (David Hume's father), 69

Hooker, C. A., 179, 200

Hospers, John, 13, 108, 143, 177, 179, 187, 196

Huet, Pierre-Daniel, 145, 158, 160

Hume, David (David's nephew, son of John Home), 58

Hutcheson, Francis, 145

Immerwahr, John, 7, 176, 197

Jastrow, Robert, 24

Jessop, T. E., 59, 184, 197, 200

Jodl, Friedrich, 186, 197

Jones, W. T., 5, 175, 197

Kames, Henry Home (Lord), 180, 190

Kant, Immanuel, 2, 3, 5, 115, 143, 147, 172, 188, 193

Kekes, John, 178, 179, 196, 197

Kenny, Anthony, 178, 197

Keynes, J. M., xi, 196

Khatchadourian, Haig, 178, 198

Kierkegaard, Søren, 9, 11, 21, 48, 172

King, James T., 70, 177, 198, 199

Kirk, R., 178, 198

Klibansky, Raymond, 180, 190, 198

Kuhn, Thomas S., 24

Laing, John, 182, 198

Laird, John, 171, 184, 197, 200

Leibniz, Gottfried, W. von, 146, 149, 159, 161, 190, 198

Leroy, André, 182, 198

Livingston, Donald, 15, 68-70, 78, 86, 105, 122, 175, 177, 184-187, 198, 199

Locke, John, 1, 2, 5, 12, 47, 76, 77, 129, 138, 143, 145, 149, 160

Luther, Martin, 11, 20, 21

MacGregor, Geddes, 49, 183, 198

MacNabb, D. G. C., 6, 195

Maimonides, Moses, 160

Malebranche, Nicholas, 146-149, 160

Mallet, (Mrs.) David, 81

Mandeville, Bernard de, 161

Metz, Rudolf, 182, 198

Michalos, A. C., 179, 200

Montaigne, Michel Eyquem de, 11, 15, 78, 84, 144, 145, 147, 148, 158, 165, 169

Morice, G. P., 70

Mossner, Ernest Campbell, 5, 29, 59, 70, 144, 150, 175, 180-182, 184, 185, 190, 194, 197, 198

Newman, John Henry, 177, 195

Newton, Isaac, 2, 64, 104, 131, 143, 160

Nidditch, P. H., xi, 196, 197

Nielsen, Kai, 179

Norton, David Fate, 70, 176, 188, 193-195, 197-200

Noxon, James, 36, 40, 59, 181, 182, 184, 199

Pap, Arthur, 176, 195

Pascal, Blaise, 11, 172

Passmore, John, 70

Patterson, Robert Leet, 178

Pears, David, 146-148, 189, 199

Penelhum, Terence, 10, 11, 13, 14, 16, 17, 21, 70, 146, 174, 176-178, 189, 199

Pike, Nelson, 70

Plass, E. M., 178, 199

Plato, 73

Popkin, Richard H., 2, 3, 7, 12, 15, 26, 39, 70, 80, 84, 142-144, 146, 148, 149, 157-165, 171-174, 176, 178, 182, 184, 185, 189, 190, 191, 195, 197, 199

Popper, Karl R., 24

Pottle, Frederick A., 185, 193

Price, John Valdimir, xi, 56, 59, 182-184, 197, 199

Pringle-Pattison, A. S., 181, 199

Putnam, Hilary, 24, 179, 199

Randall, John Herman, 29, 175, 180, 199

Reid, J. K. S., 183, 194

Reid, Thomas, 13, 65, 144, 177, 184, 195

Robinson, J. A., 114, 115, 117, 187, 189, 199

Robison, Wade L., 14, 15, 176, 177, 188, 193-195, 197-200

Rousseau, Jean-Jacques, 2

Russell, Bertrand, 12, 147, 177, 200

Schofield, Malcolm, 191, 200

Scott, Geoffrey, 185, 193

Sebond, Raimond de, 165

Selby-Bigge, L. A., xi, 196

Sextus Empiricus, 2, 7, 26, 147, 157, 163, 165, 171, 176, 189, 190, 200

Shaftesbury, Anthony Ashley Cooper, 3d Earl of, 1, 161

Skolimowski, Henryk, 179, 200

Smith, Adam, 43, 70, 75, 76

Smith, Norman Kemp, xi, 13-15, 38-40, 49-52, 54-56, 59, 66, 70, 101, 143-145, 171, 174, 177, 181-183, 185, 187, 188, 193, 196, 200

Sorbiere, Samuel, 158, 160

Index of Names

Spinoza, Baruch, 1, 147, 159, 160

Sraffa, P., xi, 196

Steinberg, Eric, 185, 197

Stewart, Dugald, 39, 143, 144, 181, 184

Stewart, John, 105, 187

Stewart, M. A., 180, 200, 201

Stillingfleet, Edward, 161

Stough, C. L., 148

Stove, D. C., 6, 176, 200

Strawson, Galen, 88, 106, 118, 122, 124, 186-188, 200

Stroud, Barry, 5, 70, 94, 103, 116, 175, 186, 187, 200

Swinburne, Richard, 24, 178, 179, 200

Taylor, A. E., 29, 30, 32, 33, 180, 182, 184, 196, 197, 200

Tillotson, John, 32, 36

Torrance, Thomas F., 181, 194

Troeltsch, Ernst, 47

Tufts, James H., 182, 201

Van Evra, J. W., 179, 200

Vespasian, 31

Voltaire, François M. A., 171

Warburton, William, 46, 144, 175

Wartofsky, Marx W., 179, 200

Watson, Richard A., 176, 189, 199

Wesley, John, 48

Wesley, Samuel, 48

Wilkes, John, 29

Wilkins, John, 177, 195

William of Occam, 20, 178, 201

Wilson, Bryan R., 179, 201

Windelband, Wilhelm, 182, 201

Wittgenstein, Ludwig, 147

Wootton, David, 30, 180, 201

Wright, William Kelley, 5, 175, 201

Zeno (Eleatic), 159

Revisioning Philosophy

The series seeks innovative and explorative thought in the foundation, aim, and objectives of philosophy. Preference will be given to approaches to world philosophy and to the repositioning of traditional viewpoints. New understandings of knowledge and being in the history of philosophy will be considered. Works may take the form of monographs, collected essays, and translations which demonstrate the imaginative flair of examining foundational questions.

The series editor is:

David Appelbaum
Department of Philosophy
The College at New Paltz
New Paltz, NY 12561

DATE DUE			
JUN 0 5 2007			

HIGHSMITH 45-220